Praise for *The American*

"*They* may have Blackwater/Xe, Halliburton, aircraft carrier ba.... g deadly drones by the score and the world's largest military budget, but *we* have Tom Engelhardt—and a more powerful truth-seeking missile has seldom been invented. Longtime fans like me will be happy to see some of his most memorable pieces reprinted here, although woven together in a way that makes them still stronger; for anyone not yet familiar with his work, this is your chance to meet one of the most forceful analysts alive of our country's dangerous, costly addiction to all things military."

—Adam Hochschild, author of *Bury the Chains* and *King Leopold's Ghost*

"Tom Engelhardt is the I. F. Stone of the post-9/11 age—seeing what others miss, calling attention to contradictions that others willfully ignore, insisting that Americans examine in full precisely those things that make us most uncomfortable."

—Andrew J. Bacevich, author of
Washington Rules: America's Path to Permanent War

"Tom Engelhardt is among our most trenchant critics of American perpetual war. Like I. F. Stone in the 1960s, he has an uncanny ability to ferret out and see clearly the ugly truths hidden in government reports and statistics. No cynic, he always measures the sordid reality against a bright vision of an America that lives up to its highest ideals."

—Juan R. Cole, Professor of History at the University of Michigan

"There are a lot of ways to describe Tom Engelhardt's astonishing service to this country's conscience and imagination: you could portray him as our generation's Orwell, standing aside from all conventional framings to see afresh our dilemmas and blind spots, as the diligent little boy sending in regular dispatches on the nakedness of the emperor and his empire, as a bodhisattva dedicated to saving all beings through compassion and awareness, but analogies don't really describe the mix of clear and sometimes hilarious writing, deep insight, superb information, empathy, and outrage that has been the core of Tom's TomDispatches for almost a decade, or the extraordinary contribution they've made to the American dialogue. Check out this bundle of some of the best from that time span."

—Rebecca Solnit, author of *Hope in the Dark* and *A Paradise Built in Hell*

The American Way of War
How Bush's Wars Became Obama's

TOM ENGELHARDT

Haymarket Books
Chicago, Illinois

For Chalmers Johnson, the most astute observer of the American way of war I know. He broke the ground and made the difference.

First published by Haymarket Books in 2010
© 2010 Tom Engelhardt

Haymarket Books
P.O. Box 180165,
Chicago, IL 60618
773-583-7884
info@haymarketbooks.org
www.haymarketbooks.org

ISBN: 978-1-608460-71-7

Trade distribution:
In the U.S. through Consortium Book Sales and Distribution, www.cbsd.com
In Canada through Publishers Group Canada, www.pgcbooks.ca/home.html
In the UK, Turnaround Publisher Services, www.turnaround-psl.com
In Australia, Palgrave Macmillan, www.palgravemacmillan.com.au
All other countries, Publishers Group Worldwide, www.pgw.com

Special discounts are available for bulk purchases by organizations and institutions.
Please contact Haymarket Books for more information at 773-583-7884 or
info@haymarketbooks.org.

This book was published with the generous support of Lannan Foundation
and the Wallace Global Fund.

Cover design by Eric Ruder.

Printed in Canada by union labor on recycled paper containing 100 percent
post-consumer waste in accordance with the guidelines of the Green Press
Initiative, www.greenpressinitiative.org.

Library of Congress CIP Data is available.

2 4 6 8 10 9 7 5 3

CONTENTS

INTRODUCTION

Is America Hooked on War?

"War is peace" was one of the memorable slogans on the facade of the Ministry of Truth, or Minitrue in "Newspeak," the language invented by George Orwell in 1948 for his dystopian novel *1984*. Some sixty years later, a quarter century after Orwell's imagined future bit the dust, the phrase is, in a number of ways, eerily applicable to the United States.

On September 10, 2009, for instance, a *New York Times* front-page story by Eric Schmitt and David E. Sanger was headlined "Obama Is Facing Doubts in Party on Afghanistan, Troop Buildup at Issue." It offered a modern version of journalistic Newspeak.

"Doubts," of course, imply dissent, and in fact just the week before there had been a major break in Washington's ranks, though not among Democrats. The conservative columnist George Will wrote a piece offering blunt advice to the Obama administration, summed up in its headline: "Time to Get Out of Afghanistan." In our age of political and audience fragmentation and polarization, think of this as the Afghan version of Vietnam's Walter Cronkite moment.

The *Times* report on those Democratic doubts, on the other hand, represented a more typical Washington moment. Ignored, for instance, was Wisconsin senator Russ Feingold's call for the president to develop an Afghan withdrawal timetable. The focus of the piece was instead a

1

planned speech by Michigan senator Carl Levin, chairman of the Armed Services Committee. He was, Schmitt and Sanger reported, hoping to push back against well-placed leaks (in the *Times*, among other places) indicating that war commander General Stanley McChrystal was urging the president to commit fifteen thousand to forty-five thousand more American troops to the Afghan War.

Here, according to the two reporters, was the gist of Levin's message about what everyone agreed was a "deteriorating" U.S. position: "[H]e was against sending more American combat troops to Afghanistan until the United States speeded up the training and equipping of more Afghan security forces."

Think of this as the line in the sand within the Democratic Party. Both positions could be summed up with the same word: More.

The essence of this "debate" came down to: More of them versus more of us (and keep in mind that more of "them"—an expanded training program for the Afghan National Army—actually meant more of "us" in the form of extra trainers and advisers). In other words, however contentious the disputes in Washington, however dismally the public viewed the war, however much the president's war coalition might threaten to crack open, the only choices were between more and more.

In such a situation, no alternatives are likely to get a real hearing. Few alternative policy proposals even exist because alternatives that don't fit with "more" have ceased to be part of Washington's war culture. No serious thought, effort, or investment goes into them. Clearly referring to Will's column, one of the unnamed "senior officials" who swarm through our major newspapers made the administration's position clear, saying sardonically, according to the *Washington Post*, "I don't anticipate that the briefing books for the [administration] principals on these debates over the next weeks and months will be filled with submissions from opinion columnists.... I do anticipate they will be filled with vigorous discussion...of how successful we've been to date."

State of War

Because the United States does not look like a militarized country, it's hard for Americans to grasp that Washington is a war capital, that the

United States is a war state, that it garrisons much of the planet, and that the norm for us is to be at war somewhere (usually, in fact, many places) at any moment. Similarly, we've become used to the idea that, when various forms of force (or threats of force) don't work, our response, as in Afghanistan, is to recalibrate and apply some alternate version of the same under a new or rebranded name—the hot one now being "counterinsurgency," or COIN—in a marginally different manner. When it comes to war, as well as preparations for war, more is now generally the order of the day.

This wasn't always the case. The early Republic that the most hawkish conservatives love to cite was a land whose leaders looked with suspicion on the very idea of a standing army. They would have viewed our hundreds of global garrisons, our vast network of spies, agents, Special Forces teams, surveillance operatives, interrogators, rent-a-guns, and mercenary corporations—as well as our staggering Pentagon budget and the constant future-war gaming and planning that accompanies it—with genuine horror.

The question is: What kind of country do we actually live in when the so-called U.S. Intelligence Community lists seventeen intelligence services ranging from Air Force Intelligence, the Central Intelligence Agency, and the Defense Intelligence Agency to the National Reconnaissance Office and the National Security Agency? What could "intelligence" mean once spread over seventeen sizeable, bureaucratic, often competing outfits with a cumulative 2009 budget estimated at more than $55 billion (a startling percentage of which is controlled by the Pentagon)? What exactly is so intelligent about all that? And why does no one think it even mildly strange or in any way out of the ordinary?

What does it mean when the most military-obsessed administration in our history, which, year after year, submitted ever more bloated Pentagon budgets to Congress, is succeeded by one headed by a president who ran, at least partially, on an antiwar platform, and who then submitted an even larger Pentagon budget? What does this tell you about Washington and about the viability of nonmilitarized alternatives to the path George W. Bush took? What does it mean when the new administration, surveying nearly eight years and two wars' worth of disasters, decides to expand the U.S. Armed Forces rather than shrink the U.S. global mission?

What kind of a world do we inhabit when, at a time of mass unemployment, the American taxpayer is financing the building of a three-story, exceedingly permanent-looking $17 million troop barracks at Bagram Air Base in Afghanistan? This, in turn, is part of a taxpayer-funded $220 million upgrade of the base that includes new "water treatment plants, headquarters buildings, fuel farms, and power generating plants." And what about the U.S. air base built at Balad, north of Baghdad, that has fifteen bus routes, two fire stations, two water treatment plants, two sewage treatment plants, two power plants, a water bottling plant, and the requisite set of fast-food outlets, PXes, and so on, as well as air traffic levels sometimes compared to those at Chicago's O'Hare International?

What kind of world are we living in when a plan to withdraw most U.S. troops from Iraq involves the removal of more than 1.5 million pieces of equipment? Or in which the possibility of withdrawal leads the Pentagon to issue nearly billion-dollar contracts (new ones!) to increase the number of private security contractors in that country?

What do you make of a world in which the U.S. military has robot assassins in the skies over its war zones, 24/7, and the "pilots" who control them from thousands of miles away are ready on a moment's notice to launch missiles—"Hellfire" missiles at that—into Pashtun peasant villages in the wild, mountainous borderlands of Pakistan and Afghanistan? What does it mean when American pilots can be at war "in" Afghanistan, 9 to 5, by remote control, while their bodies remain at a base outside Las Vegas, and then they can head home past a sign that warns them to drive carefully because this is "the most dangerous part of your day"?

What does it mean when, for our security and future safety, the Pentagon funds the wildest ideas imaginable for developing high-tech weapons systems, many of which sound as if they came straight out of the pages of sci-fi novels? Take, for example, Boeing's advanced coordinated system of handheld drones, robots, sensors, and other battlefield surveillance equipment slated for seven army brigades within the next two years at a cost of $2 billion and for the full army by 2025; or the Next Generation Bomber, an advanced "platform" slated for 2018; or a truly futuristic bomber, "a suborbital semi-spacecraft able to move at hypersonic speed along the edge of the atmosphere," for 2035? What does it mean about our world when those people in our government peering deepest into a blue-skies future are planning ways to send armed "platforms" up into those skies and kill more than a quarter century from now?

And do you ever wonder about this: If such weaponry is being end-lessly developed for our safety and security, and that of our children and grandchildren, why is it that one of our most successful businesses in-volves the sale of the same weaponry to other countries? Few Americans are comfortable thinking about this, which may explain why global-arms-trade pieces don't tend to make it onto the front pages of our news-papers. In September 2009, the *Times* Pentagon correspondent Thom Shanker, for instance, wrote a rare piece on the subject, but it appeared inside the paper on a quiet Labor Day. "Despite Slump, U.S. Role as Top Arms Supplier Grows" was the headline. Perhaps Shanker, too, felt un-comfortable with his subject, because he included the following generic description: "In the highly competitive global arms market, nations vie for both profit and political influence through weapons sales, in partic-ular to developing nations." The figures he cited from a congressional study of that "highly competitive" market told a different story: The United States, with $37.8 billion in arms sales (up $12.4 billion from 2007), controlled 68.4 percent of the global arms market in 2008. Highly competitively speaking, Italy came "a distant second" with $3.7 billion. In sales to "developing nations," the United States inked $29.6 billion in weapons agreements or 70.1 percent of the market. Russia was a vanish-ingly distant second at $3.3 billion, or 7.8 percent of the market. In other words, with 70 percent of the market, the United States actually has what, in any other field, would qualify as a monopoly position—in this case, in things that go boom in the night. With the American car industry in a ditch, it seems that this (along with Hollywood films that go boom in the night) is what we now do best, as befits a war, if not warrior, state. Is that an American accomplishment you're comfortable with?

Consider this: War is now the American way, even if peace is what most Americans experience while their proxies fight in distant lands. Any serious alternative to war, which means our "security," is increasingly in-conceivable. In Orwellian terms then, war is indeed peace in the United States—and peace is war.

American Newspeak

Newspeak, as Orwell imagined it, was an ever more constricted form of English that would, sooner or later, make "all other modes of thought impossible." "It was intended," he wrote in an appendix to his novel, "that when Newspeak had been adopted once and for all and Oldspeak forgotten, a heretical thought...should be literally unthinkable."

When it comes to war (and peace), we live in a world of American Newspeak in which alternatives to a state of war are not only ever more unacceptable, but ever harder to imagine. If war is now our permanent situation, it has also been sundered from a set of words that once accompanied it. It lacks, for instance, "victory." After all, when was the last time the United States actually won a war (unless you include our "victories" over small countries incapable of defending themselves, like the tiny Caribbean island of Grenada in 1983 or powerless Panama in 1989)? The smashing "victory" over Saddam Hussein in the First Gulf War only led to a stop-and-start conflict now almost two decades old that has proved a catastrophe.

Keep heading backward through the Vietnam and Korean Wars, and the U.S. military was last truly victorious in 1945. But achieving victory no longer seems to matter. War American-style is now conceptually unending, as are preparations for it. When George W. Bush proclaimed a Global War on Terror (aka World War IV), conceived as a "generational struggle" like the cold war, he caught a certain American reality. In a sense, the ongoing war system can't absorb victory. Any such endpoint might indeed prove to be a kind of defeat.

No longer has war anything to do with the taking of territory either, or even with direct conquest. War is increasingly a state of being, not a process with a beginning, an end, and an actual geography.

Similarly drained of its traditional meaning has been the word "security"—though it has moved from a state of being (secure) to an eternal, immensely profitable process whose endpoint is unachievable. If we ever decided we were either secure enough, or more willing to live without the unreachable idea of total security, the American way of war and the national security state would lose much of their meaning. In other words, in our world, security is insecurity.

As for "peace"—war's companion and theoretical opposite—it, too, has been emptied of meaning and all but discredited. Appropriately enough, diplomacy, the part of government that classically would have been associated with peace, or at least with the pursuit of the goals of war by other means, has been dwarfed by, subordinated to, or even subsumed by the Pentagon. In recent years, the U.S. military, with its vast funds, has taken over, or encroached upon, a range of activities that once would have been left to an underfunded State Department, especially humanitarian aid operations, foreign aid, and what's now called nation-building.

Diplomacy itself has been militarized and, like our country, is now hidden behind massive fortifications, and has been placed under *Lord of the Flies*–style guard. The State Department's embassies are now bunkers and military-style headquarters for the prosecution of war policies. Its officials, when enough of them can be found, are now sent out into the provinces in war zones to do "civilian" things.

And peace itself? Simply put, there's no money in it. Of the nearly trillion dollars the United States invests in war and war-related activities, nothing goes to peace. No money, no effort, no thought. The very idea that there might be peaceful alternatives to endless war is so discredited that it's left to utopians, bleeding hearts, and feathered doves. As in Orwell's Newspeak, while "peace" remains with us, it's largely been shorn of its possibilities. No longer the opposite of war, it's just a rhetorical flourish embedded, like one of our reporters, in Warspeak.

What a world might be like in which we began not just to withdraw our troops from one war to fight another, but to seriously scale down the American global mission, close those hundreds of bases—as of 2010, there were almost four hundred of them, macro to micro, in Afghanistan alone—and bring our military home is beyond imagining. To discuss such obviously absurd possibilities makes you an apostate to America's true religion and addiction, which is force. However much it might seem that most of us are peaceably watching our TV sets or computer screens or iPhones, we Americans are also—always—marching as to war. We may not all bother to attend the church of our new religion, but we all tithe. We all partake. In this sense, we live peaceably in a state of war.

ONE

Shock and Awe: How We Got Hit

The World Before September 11

September 2001. The "usually disengaged" president, as columnist Maureen Dowd labeled him, had just returned from a prolonged, brush-cutting Crawford vacation to much criticism and a nation in trouble. One Republican congressman complained that "it was hard for Mr. Bush to get his message out if the White House lectern had a 'Gone Fishing' sign on it."

Democrats were on the attack. Journalistic coverage seemed to grow ever bolder. George W. Bush's poll figures were dropping. A dozen prominent Republicans, fearful of a president out of touch with the national mood, gathered for a private dinner with Karl Rove to "offer an unvarnished critique of Bush's style and strategy." Next year's congressional elections suddenly seemed up for grabs. The president's aides were desperately scrambling to reposition him as a more "commanding" figure, while, according to the polls, a majority of Americans felt the country was headed in the wrong direction. At the Pentagon, Donald Rumsfeld had "cratered"; in the Middle East "violence was rising."

An editorial in the *New York Times* caught the moment this way in its opening sentence: "A simple truth of human existence is that it is vastly easier to amplify fear than it is to assuage it." Now, there was a post-9/11 truth—except that the editorial was headlined "The Statistical

Shark" and its next sentence wasn't about planes smashing into buildings or the way the Bush administration had since wielded the fear card, but another hot-button issue entirely. It went: "Consider the shark attacks that have occurred in Florida, Virginia and North Carolina this summer."

This was, in fact, September 6, 2001, the waning days of a man-bites-dog summer in which headlines had been dominated by the deaths of David Peltier, a 10-year-old boy in Florida, and Sergei Zaloukaev, a 28-year-old in North Carolina, in fatal shark attacks. Just the day before, in fact, the *Times* had carried a piece by William J. Broad reassuring readers that scientists did not believe the world was facing a shark "rampage." "If anything," Broad concluded, "the recent global trend in shark attacks is down."

It was just past Labor Day. Congress was barely back in session. Heywood Hale Broun, the sportswriter, would die at eighty-three that relatively quiet week, while Mexican president Vicente Fox swept triumphantly into Washington, and a new book, featured on *Newsweek*'s cover, would carry the title, *The Accidental President*. The Sunday *New York Times* Arts & Leisure section was promoting "the new season" in entertainment, while that night a highly publicized ten-part miniseries was premiering on HBO—*Band of Brothers*, a Tom Hanks and Steven Spielberg production that followed a platoon of "greatest generation" soldiers deep into Germany. If World War II nostalgia was on the tube, war elsewhere in the American world was also largely on screen. On September 7, *Times* journalist Thom Shanker reported on a classified war game, a computer-generated simulation played out by "the nation's senior commanders" which determined that the U.S. military could "decisively defeat one potential adversary, North Korea, while repelling an attack from Iraq"—even if "terrorists [attacked] New York City with chemical weapons."

All in all, that week before September 11 was a modestly uneventful one. An afternoon spent revisiting the version of it in the *New York Times*, via a library microfiche machine, making my way through that paper, day by day, section by section, plunged me into a nearly forgotten world in which the Democrats still controlled the Senate by a single vote and key Republican senators—it was Texan Phil Gramm's turn to announce his retirement that week—were going down like bowling pins. (Jesse Helms and Strom Thurmond had preceded Gramm, "adding a new element of uncertainty to the 2002 race.") The president had been met by exceedingly gloomy economic news as the unemployment rate jumped that Saturday to 4.9 percent—another 100,000 jobs lost—a full point above election day, ten months earlier; and Wall Street responded with a sell-off that dropped the Dow Jones to 9,600. Republicans were "panicked," the administration adrift, and we wouldn't see the likes of it again for four years.

Eerie Resonances

A number of post-9/11 subjects were in the paper that week:

Torture was in the headlines—leading off the culture page that Saturday ("Torture Charge Pits Professor vs. Professor") in a memory piece, datelined Santiago, on Augusto Pinochet's brutal military rule in Chile. (The anniversary of his bloody coup, September 11, 1973, was approaching.)

Then, too, an American citizen had been imprisoned without charges for eighteen months—but it was electrical engineer Fuming Fong and China was holding him.

Anthrax made the op-ed page—but only because Russian scientists had developed a new type that could "overcome the standard Russian and American vaccines."

Terrorism in the United States was in the news—an Oklahoma prosecutor was seeking the death penalty for Terry L. Nichols in the Oklahoma City Murrah Federal Building bombing.

"Violence in the Middle East" was on the front page—but in that week, it had only one meaning: the endless Israeli/Palestinian conflict. (The first Israeli-Arab suicide bomber had just struck.)

The Taliban could be found on the front page on September 7 (and inside on subsequent days)—but only because the mullahs were trying eight foreign aid workers for preaching Christianity. The bemused articles ("Another Strange Kabul Problem: Finding a Lawyer") were of the weird-foreigners variety.

Military recruitment was a topic of interest then as now—the army, after switching ad agencies and slogans ("Army of One" for "Be All You Can Be") had just conducted an "elaborate event" at the Pentagon, swearing into service its 75,800th recruit of the year, nineteen-year-old Rodrigo

Vasquez III of Karnes City, Texas, in order to highlight meeting its recruitment goals a month ahead of schedule in the "most successful recruiting
year since at least 1997."

Howard Dean made the inside pages of the paper that week—the
little-known Vermont governor (tagged with "fiscal conservativism/social
liberalism") announced that he would not seek reelection to his fifth two-
year term. There was "speculation" that he might even "run for the Democratic nomination for President."

Missing in Action

And then there were—in terms of what we've been used to ever
since—the missing, or almost missing issues. Saddam Hussein didn't
make it into the paper that week. Kim Jong-il was nowhere in sight.
Osama bin Laden barely slipped into print—twice deep into articles—
as "the accused terrorist" being hosted by the strange Taliban government. The Axis of Evil, of course, did not exist, nor did the Global War
on Terror, and the potential enemy of the week, pushed by Donald Rumsfeld (himself on the defensive over the military budget and arguments
with his generals), was "the rising China threat."

Iran was scarcely a blip on the news radar screen; Syria rated not a
mention. Also missing were just about any of the names we came to consider second nature to the post-9/11 news. No "Scooter" Libby. No Valerie
Plame. No Paul Wolfowitz, John Bolton, or Douglas Feith. In fact, not a
neocon made it into the pages of the paper over those seven days, and
Judy Miller, the neocons' future dream reporter, who would soon enough
storm the front page of the *Times* and take it for her own, had two pieces
that week: a September 5 article on page 5 about a former Arms Control
and Disarmament Agency general counsel challenging the administration's "assertion that the global treaty banning biological weapons per-
mits nations to test such arms for defensive purposes"; and, two days later,
a tiny Israel piece tucked away at the bottom of page 15 on "the alleged
[online] support for terrorism" by Islamic groups and charities.

The vice president, silently at the president's side at a "hastily arranged"
and awkward "appearance" on the White House grounds after the unemployment figures broke, was otherwise nowhere to be seen, though the *Times*

speculated on its editorial page ("The Bush Merry-Go-Round") that he was "losing influence." ("Mr. Cheney's heart problems and his ardent embrace of the coal, oil and gas industries seem to have hobbled him.")

Though the sharks in the world's oceans that week were feeding on something other than humans, there were still "sharks" around. Allison Mitchell began a Sunday lead Week in Review piece ("Face Off: Which Way to Win Control of Congress?") this way: "Talk about shark season. Congress came back into session last week and the Democrats were circling, sensing blood in the political waters." Little wonder. This was, after all, a non-majoritarian president who had, as *Times* writers didn't hesitate to remind people, just squeaked through with a helping hand from the Supreme Court. After managing to get one massive tax cut by Congress, he began to drift like a lost lifeboat at sea, while his advisers fretted over polls "showing that many people still view Mr. Bush not as decisive but as tentative and perhaps overly scripted." He was, as a front-page piece by Richard L. Berke and David E. Sanger put it on September 9, "essentially out of economic ammunition."

The nature of politics in Washington that week could be caught in lines like: "Democrats go on the attack" and "Democrats intensified their attacks against Mr. Bush." Less than a year into a Bush presidency, columnist Tom Friedman was already offering the faltering leader heartfelt advice on how not to lose the next election. Be "Clinton-minus," not "Reagan-squared" was the formula he offered. As the Mitchell piece made clear, this was a presidency under siege, as well as a Republican Party—so "everyone" in Washington agreed—"in peril." In the sort of action not to be seen again for years, a Senate committee actually cut money from the defense budget that week, an act Shanker of the *Times* termed "another stark challenge" from committee chairman Carl Levin of Michigan. The political failure of the president's father was evidently on Washington minds as well, and so the paper in a number of pieces linked father and son. The father's bid for reelection had, after all, gone down in flames in the nation's previous recession, or, as the headline of one story put it, "Like Father, Bush Is Caught in a Politically Perilous Budget Squeeze."

A few aspects of our post-9/11 political world were quite recognizable even then. That week, the Bush administration was easing up on Big

Tobacco ("Justice Official Denies Pressure to Settle Tobacco Suit") and Big Computer ("U.S. Abandoning Its Effort to Break Apart Microsoft"), while preparing to bail from the Anti-Ballistic Missile Treaty. And as the administration pushed for legislation to open the Arctic National Wildlife Refuge, a "hobbled" Dick Cheney was already stonewalling about what had occurred when his Energy Task Force of Big Oil met earlier in 2001.

The two days before 9/11 were so quiet that you could practically hear a news pin drop. In the *Times* of September 11—in that moment before the Internet took full possession of us, a day's lag between events and the news was a print norm—the major story ("Key Leaders Talk of Possible Deals to Revive Economy, Bush Is Under Pressure") indicated that "some Republicans" were anxiously bringing up 1982 when President Reagan "told the nation to 'stay the course' in a recession" and the party dropped numerous House seats in the midterm elections.

At the bottom of the front page was a plane hijacking story, though it was thirty years old ("Traced on Internet, Teacher Is Charged in '71 Jet Hijacking"). Across the rest of the page-bottom on that final morning were "In a Nation of Early Risers, Morning TV Is a Hot Market" and "School Dress Codes vs. a Sea of Bare Flesh."

For intimations of what was to come, you would have had to move inside. On page 3, Douglas Frantz reported, "Suicide Bomb Kills 2 Police Officers in Istanbul," a bombing for which no one took credit and which was automatically attributed to "a leftist terrorist group" (something that would not happen again soon). On the next page, you could find Barry Bearak and James Risen's piece "Reports Disagree on Fate of Anti-Taliban Rebel Chief" about the assassination of Ahmed Shah Massoud, an anti-Taliban warlord, by two Arabs posing as journalists (which we now know was connected to the September 11 plot). In its penultimate paragraph was this: "If the would-be assassins were indeed Arabs…the fact would lend credibility to those who contend that foreigners, including Osama bin Laden, are playing an ever bigger decision-making role among the Taliban."

Peering further into the future, on page 8, under World Briefs, was a throwaway paragraph on the low-level air war even then being conducted against Saddam Hussein's Iraq: "Iraq said eight civilians were killed and three wounded when Western planes attacked farms 100 miles southeast of Baghdad. The Pentagon said American and British warplanes attacked three surface-to-air missile sites in the so-called no-fly zone." Another article, "Iran: Denial on Nuclear Weapons," began: "The government rejected charges by the United States that it was seeking nuclear weapons."

And then, of course, there was nothing to do but oh-so-slowly turn the microfiche dial and, after a pitch-black break between days, stumble into those mile-high headlines—"U.S. Attacked, Hijacked Jets Destroy Twin Towers and Hit Pentagon in Day of Terror"—and, despite yourself, experience with a kind of gasp the sky in your brain filling with falling bodies.

Here, by the way, is how that September 6 *Times* shark editorial ended. If it doesn't give you a little chill for what we've lost, I don't know what will: "Life is full of things that carry more risk than swimming in the ocean. Most of them are inevitably the byproducts of daily life, like falling televisions and car accidents, because daily life is where we spend most of our time. It may lack the visceral fears aroused by the unlikely threat of a shark attack, but it is also far more lethal."

Only five days after that was written, almost three thousand New Yorkers, some adopted from countries around the globe, would face a danger far more shocking—and, until that moment, far less imaginable to most of us—than any shark attack. Things would indeed fall from the sky—and from a history so many Americans knew nothing about—and visceral fears would be aroused that would drive us, like the Pearl Harbor–style headlines that greeted the audacious act not of a major power but of nineteen fanatics in four planes prepared to die, into a future even more unimaginable.

Put another way, an afternoon spent in the lost world of September 5–10, 2001, reminds us that the savage attacks of the following day would, in fact, buy a faltering, confused, and weak administration, as well as a dazed and disengaged president, a new life, a "calling" as he would put it, and almost four years to do its damnedest. It would be 2004 before the president's polling figures settled back to the levels of that long-lost September 10. It would be the summer of 2005—and the administration's disastrous handling of hurricanes Katrina and Iraq—before the president would again be criticized for his "gone fishing" summer vacation; before the Democrats would again begin to attack; before newspapers would again be relatively uncowed; before the Republicans would again gather in those private (and then public) places and begin to complain; before Congress would again be up for grabs. Four long years to make it back to September 10, 2001, in an American world now filled to the brim with horrors, a United States that was no longer a "country," but a "homeland" and a Homeland Security State.

9/11 in a Movie-Made World

We knew it was coming. Not, as conspiracy theorists imagine, just a few top officials among us, but all of us—and not for weeks or months, but for more than half a century before September 11, 2001.

That's why, for all the shock, it was, in a sense, so familiar. Americans were already imagining versions of September 11 soon after the dropping of the first atomic bomb on Hiroshima on August 6, 1945. That event set the American imagination boiling. Within weeks of the destruction of Hiroshima and Nagasaki, as scholar Paul Boyer has shown, all the familiar signs of nuclear fear were already in place: newspapers were drawing concentric circles of atomic destruction outward from fantasy Ground Zeroes in American cities, and magazines were offering visions of our country as a vaporized wasteland, while imagining millions of American dead.

And then, suddenly, one clear morning it seemed to arrive—by air, complete with images of the destruction of the mightiest monuments to our power, and (just as previously experienced) as an onscreen spectacle. At one point that day, it could be viewed on more than thirty channels, including some never previously involved with breaking news, and most of the country was watching.

Only relatively small numbers of New Yorkers actually experienced 9/11 firsthand: those at the tip of Manhattan or close enough to watch the two planes smash into the World Trade Center towers, to watch (as some schoolchildren did) people leaping or falling from the upper floors of those buildings, to be enveloped in the vast cloud of smoke and ash, in the tens of thousands of pulverized computers and copying machines, the asbestos and flesh and plane, the shredded remains of millions of sheets of paper, of financial and office life as we know it. For most Americans, even those like me who were living in Manhattan, 9/11 arrived on the television screen. This is why what leapt to mind—and instantaneously filled our papers and TV reporting—was previous screen life, the movies.

In the immediate aftermath of the attacks, the news was peppered with comments about, thoughts about, and references to films. Reporters, as Caryn James wrote in the *New York Times* that first day, "compared the events to Hollywood action movies"; as did op-ed writers ("The scenes exceeded the worst of Hollywood's disaster movies"); columnists ("On TV, two national landmarks...look like the aftermath in the film *Independence Day*"); and eyewitnesses ("It was like one of them *Godzilla* movies"; "And then I saw an explosion straight out of *The Towering Inferno*"). Meanwhile, in an irony of the moment, Hollywood scrambled to excise from upcoming big- and small-screen life anything that might bring to mind thoughts of 9/11, including, in the case of Fox, promotion for the premiere episode of *24*, in which "a terrorist blows up an airplane."

In our guts, we had always known it was coming. Like any errant offspring, Little Boy and Fat Man, those two atomic packages with which we had paid *them* back for Pearl Harbor, were destined to return home someday. No wonder the single, omnipresent historical reference in the media in the wake of the attacks was Pearl Harbor or, as screaming headlines had it, INFAMY, or A NEW DAY OF INFAMY. We had just experienced "the Pearl Harbor of the 21st Century," or, as R. James Woolsey, former CIA director (and neocon), said in the *Washington Post* that first day, "It is clear now, as it was on December 7, 1941, that the United States is at war.... The question is: with whom?"

The Day After

No wonder what came instantly to mind was a nuclear event. No wonder, according to a *New York Times* piece, Tom Brokaw, then chairing NBC's nonstop news coverage, "may have captured it best when he looked at videotape of people on a street, everything and everyone so covered with ash...[and said] it looked 'like a nuclear winter in lower Manhattan.'" No wonder the *Tennessean* and the *Topeka Capital-Journal* both used the headline "The Day After," lifted from a famous 1983 TV movie about nuclear Armageddon.

No wonder the area where the two towers fell was quickly dubbed "Ground Zero," a term previously reserved for the spot where an atomic explosion had occurred. On September 12, for example, the *Los Angeles Times* published a full-page series of illustrations of the attacks on the towers headlined: "Ground Zero." By week's end, it had become the only name for "the collapse site," as in a September 18 *New York Times* headline, "Many Come to Bear Witness at Ground Zero."

No wonder the events seemed so strangely familiar. We had been living with the possible return of our most powerful weaponry via TV and the movies, novels and our own dream-life, in the past, the future, and even—thanks to a John F. Kennedy TV appearance on October 22, 1962, during the Cuban missile crisis to tell us that our world might end tomorrow—in something like the almost-present.

So many streams of popular culture had fed into this. So many "previews" had been offered. Everywhere in those decades, you could see yourself or your compatriots or the enemy "Hiroshimated" (as *Variety* termed it back in 1947). Even when Arnold Schwarzenegger wasn't kissing Jamie Lee Curtis in *True Lies* as an atomic explosion went off somewhere in the Florida Keys or a playground filled with American kids wasn't being atomically blistered in *Terminator 2: Judgment Day*, even when it wasn't literally nuclear, that apocalyptic sense of destruction lingered as the train, bus, blimp, explosively armed, headed for us in our unknowing innocence; as the towering inferno, airport, city, White House was blasted away, as we were offered Pompeii-scapes of futuristic destruction in what would, post-9/11, come to be known as "the homeland."

Sometimes it came from outer space armed with strange city-blasting rays; other times irradiated monsters rose from the depths to stomp our cities (in the 1998 remake of *Godzilla*—New York City, no less). After Darth Vader used his Death Star to pulverize a whole planet in *Star Wars*, planets were regularly nuclearized in Saturday-morning TV cartoons. In our imaginations, post-1945, we were always at planetary Ground Zero.

Dystopian Serendipity

Increasingly, from Hamburg to Saudi Arabia to Afghanistan, others were also watching our spectaculars, our catastrophes, our previews; and so, as Hollywood historian Neal Gabler would write in the *New York Times* only days after 9/11, they were ready to deliver what we had long dreamed of with the kind of timing—insuring, for instance, that the second plane arrived "at a decent interval" after the first, so that the cameras could be in place—and in a visual language American viewers would understand.

But here's the catch: What came, when it came, on September 11, 2001, wasn't what we thought came. There was no Ground Zero, because there was nothing faintly atomic about the attacks. It wasn't the apocalypse at all. Except in its success, it hardly differed from the 1993 attack on the World Trade Center, the one that almost toppled one tower with a rented Ryder van and a homemade bomb.

What "changed everything," as the phrase would soon go, was a bit of dystopian serendipity for al-Qaeda: Nineteen men of much conviction and middling skills, armed with exceedingly low-tech weaponry and two hijacked jets, managed to create an apocalyptic look that, in another context, would have made the special-effects masters of George Lucas's Industrial Light & Magic proud. And from that—and the Bush administration's reaction to it—everything else would follow.

The tiny band of fanatics who planned September 11 essentially lucked out. If the testimony, under CIA interrogation techniques, of al-Qaeda's master planner Khalid Shaikh Mohammed is to be believed, what happened stunned even him. ("According to the [CIA] summary, he said he 'had no idea that the damage of the first attack would be as catastrophic as it was.'") Those two mighty towers came crumbling down in that vast, roiling, near-mushroom cloud of white smoke before the cameras, in the fashion of the ultimate Hollywood action film (imagery multiplied in its traumatizing power by thousands of replays over a record-setting more than ninety straight hours of TV coverage). And that imagery fit perfectly the secret expectations of Americans—just as it fit the needs of both al-Qaeda and the Bush administration.

That's undoubtedly why other parts of the story of that moment faded from sight. For example, take American Flight 77, which plowed into the Pentagon. That destructive but non-apocalyptic-looking attack didn't satisfy the same built-in expectations. Though the term "ground zero Washington" initially floated through the media ether, it never stuck. Similarly, the unsolved anthrax murders-by-mail of almost the same moment, which caused a collective shudder of horror, are now forgotten. (According to a LexisNexis search, between October 4 and December 4, 2001, 260 stories appeared in the *New York Times* and 246 in the *Washington Post* with "anthrax" in the headline. That's the news equivalent of a high-pitched scream of horror.) Those envelopes, spilling highly refined anthrax powder and containing letters dated "9/11/01" with lines like "Death to America, Death to Israel, Allah Is Great," represented the only use of a weapon of mass destruction (WMD) in this period, yet they were slowly eradicated from our collective (and media) memory once it became clearer that the perpetrator or perpetrators were probably homegrown, possibly out of the very cold war U.S. weapons labs that produced so many WMD in the first place.

The 36-Hour War

Indulge me, then, for a moment on an otherwise grim subject. I've always been a fan of what-if history and science fiction, which led me to take my own modest time machine—the IRT subway—back to September 11, 2001, via the New York Public Library, a building that—in the realm where sci-fi and what-if history meld—suffered its own monstrous "damage," its own 9/11, only months after the A-bombing of Hiroshima.

In November 1945, *Life* magazine published "The 36-Hour War," an overheated what-if tale in which an unnamed enemy in "equatorial Africa" launched a surprise atomic missile attack on the United States, resulting in ten million deaths. A dramatic illustration accompanying the piece showed the library's two pockmarked stone lions still standing, guarding a ground-zero scene of almost total destruction, while heavily shielded technicians tested "the rubble of the shattered city for radioactivity."

I passed those same majestic lions, still standing (as was the library), entered the microfiche room and began reading the *New York Times* starting with the September 12, 2001, issue. Immediately I was plunged into an apocalypse: "gates of hell," "the unthinkable," "nightmare world of Hieronymus Bosch," "hellish storm of ash, glass, smoke, and leaping victims," "clamorous inferno," "an ashen shell of itself, all but a Pompeii." But one of the most common words in the *Times* and elsewhere was "vulnerable" (or as a *Times* piece put it, "nowhere was safe"). The front page

of the *Chicago Tribune* caught this mood in a headline, "Feeling of In-
vincibility Suddenly Shattered," and a lead sentence, "On Tuesday, America the invincible became America the vulnerable." We had faced "the
kamikazes of the 21st century"—a Pearl Harborish phrase that would
gain traction—and we had lost.

A what-if thought came to mind as I slowly rolled that grainy microfiche; as I passed the photo of a man, in midair, falling headfirst from a
World Trade Center tower; as I read this observation from a Pearl Harbor
survivor interviewed by the *Tribune*: "Things will never be the same again
in this country"; as I reeled section by section, day by day toward our distinctly changed present; as I read all those words that boiled up like a lin-
guistic storm around the photos of those white clouds; as I considered all
the op-eds and columns filled with instant opinions that poured into the
pages of our papers before there was time to think; as I noted, buried in
their pages, a raft of words and phrases—"preempt," "a new Department
of Pre-emption [at the Pentagon]," "homeland defenses," "homeland security agency"—readying themselves to be noticed.

Among them all, the word that surfaced fastest on the heels of that
"new Day of Infamy," and to deadliest effect, was "war." Senator John
McCain, among many others, labeled the attacks "an act of war" on the
spot, just as Republican senator Richard Shelby insisted that "this is total
war," just as *Washington Post* columnist Charles Krauthammer started
his first editorial that first day, "This is not crime. This is war."

On the night of September 11, the president himself, addressing the
nation, already spoke of winning "the war against terrorism." By day two,
he was using the phrase "acts of war"; by day three, "the first war of the
twenty-first century" (while the *Times* reported "a drumbeat for war" on
television); by week's end, "the long war"; and the following week, in an
address to a joint session of Congress, while announcing the creation of a
cabinet-level Office of Homeland Security, he wielded "war" twelve times.
("Our war on terror begins with Al Qaeda, but it does not end there.")

What If?

What if the two hijacked planes, American Flight 11 and United Flight
175, had plunged into those north and south towers at 8:46 and 9:03,

killing all aboard, causing extensive damage and significant death tolls, but neither tower had come down? What if, as a *Tribune* columnist called it, photogenic "scenes of apocalypse" had not been produced? What if, despite two gaping holes and the smoke and flames pouring out of the towers, the imagery had been closer to that of 1993? What if there had been no giant cloud of destruction capable of bringing to mind the look of "the day after," no images of crumbling towers worthy of *Independence Day*?

We would surely have had blazing headlines, but would they have commonly had "war" or "infamy" in them, as if we had been attacked by another state? Would the last superpower have gone from "invincible" to "vulnerable" in a split second? Would our newspapers instantly have been writing "before" and "after" editorials, or insisting that this moment was the ultimate "test" of George W. Bush's until-then languishing presidency? Would we instantaneously have been considering taking what CIA director George Tenet would soon call "the shackles" off our intelligence agencies and the military? Would we have been reconsidering, as Florida's Democratic senator Bob Graham suggested that first day, rescinding the congressional ban on the assassination of foreign officials and heads of state? Would a *Washington Post* journalist have been trying within hours to name the kind of "war" we were in? (He provisionally labeled it "the Gray War.") Would *New York Times* columnist Tom Friedman on the third day have had us deep into "World War III"? Would the *Times* have been headlining and quoting Deputy Defense Secretary Paul Wolfowitz on its front page on September 14, insisting that "it's not simply a matter of capturing people and holding them accountable, but removing the sanctuaries, removing the support systems, ending states who sponsor terrorism." (The *Times* editorial writers certainly noticed that ominous "s" on "states" and wrote the next day: "but we trust [Wolfowitz] does not have in mind invading Iraq, Iran, Syria and Sudan as well as Afghanistan.")

Would state-to-state "war" and "acts of terror" have been so quickly conjoined in the media as a "war on terror" and would that phrase have made it, in just over a week, into a major presidential address? Could the *Los Angeles Daily News* have produced the following four-day series of screaming headlines, beating even the president to the punch: "Terror"/ "Horror!"/"'This Is War'"/"War on Terror"?

If it all hadn't seemed so familiar, wouldn't we have noticed what was actually new in the attacks of September 11? Wouldn't more people have been as puzzled as the reporter who asked White House press secretary Ari Fleischer, "You don't declare war against an individual, surely"? Wouldn't Congress have balked at passing, three days later, an almost totally open-ended resolution granting the president the right to use force not against one nation (Afghanistan) but against "nations," plural and unnamed?

And how well would the Bush administration's fear-inspired nuclear agenda have worked, if those buildings hadn't come down? Would Saddam Hussein's supposed nuclear program and stores of WMD have had the same impact? Would the endless linking of the Iraqi dictator, al-Qaeda, and 9/11 have penetrated so deeply that, in 2006, half of all Americans, according to a Harris poll, still believed Saddam had WMD when the U.S. invasion began, and 85 percent of American troops stationed in Iraq, according to a Zogby poll, believed the U.S. mission there was mainly "to retaliate for Saddam's role in the 9-11 attacks"?

Without that apocalyptic 9/11 imagery, would those fantasy Iraqi mushroom clouds pictured by administration officials rising over American cities, or those fantasy Iraqi unmanned aerial vehicles capable of spraying our East Coast with chemical or biological weapons, or Saddam Hussein's supposed search for African yellowcake (or even, today, the Iranian "bomb" that won't exist for perhaps another decade, if at all) have so dominated American consciousness?

Would Osama bin Laden and Ayman al-Zawahiri be sitting in jail cells or be on trial by now? Would so many things have happened differently?

The Opportunity of a Lifetime

What if the attacks on September 11, 2001, had not been seen as a new Pearl Harbor? Only three months earlier, after all, Disney's *Pearl Harbor* (the "sanitized" version, as *Times* columnist Frank Rich labeled it), a blockbuster made with extensive Pentagon help, had performed disappointingly at the multiplexes. As an event, it seemed irrelevant to American audiences until 9/11, when that ancient history—and the ancient retribution that went with it—wiped from the American brain the actual history of recent decades, including our massive covert anti-Soviet war in Afghanistan, out of which Osama bin Laden emerged.

Here's the greatest irony: From that time of triumph in 1945, Americans had always secretly suspected that they were not "invincible" but exceedingly vulnerable, something both pop culture and the deepest fears of the cold war era only reinforced. Confirmation of that fact arrived with such immediacy on September 11 largely because it was already a gut truth. The ambulance chasers of the Bush administration, who spotted such opportunity in the attacks, were perhaps the last Americans who hadn't absorbed this reality. As that New Day of Infamy scenario played out, the horrific but actual scale of the damage inflicted in New York and Washington (and to the U.S. economy) would essentially recede. The attack had been relatively small, limited in its means and massive only in its daring and luck—abetted by the fact that the Bush administration was looking for nothing like such an attack, despite that CIA briefing given to Bush on a lazy August day in Crawford ("Bin Ladin Determined to Strike in US") and so many other clues.

Only the week before 9/11, the Bush administration had been in the doldrums with a "detached," floundering president criticized by worried members of his own party for vacationing far too long at his Texas ranch while the nation drifted. Moreover, there was only one group before September 11 with a "new Pearl Harbor" scenario on the brain. Major administration figures, including Vice President Dick Cheney, Defense Secretary Donald Rumsfeld, and Deputy Defense Secretary Wolfowitz, had wanted for years to radically increase the power of the president and the Pentagon, to roll back the power of Congress (especially any congressional restraints on the presidency left over from the Vietnam and Watergate era), and to complete the overthrow of Saddam Hussein ("regime change") aborted by the first Bush administration in 1991.

We know as well that some of those plans were on the table in the 1990s and that those who held them and promoted them, at the Project for the New American Century in particular, actually wrote that "the process of transformation [of the Pentagon], even if it brings revolutionary change, is likely to be a long one, absent some catastrophic and catalyzing event—like a new Pearl Harbor."

We also know that within hours of the 9/11 attacks, many of the same people were at work on the war of their dreams. Within five hours of the attack on the Pentagon, Rumsfeld was urging his aides to come up with plans for striking Iraq. (Notes by an aide transcribe his wishes this way: "best info fast. Judge whether good enough hit S.H. [Saddam Hussein] at same time. Not only UBL [Osama bin Laden].... Go massive. Sweep it all up. Things related and not.")

We know that by September 12, the president himself had collared his top counterterrorism adviser on the National Security Council, Richard Clarke, in a conference room next to the White House Situation Room and demanded linkages. ("'Look under every rock and do due diligence.' It was a very intimidating message which said, 'Iraq. Give me a memo about Iraq and 9/11.'") We know that by November, the top officials of the administration were already deep into operational planning for an invasion of Iraq.

And they weren't alone. Others were working feverishly. Only eight days after the attacks, for instance, the complex 342-page Patriot Act would be rushed over to Congress by Attorney General John Ashcroft, passed through a cowed Senate in the dead of night on October 11, unread by at least some of our representatives, and signed into law on October 26. As its instant appearance indicated, it was made up of a set of already existing right-wing hobbyhorses, quickly drafted provisions, and expansions of law-enforcement powers taken off an FBI "wish list" (previously rejected by Congress). All these were swept together by people who, like the president's men on Iraq, saw their main chance when those buildings went down. As such, it stands in for much of what happened "in response" to 9/11.

But what if we hadn't been waiting so long for our own 36-hour war in the most victorious nation on the planet, its sole "hyperpower," its new Rome? What if those preexisting frameworks hadn't been quite so well primed to emerge in no time at all? What if we (and our enemies as well) hadn't been at the movies all those years?

Planet of the Apes

Among other things, we've been left with a misbegotten memorial to the attacks of 9/11 planned for New York's Ground Zero and sporting the kinds of cost overruns otherwise associated with the occupation of Iraq. In its ambitions, what it will really memorialize is the Bush administration's oversized, crusading moment that followed the attacks.

Too late now—and no one asked me anyway—but I know what my memorial would have been.

A few days after 9/11, my daughter and I took a trip as close to "Ground Zero" as you could get. With the air still rubbing our throats raw, we wandered block after block, peering down side streets to catch glimpses of the sheer enormity of the destruction. And indeed, in a way that no small screen could communicate, it did have the look of the apocalyptic, especially those giant shards of fallen building sticking up like— remember, I'm a typical movie-made American on an increasingly movie-made planet and had movies on the brain that week—the image of the wrecked Statue of Liberty that chillingly ends the first *Planet of the Apes* film, that cinematic memorial to humanity's nuclear folly. Left there as it was, that would have been a sobering monument for the ages, not just to the slaughter that was 9/11, but to what we had awaited for so long—and what, sadly, we still wait for; what, in the world that George W. Bush produced, has become ever more, rather than less, likely. And imagine our reaction then.

Safer? Don't be ridiculous.

The Billion-Dollar Gravestone

According to a report commissioned by the foundation charged with building Reflecting Absence, the memorial to the dead in the attack on the World Trade Center, its projected cost was, at one point, estimated at about a billion dollars. For that billion, Reflecting Absence was to have two huge "reflecting pools"—"two voids that reside in the original footprints of the Twin Towers"—fed by waterfalls "from all sides" and surrounded by a "forest" of oak trees. A visitor would then be able to descend thirty feet to galleries under the falls "inscribed with the names of those who died." There was to be an adjacent, 100,000-square-foot underground memorial museum to "retell the events of the day, display powerful artifacts, and celebrate the lives of those who died." All of this, as the website for the memorial stated, would vividly convey "the enormity of the buildings and the enormity of the loss." The near-billion-dollar figure did not even include $80 million for a planned visitor's center or the estimated $50–$60 million annual cost of running such an elaborate memorial and museum.

So what was Reflecting Absence going to reflect? For one thing, it would mirror its gargantuan twin, the building that is to symbolically replace the World Trade Center—the Freedom Tower. As the Memorial was to be driven deep into the scarred earth of Ground Zero, so the Freedom Tower was to soar above it, scaling the imperial heights. To be precise, it was to reach exactly 1,776 feet into the heavens, a numerical tribute to the founding spirit of the Declaration of Independence and the nation that emerged from it. Its spire would even emit light—"a new beacon of freedom"—for all the world to see and admire. Its observation deck would rise a carefully planned seven feet above that of the old World Trade Center, and with spire and antennae, it was meant to be the tallest office building on the planet.

The revelation of that staggering billion-dollar price tag for a memorial, whose design has grown ever larger and more complex, caused the *New York Times* to editorialize, "The only thing a $1 billion memorial would memorialize is a complete collapse of political and private leadership in Lower Manhattan." Because the subject is such a touchy one, however, no one went further and explored the obvious—that, even in victimhood, Americans have in recent years exhibited an unseemly imperial hubris. Whether the price tag proves to be half a billion or a billion dollars, one thing can be predicted: the memorial will prove less a reminder of how many Americans happened to be in the wrong place at the wrong time on that September day, or how many—firefighters, police officers, bystanders who stayed to aid others—sacrificed their lives, than of the terrible path this country ventured down in the wake of 9/11.

Consider the prospective 9/11 memorial in this context:

- The National World War II Memorial (405,000 American dead): $182 million for all costs
- The Vietnam Memorial (56,000 American dead):$4.2 million for construction

- The Korean War Veterans Memorial (54,000 American dead): $6 million
- The USS *Arizona* Memorial at Pearl Harbor (2,390 American dead; 1,177 from the *Arizona*): $532,000
- The Oklahoma City National Memorial (168 American dead): $29 million
- The 1915 USS *Maine* Mast Memorial at Arlington Cemetery (260 American dead): $56,147.94
- The Holocaust Museum in Washington (approximately 6 million dead): $90 million for construction/$78 million for exhibitions

Or, imagine a listing of global Ground Zeros that might go something like this:

- Amount spent on a memorial for the Vietnamese dead of the Vietnam wars (approximately 3 million): $0
- Amount spent on a memorial to the Afghan dead in the civil war between competing warlords over who would control the capital of Kabul in the mid-1990s (unknown numbers of dead, a city reduced to rubble): $0
- Amount spent on a memorial to the victims of the December 26, 2004, earthquake and tsunami in the Pacific and Indian Oceans (at least 188,000 dead): $0
- Amount spent on a memorial to Iraqis confirmed dead, many with signs of execution and torture marks, just in the month of April 2006 in Baghdad alone (almost 1,100), or the Iraqis confirmed killed countrywide "in war-related violence" from January through April of that year (3,525): $0

The Victors Are the Victims

The dead, those dear to us, our wives or husbands, brothers, sisters, parents, children, relatives, friends, those who acted for us or suffered in our place, should be remembered. This is an essential human task, almost a duty. What could be more powerful than the urge to hold onto those taken from us, especially when their deaths happen in an unexpected, untimely, and visibly unjust way (only emphasizing the deeper untimeliness and injustice of death itself). But where exactly do we remember the dead? The truth: We remember them in our hearts, which makes a memorial a living thing only so long as the dead still live within us.

As an experiment, visit one of the old Civil War or World War I memorials that dot so many cities and towns. You might (or might not) admire the fountain, or the elaborate statue of soldiers or a general or any other set of icons chosen to stand in for the hallowed dead and their sacrifices. The Grand Army Plaza, designed by Augustus Saint-Gaudens and dedicated to the Union Army, that fronts on Central Park in New York City, my hometown, has always attracted me, but it is in a sense no longer a memorial. Decades ago, it turned back into a somewhat gaudy, golden decoration, a statue— as all memorials, in the end, must. Few today visit it to remember what some specific individual did or how he died. To the extent that we remember, we remember first individually in our hearts in our own lifetimes—and later, collectively, in our history books.

And, of course, for most human beings in most places, especially those who are not the victors in wars, or simply not the victors on this planet, no matter how unfairly or horrifically or bravely or fruitlessly their loved ones might be taken from them, there is only the heart. For those dying in Kabul or Baghdad, Chechnya, Darfur, the Congo, or Uzbekistan, the emotions released may be no less strong, but there will be no statues, no reflecting pools, no sunken terraces, no walls with carefully etched names.

There has, in American journalism, been an unspoken calculus of the value of a life and a death on this planet in terms of newsworthiness (which is also a kind of memorializing, a kind of remembering). Crudely put, it would go something like: one kidnapped and murdered blond white child in California equals three hundred Egyptians drowned in a ferry accident, three thousand Bangladeshis swept away in a monsoon flood, three hundred thousand Congolese killed in a bloodletting civil war.

It's also true that, as the recent World War II Memorial on the Washington Mall indicates, Americans have gained something of a taste for Roman imperial-style memorialization. (To my mind, that huge construction catches little of the modesty and stoicism of the veterans of that war who, like my father, did not come home trumpeting what they had done.)

Reflecting Absence and the Freedom Tower go well beyond that. Their particular form of excess, in which money, elaborateness, and size stand in for memory, is intimately connected not so much with September 11, 2001, as with the days, weeks, even years after that shock.

The Greatest Victim, Survivor, and Dominator

To grasp this, it's necessary to return to those now almost forgotten moments after 9/11, after the president had frozen in an elementary school classroom in Florida while reading *The Pet Goat*; after a panicky crew of his people had headed Air Force One in the wrong direction, away from Washington; after Donald Rumsfeld and George W. Bush (according to former counterterrorism tsar Richard Clarke) started rounding up the usual suspects—i.e., Saddam Hussein—on September 11 and 12; after the president insisted, "I don't care what the international lawyers say, we are going to kick some ass"; after he took that bullhorn at Ground Zero on September 14, and—to chants of "USA! USA! USA!"—promised Americans that "the people who knocked these buildings down will hear all of us soon"; after his associates promptly began to formulate the plans, the "intelligence," the lies, and the tall tales that would take us into Iraq.

It was in that unformed but quickly forming moment that, under the shock not just of the murder of almost three thousand people, but of the apocalyptic images of those two towers crumbling, an American imperial culture of revenge and domination was briefly brought to full flower. It was a moment that reached its zenith when the president strutted across the deck of the USS *Abraham Lincoln* on May 1, 2003, and, with that Mission Accomplished banner over his shoulder, declared "major combat operations" ended in Iraq.

The gargantuan Freedom Tower and the gargantuan sunken memorial to the dead of 9/11 are really monuments to that brief year and a half, each project now hardly less embattled in controversy, cost overruns, and ineptitude than were the war in Iraq or the post-Katrina rescue-and-reconstruction mission. Each project—as yet unbuilt—is already an increasingly controversial leftover from that extended moment when so many pundits pictured us proudly as a wounded Imperial Rome or the inheritor of the glories of the British Empire, while the administration, with its attendant neocon cheering squad in tow, all of them dazzled by our "hyperpower," gained confidence that this was their moment, the one that would take them over the top, that would make the United States a Republican Party possession for years, if not generations; the Middle East an American gas station; the world an American military preserve; and a "unitary" commander-in-chief presidency the recipient of untrammeled powers previously reserved for kings and emperors. These were dreams of gargantuan proportions, fantasies of power and planetary rule worthy of a tower at least 1,776 feet high that would obliterate the memory of all other buildings anywhere, and of the largest, most expensive gravestone on Earth that would quite literally put the sufferings of all other victims in the shade.

As those two enormous reflecting pools were meant to mirror the soaring "beacon" of the Freedom Tower, so the American people, under the shock of loss, experiencing a sense of violation that can only come to the victors in this world, mirrored the administration's attitude. In a country where New York City had always been Sodom to Los Angeles' Gomorrah, everyone suddenly donned "I ♥ New York" hats or T-shirts and became involved in a series of repetitive rites of mourning that, in arenas nationwide, on every television screen, went on not for days or weeks but months on end.

From these ceremonies, a clear and simple message emerged. In its suffering, the United States was the greatest victim, the greatest survivor, and the greatest dominator the globe had ever seen. Implicitly, the rest of the world's dead were, in the Pentagon's classic phrase, "collateral damage." In those months, in our all-American version of the global drama, we swept up and repossessed all the emotional roles available—with the sole exception of Greatest Evil One. That, then, was the phantasmagoric path to invasion, war, and disaster upon which the Bush administration, with a mighty helping hand from al-Qaeda, pulled back the curtain; that is the drama still being played out at Ground Zero in New York City.

But those 2,752 dead can no longer stand in—not even in the American mind—for all the dead everywhere, not even for the American dead in Iraq and Afghanistan. Perhaps it's finally time to take a breath and approach the untimely dead—our own as well as those of others around the world—with some genuine humility.

I know that for some, those reflecting pools will someday touch the heart, but unfortunately they will mainly memorialize a post-9/11 America that should not have been using the numbers 1776. Facing a building so tall, who would even have the need to approach a declaration so modest—of only 1,322 words—so tiny as to be able to fit on a single page, so iconic that just about no one bothers to pay attention to what it says anymore. But perhaps it's worth quoting a few of the words those men wrote back in the year 1776 and remembering what the American dead of that time actually stood for. Here then are some passages about another George's imperial hubris, less well remembered than the declaration's classic beginning:

> The history of the present King of Great Britain is a history of repeated injuries and usurpations, all having in direct object the establishment of an absolute Tyranny over these States.... He has erected a multitude of New Offices, and sent hither swarms of Officers to harass our people and eat out their substance. He has kept among us, in times of peace, Standing Armies without the Consent of our legislatures. He has affected to render the Military independent of and superior to the Civil power. He has combined with others to subject us to a jurisdiction foreign to our constitution, and unacknowledged by our laws; giving his Assent to their Acts of pretended Legislation.... For depriving us in many cases, of the benefit of Trial by Jury: For transporting us beyond Seas to be tried for pretended offences.... For suspending our own Legislatures, and declaring themselves invested with power to legislate for us in all cases whatsoever.

Looking Forward, Looking Backward

Given the last eight years of disaster piled on catastrophe, who in our American world would want to look backward? The urge to turn the page in this country is palpable, but just for a moment let's not.

Admittedly, we're a people who don't really believe in history—so messy, so discomforting, so old. Even the recent past is regularly wiped away as the media plunge us repeatedly into various overblown crises of the moment, a 24/7 cornucopia of news, non-news, rumor, punditry, gossip, and plain old blabbing. In turn, any sense of the larger picture surrounding each flap is, soon enough, dismantled by a media focus on a fairly limited set of questions: Was Congress adequately informed? Should the president have suppressed those photos?

The flaps, in other words, never add up to a single Imax Flap-o-rama of a spectacle. We seldom see the full scope of the legacy that we—not just the Obama administration—have inherited. Though we all know that terrible things happened in recent years, the fact is that, these days, they are seldom to be found in a single place, no less the same paragraph. Connecting the dots, or even simply putting everything in the same vicinity, just hasn't been part of the definitional role of the media in our era. So let me give it a little shot.

As a start, remind me: What didn't we do? Let's review for a moment.

In the name of everything reasonable, and in the face of acts of evil by terrible people, we tortured wantonly and profligately, and some of these torture techniques—known to the previous administration and most of the media as "enhanced interrogation techniques"—were actually demonstrated to an array of top officials, including the national security adviser, the attorney general, and the secretary of state, within the White House. We imprisoned secretly at "black sites" offshore and beyond the reach of the American legal system, holding prisoners without hope of trial or, often, release; we disappeared people; we murdered prisoners; we committed strange acts of extreme abuse and humiliation; we kidnapped terror suspects off the global streets and turned some of them over to some of the worst people who ran the worst dungeons and torture chambers on the planet. Unknown but not insignificant numbers of those kidnapped, abused, tortured, imprisoned, and/or murdered were actually innocent of any crimes against us. We invaded without pretext, based on a series of lies and the manipulation of Congress and the public. We occupied two countries with no clear intent to depart and built major networks of military bases in both. Our soldiers gunned down unknown numbers of civilians at checkpoints and, in each country, arrested thousands of people, some again innocent of any acts against us, imprisoning them often without trial or sometimes hope of release. Our Air Force repeatedly wiped out wedding parties and funerals in its Global War on

Terror. It killed civilians in significant numbers. In the process of prosecuting two major invasions, wars, and occupations, hundreds of thousands of Iraqis and Afghans have died. In Iraq, we touched off a sectarian struggle of epic proportions that involved the "cleansing" of whole communities and major parts of cities, while unleashing a humanitarian crisis of remarkable size, involving the uprooting of more than four million people who fled into exile or became internal refugees. In these same years, our special forces operatives and our drone aircraft carried out—and still carry out—assassinations globally, acting as judge, jury, and executioner, sometimes of innocent civilians. We spied on, and electronically eavesdropped on, our own citizenry and much of the rest of the world on a massive scale whose dimensions we may not yet faintly know. We pretzeled the English language, creating an Orwellian terminology that, among other things, essentially defined "torture" out of existence (or, at the very least, left its definitional status to the torturer).

And don't think that that's anything like a full list. Not by a long shot. It's only what comes to my mind on a first pass through the subject. In addition, even if I could remember everything done in these years, it would represent only what has been made public. Former Secretary of Defense Donald Rumsfeld was regularly mocked for saying: "There are known knowns. These are things we know that we know. There are known unknowns. That is to say, there are things that we know we don't know. But there are also unknown unknowns. There are things we don't know we don't know."

Actually, he had a point seldom thought about these days. By definition, we know a good deal about the known knowns, and we have a sense of an even darker world of known unknowns. We have no idea, however, what's missing from a list like the one above, because so much may indeed remain in the unknown-unknowns category. If, however, you think that everything done by Washington or the U.S. military or the CIA in these last years has already been leaked, think again. It's a reasonable bet that the unknown unknowns the Obama administration inherited would curl your toes.

Nonetheless, what is already known, when thought about in one place rather than divided up into separate flaps and argued about separately, is horrific enough. War may be hell, as people often say when try-ing to excuse what we did in these years, but it should be remembered that, in response to the attacks of 9/11, we, as a nation, were the ones who declared "war," made it a near eternal struggle (the Global War on Ter-ror), and did so much to turn parts of the world into our own private hell. Geopolitics, energy politics, vanity, greed, fear, a misreading of the nature of power, delusions of military and technological omnipotence and omniscience, and so much more drove us along the way.

Perhaps the greatest fantasy of the present moment is that there is a choice here. We can look forward or backward, turn the page on history or not. Don't believe it. History matters.

Whatever the Obama administration may want to do, or think should be done, if we don't face the record we created, if we only look forward, if we only round up the usual suspects, if we try to turn that page in history and put a paperweight atop it, we will be haunted by the Bush years until hell freezes over. This was, of course, the lesson—the only one no one ever bothers to call a lesson—of the Vietnam years. Be-cause we were so unwilling to confront what we actually did in Viet-nam—and Laos and Cambodia—because we turned the page on it so quickly and never dared take a real look back, we never, in the phrase of George H. W. Bush, "kicked the Vietnam syndrome." It still haunts us.

However busy we may be, whatever tasks await us here in this coun-try—and they remain monstrously large—we do need to make an hon-est, clear-headed assessment of what we did (and, in some cases, continue to do), of the horrors we committed in the name of…well, of us and our "safety." We need to face who we've been and just how badly we've acted, if we care to become something better.

Now, read that list again, my list of just the known knowns, and ask yourself: Aren't we the people your mother warned you about?

TWO

How to Garrison a Planet

Twenty-First-Century Gunboat Diplomacy

The wooden sailing ship mounted with cannons, the gunboat, the battleship, and finally the "airship"—historically, these proved the difference between global victory and staying at home, between empire and nothing much at all. In the first couple of centuries of Europe's burst onto the world stage, the weaponry of European armies and their foes was not generally so disparate. It was those cannons on ships that decisively tipped the balance. And they continued to do so for a long, long time. Traditionally, in fact, the modern arms race is considered to have taken off at the beginning of the twentieth century with the rush of European powers to build ever larger, ever more powerful, "all-big-gun" battleships—the "dreadnoughts" (scared of nothings).

In *"Exterminate All the Brutes,"* a remarkable travel book that takes you into the heart of European darkness (via an actual trip through Africa), the Swedish author Sven Lindqvist offers the following comments on that sixteenth-century seaborne moment when Europe was still a barbaric outcropping of Euro-Asian civilization:

> Preindustrial Europe had little that was in demand in the rest of the world. Our most important export was force. All over the rest of the

37

world, we were regarded at the time as nomadic warriors in the style of the Mongols and the Tatars. They reigned supreme from the backs of horses, we from the decks of ships.

Our cannons met little resistance among the peoples who were more advanced than we were. The Moguls in India had no ships able to withstand artillery fire or carry heavy guns.... Thus the backward and poorly resourced Europe of the sixteenth century acquired a monopoly on ocean-going ships with guns capable of spreading death and destruction across huge distances. Europeans became the gods of cannons that killed long before the weapons of their opponents could reach them.

For a while, Europeans ruled the coasts where nothing could stand up to their shipborne cannons, and then, in the mid–nineteenth century in Africa, as well as on the Asian mainland, they moved inland, taking their cannons upriver with them. For those centuries, the ship was, in modern terms, a floating military base filled with the latest in high-tech equipment. And yet ships had their limits, as indicated by a well-known passage about a French warship off the African coast from Joseph Conrad's novel about the Congo, *Heart of Darkness*:

> In the empty immensity of earth, sky, and water, there she was, incomprehensible, firing into a continent. Pop, would go one of the six-inch guns; a small flame would dart and vanish, a little white smoke would disappear, a tiny projectile would give a feeble screech—and nothing happened. Nothing could happen. There was a touch of insanity in the proceeding, a sense of lugubrious drollery in the sight.

Well, maybe it wasn't quite so droll if you happened to be on land, but the point remains. Of course, sooner or later the Europeans did make it inland with the musket, the rifle, the repeating rifle, the machine gun, artillery, and finally, by the twentieth century, the airplane filled with bombs or even, as in Iraq, poison gas. Backing up the process was often the naval vessel—as at the Battle of Omdurman in the Sudan in 1898, when somewhere between nine thousand and eleven thousand soldiers in the Mahdi's army were killed (with a British loss of forty-eight troops), thanks to mass rifle fire, Maxim machine guns, and the batteries of gunboats floating on the Nile.

Winston Churchill was a reporter with the British expeditionary force at the time. Here's part of his description of the slaughter (also from Lindqvist):

> The white flags [of the Mahdi's army] were nearly over the crest. In another minute they would become visible to the batteries. Did they realize what would come to meet them? They were in a dense mass, 2,800 yards from the 32nd Field Battery and the gunboats. The ranges were known. It was a matter of machinery.... About twenty shells struck them in the first minute. Some burst high in the air, others exactly in their faces. Others, again, plunged into the sand, and, exploding, dashed clouds of red dust, splinters, and bullets amid the ranks.... It was a terrible sight, for as yet they had not hurt us at all, and it seemed an unfair advantage to strike thus cruelly when they could not reply.

And—presto!—before you knew it, three-quarters of the world was a colony of Europe, the United States, or Japan. Not bad, all in all, for a few floating centuries. In the latter part of this period, the phrase "gunboat diplomacy" came into existence, an oxymoron that nonetheless expressed itself all too eloquently.

Our Little "Diplomats"

Today, "gunboat diplomacy" seems like a phrase from some antiquated imperial past, despite our many aircraft carrier task forces that travel the world making "friendly" house calls from time to time. But if you stop thinking about literal gunboats and try to imagine how we carry out "armed diplomacy"—and under the Bush administration the Pentagon took over much that might once have been labeled "diplomacy"—then you can begin to conjure up our own twenty-first-century version of gunboat diplomacy. But first, you have to consider exactly what the "platforms" are upon which we "export force," upon which we mount our "cannons."

What should immediately come to mind are our military bases, liberally scattered like so many vast immobile vessels over the lands of the earth. This has been especially true since the neocons of the Bush administration grabbed the reins of power at the Pentagon and set about reconceiving basing policy globally; set about, that is, creating more "mobile" versions of the military base, ever more stripped down for action, ever closer to the "arc of instability," a vast swath of lands extending from the former Yugoslavia well into northern Africa, and all the way to the Chinese border. These are areas that represent, not surprisingly, the future energy heartlands of the planet. The Pentagon's so-called lily pads strategy is meant to encircle and nail down control of this vast set of interlocking regions—the thought being that, if the occasion arises, the American frogs can leap agilely from one prepositioned pad to another, knocking off the "flies" as they go.

Thought about a certain way, the military base, particularly as reconceived in recent years, whether in Uzbekistan, Kosovo, or Qatar, is our "gunboat," a "platform" that has been ridden ever deeper into the landlocked parts of the globe—into regions like the Middle East, where our access once had some limits, or like the former Yugoslavia and the -stans of Central Asia, where the lesser superpower of the cold war era once blocked access entirely. Our new military bases are essentially the twenty-first-century version of those old European warships, the difference being that, once built, the base remains in place, while its parts—the modern equivalents of those sixteenth-century cannons—are capable of moving over land or water almost anywhere.

As Chalmers Johnson has calculated in his book *The Sorrows of Empire*, our global baseworld consists of at least seven hundred military and intelligence bases, possibly—depending on how you count them up—many more. This is our true "imperial fleet" (though, of course, we have an actual imperial fleet, our aircraft carriers alone being like small, massively armed towns). In the last decade-plus, as the pace of our foreign wars has picked up, we've left behind, after each of them, a new set of bases like the droppings of some giant beast marking the scene with its scent. Bases were dropped into Saudi Arabia and the small Gulf emirates after our first Gulf War in 1991; into the former Yugoslavia after the Kosovo air war of 1999; into Pakistan, Afghanistan, and several Central Asian states after the Afghan War of 2001; and into Iraq after the 2003 invasion.

The process speeded up under the Bush administration, but you would have had almost no way of knowing this. Basing is generally considered either a topic not worth writing about or an arcane policy matter best left to the inside pages of the newspaper for the policy wonks and news junkies. This is in part because we Americans—and by extension our journalists—don't imagine us as garrisoning or occupying the world, and certainly not as having anything faintly approaching a military empire. Generally speaking, those more than seven hundred bases, our little "diplomats" (and the rights of extraterritoriality that go with them via Status of Forces Agreements) don't even register on our media's mental map of our globe.

Enduring Camps

In Iraq, our permanent bases are endearingly referred to by the military as "enduring camps." Such bases were almost certainly planned before the 2003 invasion. After all, we were also planning to withdraw most of our troops from Saudi Arabia—Osama bin Laden had complained bitterly about the occupation of Islam's holy sites—and they weren't simply going to be shipped back to the United States.

The numbers of those potential enduring camps in Iraq are startling indeed. As one rare *Chicago Tribune* article on the topic noted, early on in the occupation of Iraq, "From the ashes of abandoned Iraqi army bases, U.S. military engineers are overseeing the building of an enhanced system of American bases designed to last for years." Some of these bases are already comparable in size and elaborateness to the ones we built in Vietnam four decades ago. Christine Spolar, who wrote the article, continues:

> As the U.S. scales back its military presence in Saudi Arabia, Iraq provides an option for an administration eager to maintain a robust military presence in the Middle East and intent on a muscular approach to seeding democracy in the region....
>
> "Is this a swap for the Saudi bases?" asked Army Brig. Gen. Robert Pollman, chief engineer for base construction in Iraq. "I don't know.... When we talk about enduring bases here, we're talking about the present operation, not in terms of America's global strategic base. But this makes sense. It makes a lot of logical sense."

And keep in mind as well that all of this construction is being done to the tune of billions of dollars under contracts controlled by the Pentagon and, as Spolar writes, quite "separate from the State Department and its Embassy in Baghdad" (which is slated to be the largest embassy in the world).

As the Pentagon planned it, and as we knew via leaks to the press soon after the invasion began, newly "liberated" Iraq, once "sovereignty" had been restored, was to have only a lightly armed military force of some forty thousand troops and no air force. The other part of this equation, the given (if unspoken) part, was that some sort of significant long-term U.S. military protection of the country would have to be put in place. And we proceeded accordingly, emplacing our "little diplomats" right at a future hub of the global energy superhighway.

But we've made sure to cover the other on- and off-ramps as well. As James Sterngold of the *San Francisco Chronicle* wrote in a rundown of some of our post-9/11 basing policies:

> [T]he administration has instituted what some experts describe as the most militarized foreign policy machine in modern history.
>
> The policy has involved not just resorting to military action, or the threat of action, but constructing an arc of new facilities in such places as Uzbekistan, Pakistan, Qatar and Djibouti that the Pentagon calls "lily pads." They are seen not merely as a means of defending the host countries—the traditional Cold War role of such installations—but as jumping-off points for future "preventive wars" and military missions.

In fact, our particular version of military empire is perhaps unique: all "gunboats," no colonies. The combination of bases we set down in any given country is referred to in the Pentagon as our "footprint" in that country. It's a term that may once have come from the idea of "boots on the ground," but now has congealed, imagistically speaking, into a single (and assumedly singular) boot print—as if, as it strode across the planet, the globe's only hyperpower was so vast that it could place but a single boot in any given country at any time, an eerie echo perhaps of that British sun which was never to set on their vast empire (until, of course, it did).

Undersecretary of Defense for Policy Douglas Feith was the main Pentagon architect of a plan to "realign" our bases so as to "forward deploy" U.S. forces into the "arc of instability." In a December 2003 speech to the Center for Strategic and International Studies, he offered a Pentagon version of sensitivity in discussing his forward deployment plans: "Realigning the U.S. posture will also help strengthen our alliances by tailoring the physical U.S. 'footprint' to suit local conditions. The goal is to reduce friction with host nations, the kind that results from accidents and other problems relating to local sensitivities." In the meantime, to ensure that there will be no consequences if the giant foot, however enclosed, happens to stamp its print in a tad clumsily, causing the odd bit of collateral damage, he added:

> For this deployability concept to work, U.S. forces must be able to move smoothly into, through, and out of host nations, which puts a premium on establishing legal and support arrangements with many friendly countries. We are negotiating or planning to negotiate with many countries legal protections for U.S. personnel, through Status of Forces Agreements and agreements (known as Article 98 agreements) limiting the jurisdiction of the International Criminal Court with respect to our forces' activities.

Bradley Graham of the *Washington Post* offered a more precise glimpse at Feith's realignment strategy, which would move us away from our cold war deployments, especially in Germany, Japan, and Korea:

> The Pentagon has drafted plans to withdraw as many as half of the 71,000 troops based in Germany as part of an extensive realignment of American military forces that moves away from large concentrations in Europe and Asia, according to U.S. officials....
> U.S. officials have said before that they intended to eliminate a number of large, full-service Cold War bases abroad and construct a network of more skeletal outposts closer to potential trouble spots in the Middle East and along the Pacific Rim.

In fact, the structure of major bases and "forward operating sites" in the arc of instability and, from Eastern Europe to the Central Asian states, inside the former Soviet empire, is already in place or, as in Iraq, in the process of being built or negotiated. As Michael Kilian of the *Chicago Tribune* writes:

> [T]he U.S. now has bases or shares military installations in Turkey, Iraq, Saudi Arabia, Kuwait, Bahrain, Qatar, the United Arab Emirates,

Oman, Ethiopia, Pakistan, Uzbekistan, Tajikistan and Kyrgyzstan, as well as on the island of Diego Garcia in the Indian Ocean.

Rumsfeld and Pentagon officials are soon expected to unveil plans for a new U.S. military "footprint" on the rest of the world. The plan is expected to include a shift of resources from the huge Cold War–era bases in Western Europe to new and smaller ones in Poland and other Eastern Europe nations as well as a relocation of U.S. troops in South Korea.

In the meantime, Pentagon strategic planning for ever more aggressive future war-fighting is likely only to intensify this process. *Los Angeles Times* military analyst William Arkin wrote of the unveiling of Secretary of Defense Rumsfeld's plan for a new military map of the globe:

> The Rumsfeld plan envisions what it labels a "1-4-2-1 defense strategy," in which war planners prepare to fully defend one country (the United States), maintain forces capable of "deterring aggression and coercion" in four "critical regions" (Europe, Northeast Asia, East Asia, and the Middle East and Southwest Asia), maintain the ability to defeat aggression in two of these regions simultaneously, and be able to "win decisively"—up to and including forcing regime change and occupying a country—in one of those conflicts "at a time and place of our choosing"....
>
> In the Clinton era, the Pentagon planned for fighting two wars simultaneously (in the Middle East and Northeast Asia). Under the new strategy, it must prepare for four....
>
> The planning model Rumsfeld and company have embraced is certainly more ambitious. It covers domestic and foreign contingencies and favors preemption over diplomacy, and military strikes over peacekeeping operations. The plan signals to the world that the United States considers nuclear weapons useful military instruments, to be employed where warranted.

Twenty-Second-Century Gunboat Diplomacy

At least as imagined in the Pentagon, twenty-second-century "gunboat diplomacy" will be conducted by what the Air Force's Space Command refers to as "space-based platforms," and the "cannons" will be a range of "exotic" weapons and delivery systems. In still unweaponized space (if you exclude the various spy satellites overhead), we plan for our future "ships" to travel the heavens alone, representatives of a singular version of gunboat diplomacy. Among the "five priorities for national security space efforts" set out by Peter B. Teets, Bush's undersecretary of the air force and director of the National Reconnaissance Office, in an article for *Air & Space Power Journal*, the most striking, if also predictable, was that of "ensuring freedom of action in space"—as in freedom of action for us, and no action at all for anyone else.

Space, long depicted as a void, is now being reimagined as the ocean of our imperial future, thanks to space weaponry on the drawing boards like the nicknamed "Rods from God." These are to be "orbiting platforms stocked with tungsten rods perhaps 20 feet long and one foot in diameter that could be satellite-guided to targets anywhere on Earth within minutes. Accurate within about 25 feet, they would strike at speeds upwards of 12,000 feet per second, enough to destroy even hardened bunkers several stories underground."

Planning among "high frontier" enthusiasts for the conquest and militarization of space began in the 1980s during the Reagan administration, but it has reached new levels of realism (of a mad sort). Theresa Hitchens of the Center for Defense Information, writing in the *San Francisco Chronicle*, described a "new U.S. Air Force Transformation Flight Plan": "The document details a stunning array of exotic weapons to be pursued over the next decade: from an air-launched missile designed to knock satellites out of low orbit, to ground- and space-based lasers for attacking both missiles and satellites, to 'hypervelocity rod bundles' (nicknamed Rods from God).... Far from being aimed solely at the protection of U.S. space capabilities, such weapons are instead intended for offensive, first-strike missions."

Ever since H. G. Wells wrote *The War of the Worlds* in 1898, we humans have been imagining scenarios in which implacable aliens with superweapons arrive from space to devastate our planet. But what if it turns out that the implacable aliens are actually us—and that, as in the sixteenth century, someday in the not-too-distant future U.S. "ships" will "burst from space" upon the "coasts" of our planet with devastation imprinted in their programs. These are, of course, the dreams of modern Mongols.

Wonders of the Imperial World

Of the seven wonders of the ancient Mediterranean world, including the Hanging Gardens of Babylon and the Colossus of Rhodes, four were destroyed by earthquakes, two by fire. Only the Great Pyramid of Giza today remains.

We no longer know who built those fabled monuments to the grandiosity of kings, pharaohs, and gods. Nowadays, at least, it's easier to identify the various wonders of our world with their architects. Maya Lin, for instance, spun the moving black marble Vietnam Memorial from her remarkable brain for the U.S. veterans of that war. Frank Gehry dreamt up his visionary titanium-covered museum in Bilbao, Spain, for the Guggenheim. The architectural firm of BDY (Berger Devine Yaeger, Inc.), previously responsible for the Sprint Corporation's world headquarters in Overland Park, Kansas, the Visitation Church in Kansas City, Missouri, and Harrah's Hotel and Casino in North Kansas City, Missouri, turns out to have designed the biggest wonder of all—an embassy large enough to embody Washington's vision of an American-reordered Middle East. We're talking, of course, about the U.S. embassy, the largest on the planet, being constructed on a 104-acre stretch of land in the heart of Baghdad's embattled Green Zone. As Patrick Lenahan, then Senior Architect and Project Manager at BDY, put it (according to the firm's website): "We understand how to involve the client most effectively as we direct our resources to make our client's vision a reality."

And what a vision it was. What a reality it's turned out to be.

Who can forget the grandiose architecture of pre–Bush administration Baghdad: Saddam Hussein's mighty vision of kitsch Orientalism melting into terror, based on which, in those last years of his rule, he reconstructed parts of the Iraqi capital? He ensured that what was soon to become the Green Zone would be dotted with overheated, Disneyesque, Arabian Nights palaces by the score, filled with every luxury imaginable in a country whose population was growing increasingly desperate under the weight of United Nations sanctions. Who can forget those vast, sculpted hands, "The Hands of Victory," supposedly modeled on Saddam Hussein's own, holding twelve-story-high giant crossed swords (over piles of Iranian helmets) on a vast Baghdad parade ground? Meant to commemorate a triumph over Iran that the despot never actually achieved, they still sit there, partially dismantled and a monument to folly.

It is worth remembering that, when the American commanders whose troops had just taken Baghdad wanted *their* victory photo snapped, they memorably seated themselves, grinning happily, behind a marble table in one of those captured palaces; that American soldiers and newly arrived officials marveled at the former tyrant's exotic symbols of power; that they swam in Saddam's pools, fed rare antelopes from his son Uday's private zoo to its lions (and elsewhere shot his herd of gazelles and ate them); and, when in need of someplace to set up an American embassy, the newly arrived occupation officials chose—are you surprised?—one of his former dream palaces. They found nothing strange in the symbolism of this (though it was carefully noted by Iraqis), even as they swore they were bringing liberation and democracy to the benighted land.

And then, as the Iraqi capital's landscape became ever more dangerous, as an insurgency gained traction while the administration's dreams of a redesigned American Middle East remained as strong as ever, its officials evidently concluded that even a palace roomy enough for a dictator wasn't faintly big enough, or safe enough, or modern enough for the representatives of the planet's New Rome.

Hence, BDY. That Midwestern firm's designers can now be classified as architects to the wildest imperial dreamers and schemers of our time. And the company seems proud of it. You could, in May 2007, go to its website and take a little tour in sketch form, a blast-resistant spin, through its particular colossus of the modern world. Imagine this: At a pricetag of at least $592 million, its proudest boast was that, unlike almost any other American construction project in that country, it was coming in on time and on budget (though, in the end, the cost overruns for the embassy would be humongous). Of course, with a 30 percent increase in staffing size since Congress first approved the project, it is estimated that being "represented" in Baghdad will cost a staggering $1.2 billion *per year.*

The BDY-designed embassy may lack the gold-plated faucets installed in some of Hussein's palaces and villas (and those of his sons), but it was planned to lack none of the amenities that Americans consider part and parcel of the good life, even in a "hardship" post. Consider, for instance, the embassy's "pool house." (There was a lovely sketch of it at the BDY website.) Note the palm trees dotted around it, the expansive lawns, and those tennis courts discretely in the background. For an American official not likely to leave the constricted, heavily fortified, four-mile square Green Zone during a year's tour of duty, practicing his or her serve (on the taxpayer's dollar) would undoubtedly be no small thing.

Admittedly, it became harder to think about taking that refreshing dip or catching a few sets of tennis in Baghdad's heat once the order for all U.S. personnel in the Green Zone to wear flak jackets and helmets at all times went into effect. Lucky then for the massive, largely window-less-looking Recreation Center, one of more than twenty blast-resistant buildings BDY planned for. Perhaps this will house the promised embassy cinema. Perhaps hours will be wiled away in the no less massive-looking, low-slung Post Exchange/Community Center, or in the promised commissary, the "retail and shopping areas," the restaurants, or even, so the BDY website assured visitors, the "schools" (though it's difficult to imagine the State Department allowing children at this particular post).

And don't forget the "fire station" (mentioned but not shown by BDY), surely so handy once the first rockets hit. Small warning: If you are among the officials staffing this post, keep in mind that the PX and commissary might be slightly understocked. The *Washington Post* reported at one point in 2007 that "virtually every bite and sip consumed [in the embassy] is imported from the United States, entering Iraq via Kuwait in huge truck convoys that bring fresh and processed food, including a full range of Baskin-Robbins ice cream flavors, every seven to 10 days."

When you look at the plans for the complex, you have to wonder: Can it, in any meaningful sense, be considered an embassy? And if so, an embassy to whom? The *Guardian*'s Jonathan Freedland more aptly termed it a "base," like our other vast, multibillion-dollar permanent bases in Iraq. It is also a headquarters. It is neither town, nor quite city-state, but it could be considered a citadel, with its own anti-missile defenses, inside the breachable citadel of the Green Zone. It may already be the last piece of ground (excepting those other bases) that the United States, surge or no, can actually claim to fully occupy and control in Iraq—and yet it already has something of the look of the Alamo (but with amenities). Someday, perhaps, it will turn out to be the "White House" (though, in BDY's sketches, its buildings look more like those prison-style schools being constructed in embattled American urban neighborhoods) for the radical cleric Moqtada al-Sadr, or some future Shiite party, or even a Sunni strongman.

What we know is that such an embassy is remarkably outsized for Iraq. Even as a headquarters for a vast, secret set of operations, it doesn't quite add up. After all, our military headquarters in Iraq are at Camp Victory, on the outskirts of Baghdad. We can certainly assume—though no one in our mainstream media world would think to say such a thing—that this new embassy will house a rousing set of CIA (and probably Pentagon) intelligence operations for the country and region, and will be a massive hive for American spooks of all sorts. But whatever its specific functions, it might best be described as the imperial Mother Ship dropping into Baghdad.

As an outpost, the vast compound reeks of one thing: imperial impunity. It was never meant to be an embassy from a democracy that had liberated an oppressed land. From the first thought, the first sketch, it was to be the sort of imperial control center suitable for the planet's sole "hyperpower," dropped into the middle of the oil heartlands of the globe. It was to be Washington's dream and Kansas City's idea of a palace fit for an embattled American proconsul—or a khan.

Completed, it will indeed be the perfect folly, as well as the perfect embassy, for a country that finds it absolutely normal to build vast base-worlds across the planet; that considers it just a regular day's work to send its aircraft carrier "strike forces" and various battleships through the Straits of Hormuz in daylight as a visible warning to a "neighboring" regional power; whose Central Intelligence Agency operatives feel free to organize and launch Baluchi tribal warriors from Pakistan into the Baluchi areas of Iran to commit acts of terror and mayhem; whose commander-in-chief president can sign a "nonlethal presidential finding" that commits our nation to a "soft power" version of the economic destabilization of Iran, involving, according to ABC News, "a coordinated campaign of propaganda, disinformation and manipulation of Iran's currency and international financial transactions"; whose vice president can appear on the deck of the USS *John C. Stennis* to address a "rally for the troops," while that aircraft carrier is on station in the Persian Gulf, readying itself to pass through those Straits, and can insist to the world: "With two carrier strike groups in the Gulf, we're sending clear messages to friends and adversaries alike. We'll keep the sea lanes open. We'll stand with our friends in opposing extremism and strategic threats. We'll disrupt attacks on our own forces.... And we'll stand with others to prevent Iran from gaining nuclear weapons and dominating this region"; whose military men can refer to Iraqi insurgents as "anti-Iraqi forces"; members of whose Congress can offer plans for the dismemberment of Iraq into three or more parts; and all of whose movers and shakers, participating in the Washington consensus, can agree that one "benchmark" the Iraqi government, also locked inside the Green Zone, must fulfill is signing off on an oil law designed in Washington and meant to turn the energy clock in the Middle East back several decades.

To recognize such imperial impunity and its symbols for what they are, all you really need to do is try to reverse any of these examples. In most cases, that's essentially inconceivable. Imagine any country building the equivalent Mother Ship "embassy" on the equivalent of two-thirds of the Washington Mall; or sailing its warships into the Gulf of Mexico and putting its second-in-command aboard the flagship of the fleet to insist on keeping the sea lanes "open"; or sending Caribbean terrorists into Florida to blow up local buses and police stations; or signing a "finding" to economically destabilize the American government; or planning the future shape of our country from a foreign capital. But you get the idea. Most of these actions, if aimed against the United States, would be treated as tantamount to acts of war, and dealt with accordingly, with unbelievable hue and cry.

When it's a matter of other countries halfway across the planet, however, we largely consider such things, even if revealed in the news, at worst as tactical errors or miscalculations. The imperial mindset goes deep. It also thinks unbearably well of itself and so, naturally, wants to memori-

alize itself, to give itself the surroundings that only the great, the super,
the hyper deserve.

Percy Bysshe Shelley's poem "Ozymandias," inspired by the arrival
in London in 1816 of an enormous statue of the Pharaoh Ramesses II,
comes to mind:

> I met a traveler from an antique land
> Who said:—Two vast and trunkless legs of stone
> Stand in the desert. Near them, on the sand,
> Half sunk a shattered visage lies, whose frown,
> And wrinkled lip, and sneer of cold command,
> Tell that its sculptor well those passions read
> Which yet survive, stamped on these lifeless things,
> The hand that mocked them and the heart that fed.
> And on the pedestal, these words appear:
> "My name is Ozymandias, King of Kings,
> Look on my works, ye mighty, and despair!"
> Nothing beside remains. Round the decay
> Of that colossal Wreck, boundless and bare,
> The lone and level sands stretch far away.

In Baghdad, Saddam Hussein's giant hands are already on the road
to ruin. In New York and Baghdad, our near billion-dollar monuments
to our imperial moment: a 9/11 memorial, as yet unbuilt, so grotesquely
expensive that, when completed, it will be a reminder only of a time, already long past, when we could imagine ourselves as the greatest victims
on the planet, and in Baghdad's Green Zone, a monument to Washington's conviction that we were also destined to be the greatest dominators
this world, and history, had ever seen.

From both of these monuments, someday those lone and level sands
will undoubtedly stretch far, far away.

How to Garrison a Planet (and Not Even Notice)

In the course of any year, there must be relatively few countries on
which U.S. soldiers do not set foot, whether with guns blazing, "humanitarian aid" in hand, or just for a friendly visit. In a startling number of

them, our soldiers not only arrive, but stay interminably, if not indefinitely. Sometimes they live on military bases built to the tune of billions
of dollars that are comparable to sizeable American towns (with accompanying amenities), sometimes on stripped-down forward operating
bases that may not even have showers. When those troops don't stay,
often American equipment does—carefully stored for further use at tiny
"cooperative security locations."

At the height of the Roman Empire, the Romans had an estimated
thirty-seven major military bases scattered around their dominions. At
the height of the British Empire, the British had thirty-six of them planet
wide. Depending on just who you listen to and how you count, we have
hundreds of bases. According to Pentagon records, in fact, there are 761
active military "sites" abroad.

The fact is: We garrison the planet north to south, east to west, and
even on the seven seas, thanks to our various fleets and our massive aircraft carriers which, with five thousand to six thousand personnel
aboard—that is, the population of an American town—are functionally
floating bases.

And here's the other half of that simple truth: We don't care to know
about it. We, the American people, aided and abetted by our politicians,
the Pentagon, and the mainstream media, are knee-deep in base denial.

Let's face it, we're on an imperial bender—and it's been a long, long
night. Even now, in the wee hours, the Pentagon continues its massive
expansion of recent years; we spend militarily as if there were no tomorrow; we're still building bases as if the world were our oyster; and we're
still in denial. Someone should phone the imperial equivalent of Alco-
holics Anonymous.

But let's start in a sunnier time, less than two decades ago, when it
seemed that there would be many tomorrows, all painted red, white, and
blue. Remember the 1990s, when the United States was hailed—or perhaps more accurately, Washington hailed itself—not just as the planet's
"sole superpower" or even its unique "hyperpower," but as its "global policeman," the only cop on the block? As it happened, our leaders took that
label seriously and our central police headquarters, that famed five-sided
building in Washington, D.C., promptly began dropping police stations—

also known as military bases—in or near the energy centers of the planet (Kosovo, Saudi Arabia, Qatar, Kuwait) after successful wars in the former Yugoslavia and the Persian Gulf.

As those bases multiplied, it seemed that we were embarking on a new, post-Soviet version of "containment." With the USSR gone, however, what we were containing grew a lot vaguer and, before 9/11, no one spoke its name. Nonetheless, it was, in essence, Muslims who happened to live on so many of the key oil lands of the planet.

Yes, for a while we also kept intact our old bases from our triumphant mega-war against Japan and Germany, and the stalemated "police action" in South Korea (1950–1953), vast structures that added up to something like an all-military American version of the old British Raj. According to the Pentagon, we still have a total of 124 bases in Japan, up to 38 on the small island of Okinawa, and 87 in South Korea. (Of course, there were setbacks. The giant bases we built in South Vietnam were lost in 1975, and we were peaceably ejected from our major bases in the Philippines in 1992.)

But imagine the hubris involved in the idea of being "global policeman" or "sheriff" and marching into a Dodge City that was nothing less than planet Earth. Naturally, with a whole passel of bad guys out there, a global "swamp" to be "drained," we armed ourselves to kill, not stun. And the police stations…well, they were often something to behold—and they still are.

Let's start with the basics: Almost seventy years after World War II, the sun is still incapable of setting on the American "empire of bases"—in Chalmers Johnson's phrase—which at this moment stretches from Australia to Italy, Japan to Qatar, Iraq to Colombia, Greenland to the Indian Ocean island of Diego Garcia, Romania to Djibouti. And new bases of various kinds are going up all the time (always with rumors of more to come).

There are 194 countries on the planet (more or less), and officially 39 are home to U.S. "facilities." But those are only the bases the Pentagon publicly acknowledges. Others simply aren't counted, either because, as in the case of Jordan, a country finds it politically preferable not to acknowledge such bases; or, as in the case of Pakistan, the American mili-

tary shares bases that are officially Pakistani. Bases in war zones, no matter how elaborate, somehow don't count either, including the approximately three hundred the United States built in Iraq, ranging from tiny
outposts to mega-bases like Balad Air Base and the ill-named Camp Victory, that house tens of thousands of troops, private contractors, Defense
Department civilians, and have bus routes, traffic lights, PXes, big-name
fast-food franchises, and so on.

Some of these bases are, in effect, "American towns" on foreign soil.
In Afghanistan, Bagram Air Base, previously used by the Soviets in their
occupation of the country, is the largest and best known. There are, however, many more, large and small, including Kandahar Airfield, located
in what was once the unofficial capital of the Taliban, which even has a
hockey rink (evidently for its Canadian contingent of troops). You would
think that all of this would be genuine news, that the establishment of
new bases would regularly generate significant news stories, that books
by the score would pour out on America's version of imperial control.
But here's the strange thing: We garrison the globe in ways that really
are—not to put too fine a point on it—unprecedented, and yet, if you
happen to live in the United States, you basically wouldn't know it; or,
thought about another way, you wouldn't have to know it.

In Washington, our garrisoning of the world is so taken for granted
that no one seems to blink when billions go into a new base in some exotic, embattled, war-torn land. There's no discussion, no debate at all.
And yet there may be no foreign-policy subject more deserving of coverage. It has always been obvious—to me, at least—that any discussion
of Iraq policy, of timelines or "time horizons," drawdowns or withdrawals, made little sense if those giant *facts on the ground* weren't taken
into account. And yet you have to search the U.S. press carefully to find
any reporting on the subject, nor have bases played any real role in debates in Washington or the nation over Iraq policy.

Of course, millions of Americans know about our bases abroad firsthand. In this sense, they may be the least well-kept secrets on the planet.
American troops, private contractors, and Defense Department civilian
employees all have spent extended periods of time on at least one U.S.
base abroad. And yet no one seems to notice the near news blackout on

our global bases or consider it the least bit strange. In the United States, military bases really only matter, and so make headlines, when the Pentagon attempts to close some of the vast numbers of them scattered across this country. Then, the fear of lost jobs and lost income in local communities leads to headlines and hubbub.

In purely practical terms, though, Americans are unlikely to be able to shoulder forever the massive global role the Pentagon and successive administrations have laid out for us. Sooner or later, cutbacks will come and the sun will slowly begin to set on our base-world abroad. In the meantime, occupying the planet, base by base, normally simply isn't news. Americans may pay no attention—and yet, of course, they do pay an enormous price.

THREE

Air War, Barbarity, and Collateral Damage

Icarus (Armed with Vipers) Over Iraq

The human imagination is quicker off the mark than any six-gun, bomb, or missile. Long before humans made it into airplanes, whole cities were being destroyed from the air—in an avalanche of popular fiction. By the late nineteenth century, London had gone down in flames more than once and New York soon would follow. Genocidal wars from the air were repeatedly imagined and described in which whole nations, whole races, were wiped out. In 1914, more than three decades before the first atomic bomb was dropped, H. G. Wells had already imagined and named "atomic weapons" in *The World Set Free*, his novel about a future atomic air war.

When it came to fantasies and fears of destruction, we knew no bounds. As the scholar Spencer Weart has written in *Nuclear Fear: A History of Images*:

> Right from the start [the] new idea of atomic weapons was linked to an even more impressive idea: the end of the world. When [scientist Frederick] Soddy first told the public about atomic energy, in May 1903, he said that our planet is "a storehouse stuffed with explosives, inconceivably more powerful than any we know of, and possibly only awaiting a suitable detonator to cause the earth to revert to chaos." This was an entirely new idea: that it might be technically possible for

someone to destroy the world deliberately. Yet the idea slipped into the public mind with suspicious ease…. For example, in 1903 the irrepressible Gustave Le Bon got into newspaper Sunday supplements in various countries by imagining a radioactive device that could "blow up the whole earth" at the touch of a button.

In fact, for almost half a century before 1945, such weapons were the property only of science fiction. In his magisterial *The Rise of American Air Power*, Michael Sherry offers this comment on the machine that delivered the first of those atomic devices of our imagination to a real city: "More than any other modern weapon, the bomber was imagined before it was invented." Should we be amazed or horrified, proud or ashamed to have so actively imagined a century or more of future horrors of our own making? The imagination worked so quickly, but at least as miraculous was how quickly the inventors and the scientists followed.

I doubt that any invention other than the airplane has so combined the wonder of creation, of defiance of obvious human limits, and of destruction so intimately and for so long. Now, it seems, the wonder and even the horror of airpower is largely gone, but the inventions, the destruction, and the carnage remain.

The odd thing is this: No sooner had we human beings risen above the earth in powered flight—think Icarus—than we expressed the wonder of that event by dropping bombs from the planes that took us into the heavens. After that, it was just a straight line up (or down?) for the next near century.

Look at it this way: The Wright Brothers' "whopper flying machine" leaves the beach at Kitty Hawk for the first time on December 17, 1903. That initial flight lasts all of 12 seconds before the plane hits the sand 120 feet away. Later the same day, the plane flies 859 feet in 59 seconds before, on a final flight, it totals itself and is no more. Only five years later, the Wright Brothers are demonstrating their new invention in the skies over Washington for the U.S. Army Signal Corps. By 1911, the plane is wedded to the bomb. According to Sven Lindqvist's *A History of Bombing*, one Lieutenant Giulio Cavotti "leaned out of his delicate monoplane and dropped the bomb—a Danish Haasen hand grenade—on the North

African oasis Tagiura, near Tripoli. Several moments later, he attacked the oasis Ain Zara. Four bombs in total, each weighing two kilos, were dropped during this first air attack." On the "natives" in the colonies, naturally enough. What better place to test a new weapon? And that first attack, as perhaps befits our temperaments, was, Lindqvist tells us, for revenge, a kind of collective punishment called down upon Arabs who had successfully resisted the advanced rationality (and occupying spirit) of the Italian army. Given where we've ended up, it would be perfectly reasonable to consider this moment the beginning of modern history, even of modernism itself.

A generation, no more, from Kitty Hawk to thousand-bomber raids over Germany. Another from the atomic bombing of Hiroshima to "shock and awe" in Iraq. No more than a blink of history's unseeing eye. Between 1911 and the end of the last bloody century, villages, towns, and cities across the earth were destroyed in copious numbers in part or in full by bombs. Their names could make up a modern chant: Chechaouen, Guernica, Shanghai, London, Coventry, Hamburg, Dresden, Tokyo, Hiroshima, Nagasaki, Damascus, Pyongyang, Haiphong, Grozny, Baghdad, and now Falluja among too many other places to name (including the colonial countryside of our planet from Kenya to Malaya). Millions and millions of tons of bombs dropped; millions and millions of dead, mostly, of course, civilians.

And from the Japanese and German cities of World War II to the devastated Korean peninsula of the early 1950s, from the ravaged southern Vietnamese countryside of the late 1960s to the "highway of death" on which much of a fleeing Iraqi army was destroyed in the First Gulf War of 1991, airpower has been America's signature way of war.

Think of the history of the development of the plane and of bombing as a giant, extremely top-heavy diamond. In 1903, one fragile plane flies 120 feet. In 1911, another only slightly less fragile plane drops a bomb. In 1945, vast air armadas take off to devastate chosen German and Japanese cities. On August 6, 1945, all the power of those armadas is compacted into the belly of the *Enola Gay*, a lone B-29, which drops its single bomb on Hiroshima, destroying the city and so many of its inhabitants. Remarkably, the man who commanded the U.S. Army Air

Forces, both the armadas and the *Enola Gay*, General Henry "Hap" Arnold (according to Robin Neillands in *The Bomber War: The Allied Air Offensive Against Nazi Germany*), "had been taught to fly by none other than Orville Wright, one of the two men credited with inventing the first viable airplane." Barely more than a generation took us from those 120 feet at Kitty Hawk to the *Enola Gay* and the destruction of one city from the air by one bomb.

Since 1945, both civilian plane flight and the killing of enormous numbers of civilians from the air (now subsumed in the term "collateral damage") have become completely normal parts of our lives. Too normal, it seems, to spend a lot of time thinking about or even writing fiction about. When we get on a plane now, we close the window shade and watch a movie on a tiny TV screen or, on certain flights, TV itself in real time, as if we were still in our living rooms. So much for either shock or awe. Today, American planes regularly bomb distant lands and no one even seems to notice. No one, not even reporters on the spot, bothers to comment. No one writes a significant word about it. Should we be amazed or horrified, proud or ashamed?

This is not to say the press does not write about the air war at all. Anodyne press reports on our ongoing air wars in Iraq, Afghanistan, and beyond appear almost daily. Normally, only a few lines are devoted to the air war against urban or rural areas, which is, by the nature of the situation, a war of terror. We almost never see any cumulative figures on air strikes in Iraq or Afghanistan per day, week, or month, maps of the reach of the air war, or more than a few photos of its results—let alone what it's been like for people in major cities and rural villages to experience such periodic attacks, or what kinds of casualties result (or who the casualties actually are), or what, if any, may be the limitations on the use of airpower.

To the extent that we know anything about the loosing of airpower on heavily populated urban areas, we only know what an uninquisitive press has been told by the military and stenographically recorded, which means we know remarkably little. During the war in Iraq, American reporters could be found embedded with tank or Bradley Fighting Vehicle units: "Captain Paul Fowler sat on the curb next to a deserted gas station," wrote Anne Barnard of the *Boston Globe*.

Behind him, smoke rose over Fallujah. His company of tanks and Bradley Fighting Vehicles had roamed the eastern third of the city for 13 days, shooting holes in every building that might pose a threat, leaving behind a landscape of half-collapsed houses and factories singed with soot.

"I really hate that it had to be destroyed. But that was the only way to root these guys out," said Fowler, 33, the son of a Baptist preacher in North Carolina. "The only way to root them out is to destroy everything in your path."

American reporters could climb aboard SURCs (Small Unit Riverine Craft), high-tech Swift Boat equivalents, as John Burns of the *New York Times* once did, to "[roar] up the Euphrates on a dawn raid." They could follow U.S. patrols as they busted down Iraqi doors looking for insurgents. The only thing they evidently couldn't do in Iraq was look up, even though the air space was populated with all kinds of jets, fearsome AC-130 Spectre gunships, Hellfire-missile-armed Predator drones, and ubiquitous Apache, Cobra, Lynx, and Puma helicopters.

On Not Looking Up

Given the history of twentieth-century war, which is, in many ways, simply the history of bombing cities, should our "war reporters" not have been prepared? Shouldn't anyone have been thinking about the destruction of cities when it's been such a commonplace? Shouldn't major papers have insisted on embedding reporters in Air Force units (if not on the planes themselves)? Shouldn't reporters have visited our air bases and talked to pilots? Does no one remember the magnitude of the air war in Vietnam (or Laos or Cambodia), no less any other major war experience of our lifetimes?

A glance at the history of American war tells us airpower is as American as apple pie and that Americans were dreaming of cities destroyed from the air long before anyone had the ability to do so. As H. Bruce Franklin tells us in his book *War Stars: The Superweapon and the American Imagination*, as early as 1881, former naval officer Park Benjamin wrote a short story called "The End of New York" that caused a sensation. In it the city was left in ruins by a Spanish naval bombardment. By 1921, air-power visionary Billy Mitchell was already flying mock sorties over New York and other East Coast cities, "pulverizing" them in "raids" sensationalized in the press, to publicize the need for an independent air force. ("The sun rose today on a city whose tallest tower lay scattered in crumbled bits," began a *New York Herald* article after Mitchell's "raid" on New York City, a line that should still send small shudders through us all and remind us how much the sensational of the previous century has become the accepted of our world.)

It would seem hard to forget that the "invasion" of Iraq began from the air—as much a demonstration of power meant for viewers around the world as for Saddam Hussein and his followers. Who could forget those cameras strategically placed on the balconies of Baghdad hotels for the shock-and-awe *son-et-lumière* show—dramatic explosions in the night (only lacking a score to go with it). Does no one remember air force claims that airpower alone could win wars?

Is there some secret I'm missing here? Doesn't anyone find it strange that, back in 1995, our papers—from their front pages to their editorial and op-ed pages—were convulsed by a single contested air-war exhibit being mounted at the Smithsonian National Air and Space Museum on the bombing of Hiroshima? A historical argument about the use of air power half a century ago merited such treatment, but the actual—and potentially hardly less controversial—use of airpower today doesn't merit a peep?

Near the end of 2004, I could find but a single press example of an American reporter in the air in Iraq. On November 17, 2003, the *New York Times*' Dexter Filkins wrote an article focusing on the dangers to American pilots in the Iraqi skies ("It is not a good time to be a helicopter pilot in the skies over Iraq"). That, as far as I can tell, is it. Now, it's true that any air war is harder to report on than a ground war, especially if reporters aren't allowed in planes or on helicopters (as they are on the river boats and in the Bradleys, for instance). But hardly impossible. Most reporters in Baghdad, after all, have at least been witnesses to air attacks in the capital itself. In one case, an American helicopter even fired a missile into a crowd in a Baghdad street only a few hundred yards from the heavily fortified American heartland, the capital's Green Zone, killing a reporter for al Arabiya satellite network in footage seen only briefly on American TV but repeatedly around the world.

Life under the helicopters is a story that might be written. At the very least, the subject could be investigated. Pilots could be interviewed on the ground. Victims could be found. The literature could be read because, as it happens, air force people are thinking carefully about the uses of airpower in a counterinsurgency war, even if reporters aren't. Journalists could, for instance, read Thomas F. Searle's article "Making Air Power Effective Against Guerrillas." (If I can find it, they can.) Searle, a military defense analyst with the Airpower Research Institute at Maxwell Air Force Base in Alabama, concludes:

> Airpower remains the single greatest asymmetrical advantage the United States has over its foes. However, by focusing on the demands of major combat and ignoring counterguerrilla warfare, we Airmen have marginalized ourselves in the global war on terrorism. To make airpower truly effective against guerrillas in that war, we cannot wait for the joint force commander or the ground component commander to tell us what to do. Rather, we must aggressively develop and employ airpower's counterguerrilla capabilities.

Journalists could report on the new airborne weaponry being deployed and tested by U.S. forces. After all, like other recent American battlefields, Iraq has doubled as a laboratory for the corporate development and testing of ever more advanced weaponry. A piece, for instance, could be done on the armed Unmanned Aerial Vehicle (UAV), the Hunter, being deployed alongside the Predator in Iraq. (The people who name these things have certainly seen too many sci-fi movies.) In a piece in *Defense Daily*, a "trade" publication, we read, for example:

> The Army in Iraq is poised to start operations using an unmanned aerial vehicle (UAV) armed with a precision weapon, Northrop Grumman's [NOC] Viper Strike munition, a service official said…. The Army is arming the Israel Aircraft Industries (IAI)–Northrop Grumman [NOC] Hunter UAV, under an approximately $4 million Quick Reaction Capability contract with Northrop Grumman that will be completed in December, John Miller, Northrop Grumman director of Viper Strike, told *Defense Daily*…. The Hunter can carry two Viper Strike missiles.

The Hunter UAV has been used in Iraq "since day one," [Lt. Col. Jeff] Gabbert [program manager of Medium Altitude Endurance] said. The precise Viper Strike munition is important because, "it has very low collateral damage, so it's going to be able to be employed in places where you might not use 500-pound bombs or might not use a Hellfire munition, [but] you'll be able to use the Viper Strike munition."

Of course, it would be a reportorial coup if any reporter were to go up in a plane or helicopter and survey the urban damage in Iraq, for example, as Jonathan Schell did from the back seat of a small forward air controller's plane during the Vietnam War. (From this he wrote a report for the *New Yorker* magazine, "The Military Half," which remains unparalleled in its graphic descriptions of the destruction of the Vietnamese countryside and which can be found collected in his book *The Real War*.)

But that's a lot to hope for these days. The complete absence of coverage, however, is a little harder to explain. Along with the vast permanent military base facilities the United States has been building in Iraq, the expansion of U.S. airpower is the great missing story of the post-9/11 era. Is there no reporter out there willing to cover it? Is the repeated bombing, strafing, and missiling of heavily populated civilian urban centers and the partial or total destruction of cities such a humdrum event, after the last century of destruction and threatened destruction, that no one thinks it worth the bother?

The Barbarism of War from the Air

Barbarism seems an obvious enough category. Ordinarily in our world, the barbarians are them. *They* act in ways that seem unimaginably primitive and brutal to us. For instance, they kidnap or capture someone, American or Iraqi, and cut off his head. Now, isn't that the definition of barbaric? Who does that anymore? The word *medieval* comes to mind immediately, and to the mass mind of our media even faster.

To jump a little closer to modernity, *they* strap on grenades, plastic explosives, bombs of various ingenious sorts fashioned in home labs, with nails or other bits of sharp metal added in to create instant shrapnel meant to rend human flesh, to maim, and kill. Then they approach a target—an

Israeli bus filled with civilians and perhaps some soldiers, a pizza parlor in Jerusalem, a gathering of Shiite or Sunni worshippers at or near a mosque in Iraq or Pakistan, or of unemployed potential police or army recruits in Ramadi or Baghdad, or of shoppers in an Iraqi market, or perhaps a foreigner on the streets of Kabul—and they blow themselves up. Or they arm backpacks or bags and step onto trains in London, Madrid, Mumbai, and set them off.

Or, to up the technology and modernity a bit, they wire a car to explode, put a jihadist in the driver's seat, and drive it into—well, this is now common enough that you can pick your target. Or perhaps they audaciously hijack four just-fueled jets filled with passengers and run two of them into the World Trade Center, one into the Pentagon, and another into a field in Pennsylvania. This is, of course, the very definition of barbaric.

Now, let's jump a step further into our age of technological destruction, becoming less face to face, more impersonal, without, in the end, changing things that much. *They* send rockets from southern Lebanon (or even cruder ones from the Gaza Strip) against Israeli towns and cities. These rockets can only vaguely be aimed. Some can be brought into the general vicinity of an inhabited area; others, more advanced, into specific urban neighborhoods many tens of miles away—and then they detonate, killing whoever is in the vicinity, which normally means civilians just living their lives, even, in one Hezbollah volley aimed at Nazareth, two Israeli Arab children. In this process, thousands of Israelis have been temporarily driven from their homes.

In the case of rockets by the hundreds lofted into Israel by an armed, organized militia, meant to terrorize and harm civilian populations, these are undoubtedly war crimes. Above all, they represent a kind of barbarism that—with the possible exception of some of those advanced Hezbollah rockets—feels primitive to us. Despite the explosives, cars, planes, all so basic to our modern way of life, such acts still seem redolent of less civilized times when people did especially cruel things to each other face to face.

The Religion of Airpower

That's *them*. But what about us? On our we/they planet, most groups don't consider themselves barbarians. Nonetheless, we have largely achieved non-barbaric status in an interesting way—by removing the most essential aspect of the American (and Israeli) way of war from the category of the barbaric. I'm talking, of course, about airpower, about raining destruction down on the earth from the skies, and about the belief—so common, so long-lasting, so deep-seated—that bombing others, including civilian populations, is a "strategic" thing to do, that airpower can, in relatively swift measure, break the "will" not just of the enemy, but of that enemy's society, and that such a way of war is the royal path to victory.

This set of beliefs was common to airpower advocates even before modern air war had been tested, and repeated unsuccessful attempts to put these convictions into practice have never really shaken what is essentially a war-making religion. The result has been the development of the most barbaric style of warfare imaginable, one that has seldom succeeded in breaking *any* will, though it has destroyed innumerable bodies, lives, stretches of countryside, villages, towns, and cities.

Even during the 2006 Lebanon War, Israeli military strategists were saying things that could have been put in the mouths of their airpower-loving predecessors decades ago. The *New York Times'* Steven Erlanger, for instance, quoted an unnamed senior Israeli commander this way: "He predicted that Israel would stick largely to air power for now…. 'The problem is the will to launch. We have to break the will of Hezbollah.'" Don't hold your breath is the first lesson history teaches on this particular assessment of the powers of air war. The second is that, a decade from now, some other senior commander in some other country will be saying the same thing, word for word.

When it comes to brutality, the fact is that ancient times have gotten a bad rap. Nothing in history was more brutal than the last century's style of war making—than those two world wars with their air armadas, backed by the most advanced industrial systems on the planet. Powerful countries then bent every elbow, every brain, to support the destruction of other human beings en masse, not to speak of the Holocaust (which was assembly-line warfare in another form), and the various colonial and cold war campaigns that substituted the devastation of airpower in the third world for a war between the two superpowers that might have employed the mightiest air weaponry of all to scour the earth.

It may be that the human capacity for brutality, for barbarism, hasn't changed much since the eighth century, but the industrial revolution—and in particular the rise of the airplane—opened up new landscapes to brutality. The view from behind the gun sight, then the bomb sight, and finally the missile sight slowly widened until all of humanity was taken in. From the lofty, godlike vantage point of the strategic, as well as the literal heavens, the military and the civilian began to blur on the ground. Soldiers and citizens, conscripts and refugees alike, became nothing but tiny, indistinguishable hordes of ants, or nothing at all but the structures that housed them, or even just concepts, indistinguishable one from the other.

One Plane, One Bomb

We have come far from that first bomb dropped by hand over the Italian colony of Libya. In the case of Tokyo—then constructed almost totally out of highly flammable materials—a single raid carrying incendiary bombs and napalm that began just after midnight on March 10, 1945, proved capable of incinerating or killing at least 90,000 people, possibly many more, from such a height that the dead could not be seen (though the stench of burning flesh carried up to the planes). The first American planes to arrive over the city, writes historian Michael Sherry, "carved out an X of flames across one of the world's most densely packed residential districts; followers fed and broadened it for some three hours thereafter."

What descended from the skies, as James Carroll recounts it in his book *House of War*, was "1,665 tons of pure fire…the most efficient and deliberate act of arson in history. The consequent firestorm obliterated fifteen square miles, which included both residential and industrial areas. Fires raged for four days." It was the bonfire of bonfires, and not a single American plane was shot down.

On August 6, 1945, all the power of that vast air armada was again reduced to a single bomb, "Little Boy," dropped near a single bridge in a single city, Hiroshima, which in a single moment of a sort never before experienced on the planet did what it had taken three hundred B-29s and many hours to do to Tokyo. In those two cities—as well as Dresden and other German and Japanese cities subjected to "strategic bombing"—the dead (perhaps 900,000 in Japan and 600,000 in Germany) were invariably preponderantly civilian, and far too distant to be seen by plane crews often dropping their bomb loads in the dark of night, giving the scene below the look of hell on earth.

So 1911: one plane, one bomb. 1945: one plane, one bomb—but this time at least 120,000 dead, possibly many more. Two bookmarks less than four decades apart on the first chapter of a history of the invention of a new kind of warfare, a new kind of barbarism that, by now, is the way we expect war to be made, a way that no longer strikes us as barbaric at all. This wasn't always the case.

The Shock of the New

When military airpower was in its infancy, and silent films still ruled the movie theaters, the first air-war films presented pilots as knights of the heavens, engaging in courageous, chivalric, one-on-one combat in the skies. As that image reflects, in the wake of the meat grinder of trench warfare in World War I, the medieval actually seemed far less brutal, a time much preferable to those years in which young men died by their hundreds of thousands, anonymously, from machine guns, artillery, poison gas, all the lovely inventions of industrial civilization, ground into the mud of no-man's-land, often without managing to move their lines or the enemy's more than a few hundred yards.

The image of chivalric knights in planes jousting in the skies slowly disappeared from American screens, as after the 1950s would, by and large, airpower itself, even as the war film went on (and on). It can last be found perhaps in the film *Top Gun*; in old Peanuts comics in which Snoopy imagines himself as the Red Baron; and, of course, post–*Star Wars*, in the fantasy realm of outer space, where Jedi Knights took up lethal sky-jousting in the late 1970s, X-wing fighter to X-wing fighter, and in zillions of video games to follow. In the meantime, the one-way air slaughter in South Vietnam would be largely left out of the burst of Vietnam films that started hitting the screen from the late 1970s on.

In the real, off-screen world, that courtly medieval image of airpower disappeared fast indeed. As World War II came ever closer, and it became more apparent what airpower was best at—what would now be called "collateral damage"—the shock set in. When civilians were first purposely targeted and bombed in the industrializing world rather than in colonies like Iraq, the act was widely condemned as inhuman by a startled world.

People were horrified when, during the Spanish Civil War in 1937, Hitler's Condor Legion and planes from fascist Italy repeatedly bombed the Basque town of Guernica, engulfing most of its buildings in a firestorm that killed hundreds, if not thousands, of civilians. If you want to get a sense of the power of that act to shock then, view Picasso's famous painting of protest done almost immediately in response. (When Secretary of State Colin Powell went to the United Nations in February 2003 to deliver his now infamous speech explaining what we supposedly knew about Saddam Hussein's weapons of mass destruction, UN officials covered over a tapestry of the painting that happened to be positioned where Powell would have to pass on his way to deliver his speech and where press comments would be offered afterwards.)

Later in 1937, as the Japanese began their campaign to conquer China, they bombed a number of Chinese cities. A single shot of a Chinese baby wailing amid the ruins, published in *Life* magazine, was enough to horrify Americans (even though the actual photo may have been doctored). Airpower was then seen as nothing but a new kind of barbarism. According to Sherry, "In 1937 and 1938, [President Roosevelt] had the State Department condemn Japanese bombing of civilians in China as 'barbarous' violations of the 'elementary principles' of modern morality." Meanwhile, observers checking out what effect the bombing of civilians had on the "will" of society offered nothing but bad news to the strategists of airpower. As Sherry writes,

> In the *Saturday Evening Post*, an American army officer observed that bombing had proven "disappointing to the theorists of peacetime." When Franco's rebels bombed Madrid, "Did the Madrileños sue for peace? No, they shook futile fists at the murderers in the sky and muttered, 'Swine.'" His conclusion: "Terrorism from the air has been tried and found wanting. Bombing, far from softening the civil will, hardens it."

Today, however, terms like "barbarism" and "terrorism" are unlikely to be applied to Israel's war from the heavens over Lebanon, or ours over Iraq and Afghanistan. *New York Times* correspondent Sabrina Tavernise, for instance, reported the following from the site of an apartment building destroyed by an Israeli airstrike in the bomb-shocked southern Lebanese port of Tyre in July 2006:

> Whatever the target, the result was an emotional outpouring in support of Hezbollah. Standing near a cluster of dangling electrical wires, a group of men began to chant. "By our blood and our soul, we'll fight for you, Nasrallah!" they said, referring to Hezbollah's leader, Sheik Hassan Nasrallah. In a foggy double image, another small group chanted the same thing, as if answering, on the other side of the smoke.

World War II began with the German bombing of Warsaw. On September 9, 1939, according to Carroll, President Roosevelt "beseeched the war leaders on both sides to 'under no circumstances undertake the bombardment from the air of civilian populations or of unfortified cities.'" Then came the terror-bombing of Rotterdam and Hitler's blitz against England, in which tens of thousands of British civilians died and many more were displaced, each event proving but another systemic shock to what was left of global opinion, another unimaginable act by the planet's reigning barbarians.

British civilians still retain a deserved reputation for the stiff-upper-lip-style bravery with which they comported themselves in the face of a merciless German air offensive against their cities. No wills were broken there, nor would they be in Russia (where, in 1942, perhaps forty thousand were killed in German air attacks on the city of Stalingrad alone), any more than they would be in Germany by the far more massive Allied air offensive against the German population.

All of this, of course, came before it was clear that the United States could design and churn out planes faster, in greater numbers, and with more firepower than any country on the planet and then wield airpower far more massively and brutally than anyone had previously been capable of doing. That was before the United States and Britain decided to fight fire with fire by blitz- and terror-bombing Germany and Japan. (The U.S. military moved more slowly and awkwardly than the British from "precision bombing" against targets like factories producing military equipment or oil-storage depots—campaigns that largely failed—to "area bombing" that was simply meant to annihilate vast numbers of civilians and destroy cities. But move American strategists did.) That was before Dresden and Hiroshima; before Pyongyang, along with much of the Korean peninsula, was reduced to rubble from the air in the Korean War; before the Plain of Jars was bombed back to the Stone Age in Laos in the late 1960s and early 1970s; before the B-52s were sent against the cities of Hanoi and Haiphong in the terror-bombing of Christmas 1972 to wring concessions out of the North Vietnamese at the peace table in Paris; before the First President Bush ended the First Gulf War with a "turkey shoot" on the "highway of death" as Saddam Hussein's largely conscript military fled Kuwait City in whatever vehicles were at hand; before we bombed the rubble in Afghanistan into further rubble in 2001; and before we shock-and-awed Baghdad in 2003.

Taking the Sting out of Air War

Somewhere in this process, a new language to describe air war began to develop—after, in the Vietnam era, the first "smart bombs" and "precision-guided weapons" came on line. From then on, air attacks would, for instance, be termed "surgical" and civilian casualties dismissed as "collateral damage." All of this helped removed the sting of barbarity from the form of war we had chosen to make our own (unless, of course, you happened to be one of those "collateral" people under those "surgical" strikes). Just consider, for a moment, that, with the advent of the First Gulf War, airpower—as it was being applied—essentially became entertainment, a Disney-style spectacular over Baghdad to be watched in real time on television by a population of noncombatants from thousands of miles away.

With that same war, the Pentagon started calling press briefings and screening nose-cone photography, essentially little Iraqi snuff films, in which you actually looked through the precision-guided bomb or missile sights yourself, found your target, and followed that missile or "smart bomb" right down to its explosive impact. If you were lucky, the Pentagon even let you check out the after-mission damage assessments. These films were so nifty, so like the high-tech video-game experience just then coming into being, that they were used by the Pentagon as reputation enhancers. From then on, Pentagon officials not only described their air weaponry as "surgical" in its abilities, but showed you the "surgery" (just as the Israelis did with their footage of "precision" attacks in Lebanon). What you didn't see, of course, was the "collateral damage."

And yet this new form of air war had managed to move far indeed from the image of the knightly joust, from the sense, in fact, of battle at all. In those years, except over the far north of Korea during the Korean War or over North Vietnam and some parts of South Vietnam, American pilots, unless in helicopters, went into action knowing that the dangers to them were usually minimal—or nonexistent. War from the air was in the process of becoming a one-way street of destruction.

At an extreme, with the arrival of fleets of Hellfire-missile-armed unmanned Predator drones over Iraq, the "warrior" suddenly found himself seven thousand miles away, delivering "precision" strikes that almost always, somehow, manage to kill collaterally. In such cases, war and screen war have indeed merged.

This kind of war has the allure, from a military point of view, of ever fewer casualties on one end in return for ever more on the other. It must also instill a feeling of bloodless, godlike control over those enemy "ants" (until, of course, things begin to go wrong, as they always do), as well as a sense that the world can truly be "remade" from the air, by remote control, and at a great remove. This has to be a powerful, even a transporting fantasy for strategists, however regularly it may be denied by history.

Despite the cleansed language of air war, and no matter how good the targeting intelligence or smart the bomb (neither of which can be counted on), civilians who make the mistake of simply being alive and going about their daily business die in profusion whenever war descends from the heavens. This is the deepest reality of war today.

Afghanistan, Iraq, Lebanon...

In fact, the process of removing airpower from the ranks of the barbaric, of making it, if not glorious (as in those visually startling moments when Baghdad was shock-and-awed), then completely humdrum, and so of no note whatsoever, has been remarkably successful in our world. In fact, we have loosed our airpower regularly on the countryside of Afghanistan, and especially on rebellious urban areas of Iraq in "targeted" and "precise" attacks on insurgent concentrations and "al-Qaeda safe houses" (as well as in more wholesale assaults on the Old City of Najaf and on the city of Falluja) largely without comment or criticism. In the process, significant parts of two cities in a country we occupied and supposedly "liberated" were reduced to rubble, and everywhere, civilians, not to speak of whole wedding parties, were blown away without our media paying much attention at all.

Until, in December 2005, Seymour Hersh wrote a piece from Washington for the *New Yorker*, entitled "Up in the Air," our reporters had, with rare exceptions, simply refused to look up. Yet here is an air force summary of just a single, nondescript day of operations in Iraq in July 2006, one of hundreds and hundreds of such days, some far more intense, since we invaded that country: "In total, coalition aircraft flew 46 close-air support missions for Operation Iraqi Freedom. These missions included support to coalition troops, infrastructure protection, reconstruction activities and operations to deter and disrupt terrorist activities."

And here's the summary of the same day in Afghanistan: "In total, coalition aircraft flew 32 close-air support missions in support of Operation Enduring Freedom. These missions included support to coalition and Afghan troops, reconstruction activities and route patrols." Note that, in Afghanistan, as the situation began to worsen militarily and politically, the old Vietnam-era B-52s, the carpet-bombers of that war, were called back into action, again without significant attention here.

In summer 2006, using the highest-tech American precision-guided and bunker-busting bombs, Israel launched air strike after strike, thousands of them into Lebanon. They hit an international airport, the nation's largest milk factories, a major food factory, aid convoys, Red Cross ambulances, a UN observer post, a power plant, apartment complexes, villages (claiming that they housed or supported the enemy), branches of banks (because they might facilitate Hezbollah finances), the telecommunications system (because of the messages that might pass along it), highways (because they might transport weapons to the enemy), bridges (because they might be crossed by those transporting weapons), a lighthouse in Beirut harbor (for reasons unknown), trucks (because they might be transporting those weapons, though they might also be transporting vegetables), families who just happen to be jammed into cars or minivans fleeing at the urging of the attackers, who turned at least 20 percent of all Lebanese into refugees while creating a "landscape of death" (in the phrase of the superb reporter Anthony Shadid) in the southern part of that country. In this process, civilian casualties were widespread.

As the Israelis rediscovered—though, by now, you'd think that military planners with half a brain wouldn't have to destroy a country to do so—it is impossible to "surgically" separate a movement and its supporters from the air. When you try, you invariably do the opposite, fusing them ever more closely, while creating an even larger, ever angrier base for the movement whose essence is, in any case, never literal geography, never simply a set of villages or bunkers or military supplies to be taken and destroyed.

As air wars go, the one in Lebanon in 2006 was strikingly directed against the civilian infrastructure and against society; in that, however, it was historically anything but unique. It might even be said that war from the air, since first launched in Europe's colonies early in the last century, has always been essentially directed against civilians. Air power—no matter its stated targets—almost invariably turns out to be worst for civilians and, in the end, to be aimed at society itself. In that way, its damage is anything but "collateral," never truly "surgical," and never in its overall effect "precise." Even when it doesn't start that way, the frustration of not working as planned, of not breaking the "will," tends to lead, as with the Israelis in 2006, to ever wider, ever fiercer versions of the same, which, if allowed to proceed to their logical conclusion, will bring down not society's will, but society itself.

Lebanon's prime minister may have described Israel's actions as "barbaric destruction," but, in our world, airpower has long been robbed of its barbarism. For us, air war involves dumb hits by smart bombs, collateral damage, and surgery that may do in the patient, but somehow is not barbaric. For that, you need to personally cut off a head.

An Anatomy of Collateral Damage

In a little noted passage in her book *The Dark Side*, Jane Mayer offered us a vision, just post-9/11, of the value of one. In October 2001, shaken by a nerve gas false alarm at the White House, Vice President Dick Cheney, reported Mayer, went underground. He literally bunkered himself in "a secure, undisclosed location," which she described as "one of several Cold War–era nuclear-hardened subterranean bunkers built during the Truman and Eisenhower Administrations, the nearest of which were located hundreds of feet below bedrock." That bunker would be dubbed, perhaps only half-sardonically, "The Commander in Chief's Suite."

Oh, and in that period, if Cheney had to be in transit, "he was chauffeured in an armored motorcade that varied its route to foil possible attackers." In the backseat of his car (just in case), added Mayer, "rested a duffel bag stocked with a gas mask and a biochemical survival suit." And lest danger rear its head, "Rarely did he travel without a medical doctor in tow."

When it came to leadership in troubled times, this wasn't exactly a profile in courage. Perhaps it was closer to a profile in paranoia, or simply in fear, but whatever else it might have been, it was also a strange kind of statement of self-worth. Has any wartime *president*—forget the vice president—including Abraham Lincoln when Southern armies might have marched on Washington, or Franklin D. Roosevelt at the height of World War II, ever been so bizarrely overprotected in the nation's capital? Has any administration ever placed such value on the preservation of the life of a single official?

On the other hand, the well-armored vice president and his aide David Addington played a leading role, as Mayer documented in grim detail, in loosing a Global War on Terror that was also a global war *of* terror on lands thousands of miles distant. In this new war, "the gloves came off," "the shackles were removed"—images much beloved within the administration and, in the case of those "shackles," by George Tenet's CIA. In the process, no price in human abasement or human life proved too high to pay—as long as it was paid by someone else.

The Value of None

If no level of protection was too much for Dick Cheney, then no protection at all is what Washington offers civilians who happen to live in the ever expanding "war zones" of the planet. In the Middle East, in Somalia, in Pakistan, in Afghanistan, the war—in part from the air, sometimes via pilotless unmanned aerial vehicles or drones—is, in crucial ways, aimed at civilians (though this could never be admitted).

Civilians have few doctors on hand, much less full chemical body suits or gas masks, when disaster strikes. Often they are asleep, or going about their daily business, when death makes its appearance unannounced.

We have no idea just how many civilians have been blown away by the U.S. military (and allies) in recent years, only that the "collateral damage" has been widespread and far more central than anyone here generally cares to acknowledge. Collateral damage has come in myriad ways—from artillery fire in the initial invasion of Iraq; from repeated shootings of civilians in vehicles at checkpoints; from troops (or even private mercenaries) blasting away from convoys; during raids on private homes; in village operations; and, significantly, from the air.

In Afghanistan, air strikes increased tenfold from 2004 to 2007 alone. From 2006 to 2007, civilian deaths from those air strikes nearly tripled. According to Marc Garlasco, a former Pentagon official and military analyst at Human Rights Watch, 317,000 pounds of bombs were dropped in June and 270,000 in July 2008, equaling "the total tonnage dropped in 2006."

As with all figures relating to casualties, the actual counts you get on Afghan civilian dead are approximations and probably undercounts, especially since the war against the Taliban has been taking place largely in the backlands of one (or, if you count Pakistan, two) of the poorest, most remote regions on the planet. And yet we do know something. For instance, although the media have seldom attended to the subject, we know that one subset of innocent civilians has been slaughtered repeatedly. While Americans spent days in October 2006 riveted to TV screens following the murders of five Amish girls by a madman in a one-room schoolhouse in Pennsylvania, and weeks following the mass slaughter of thirty-two college students by a mad boy at Virginia Tech in April 2007, a number of Afghan wedding parties and at least one Iraqi wedding party were largely wiped out from the air by American planes to hardly any news coverage at all.

The message of these slaughters is that if you live in areas where the Taliban exists, which is now much of Afghanistan, you'd better not gather.

Each of these events was marked by something else—the uniformity of the U.S. response: initial claims that U.S. forces had been fired on first and that those killed were the enemy; a dismissal of the slaughters as the unavoidable "collateral damage" of wartime; and, above all, an unwillingness to genuinely apologize for, or take real responsibility for, having wiped out groups of celebrating locals.

And keep in mind that such disasters are just subsets of a far larger, barely covered story. In July 2008 alone, for example, the U.S. military and NATO officials launched investigations into three air strikes in Afghanistan (including one on a wedding party) in which seventy-eight Afghan civilians were killed.

Since the Afghan War began in 2001, such "incidents" have occurred again and again. The Global War on Terror is premised on an unspoken belief that the lives of others—civilians going about their business in distant lands—are essentially of no importance when placed against American needs and desires. That, you might say, is the value of none.

Incident in Azizabad

To take one example: on the night of August 21, 2008, a memorial service was held in Azizabad, a village in the Shindand District of Afghanistan's Herat Province, for a tribal leader killed the previous year, who had been, villagers reported, anti-Taliban. Hundreds had attended, including "extended families from two tribes."

That night, a combined party of U.S. Special Forces and Afghan army troops attacked the village. They claimed they were "ambushed" and came under "intense fire." What we know is that they called in repeated air strikes. According to several investigations and the on-the-spot reporting of *New York Times* journalist Carlotta Gall, at least ninety civilians, including perhaps fifteen women and up to sixty children, died that night. As many as seventy-six members of a single extended family were killed, along with its head, Reza Khan. His compound seems to have been specially targeted.

Khan, it turns out, was no Taliban "militant," but a "wealthy businessman with construction and security contracts with the nearby American base at Shindand airport." He reportedly had a private security company that worked for the U.S. military at the airport and also owned a cell phone business in the town of Herat. He had a card "issued by an American Special Forces officer that designated [him] as a 'coordinator for the U.S.S.F.'" Eight of the other men killed that night, according to Gall, worked as guards for a private American security firm. At least two dead men had served in the Afghan police and fought against the Taliban.

The incident in Azizabad represents one of the deadliest media-verified attacks on civilians by U.S. forces since the invasion of 2001. Numerous buildings were damaged. Many bodies, including those of children, had to be dug out of the rubble. There may have been as many as sixty children among the dead. The U.S. military evidently launched its attack after being given false information by another person in the area with a grudge against Khan and his brother. As one tribal elder, who helped bury the dead, put it: "It is quite obvious, the Americans bombed the area due to wrong information. I am 100 percent confident that someone gave the information due to a tribal dispute. The Americans are foreigners and they do not understand. These people they killed were enemies of the Taliban."

Repeated U.S. air attacks resulting in civilian deaths have proven a disaster for Afghan president Hamid Karzai. He promptly denounced the strikes against Azizabad, fired two Afghan commanders, including the top-ranking officer in western Afghanistan, for "negligence and concealing facts," and ordered his own investigation of the incident. His team of investigators concluded that more than ninety Afghan civilians had indeed died. Along with the Afghan Council of Ministers, Karzai also demanded a "review" of "the presence of international forces and agreements with foreign allies, including NATO and the United States."

Ahmad Nader Nadery, commissioner of the Afghanistan Independent Human Rights Commission, similarly reported that one of the group's researchers had "found that 88 people had been killed, including 20 women." The UN mission in Afghanistan then dispatched its own investigative team from Herat to interview survivors. Its investigation "found convincing evidence, based on the testimony of eyewitnesses, and others, that some 90 civilians were killed, including 60 children, 15 women and 15 men." (The 60 children were reportedly "3 months old to 16 years old, all killed as they slept.")

The American Response

Given the weight of evidence at Azizabad, the on-site investigations, the many graves, the destroyed houses, the specificity of survivor accounts, and so on, this might have seemed like a cut-and-dried case of mistaken intelligence followed by an errant assault with disastrous consequences. But accepting such a conclusion simply isn't in the playbook of the U.S. military.

Instead, in such cases what you regularly get is a predictable U.S. narrative about what happened made up of outlandish claims (or simply lies), followed by a strategy of stonewalling, including a blame-the-victims approach in which civilian deaths are regularly dismissed as enemy-inspired "propaganda," followed—if the pressure doesn't ease up—by the announcement of an "investigation" (whose results will rarely be released), followed by an expression of "regrets" or "sorrow" for the loss of life—both weasel words that can be uttered without taking actual responsibility for what happened—never to be followed by a genuine apology.

Now, let's consider the American response to Azizabad.

The numbers: Initially, the U.S. military flatly denied that any civilians had been killed in the village. In the operation, they claimed, exactly 30 Taliban "militants" had died. ("Insurgents engaged the soldiers from multiple points within the compound using small-arms and RPG [rocket-propelled grenade] fire. The joint forces responded with small-arms fire and an air strike killing 30 militants.")

Targeted, they said, had been a single compound holding a local Taliban commander, later identified as Mullah Sadiq, who was killed. (Sadiq would subsequently call Radio Liberty to indicate that he was still very much alive and to deny that he had been in the village that night.) Quickly enough, however, military spokespeople began backing off. Brigadier General Richard Blanchette, a NATO spokesperson, said that "investigators sent to the site immediately after the bombing" had, in fact, verified the deaths of three women and two children, who were suspected of being relatives of the dead Taliban commander.

After President Karzai's angry denunciation, and the results of his team's investigation were released, the U.S. military altered its account slightly, admitting that only twenty-five Taliban fighters had actually died alongside five Afghans identified as "noncombatants," including a woman and two children. The U.S. command, however, remained "very confident" that only thirty Afghans had been killed. Later, after a military investigation had been launched, the U.S. command in Afghanistan issued a vague statement indicating that "coalition forces are aware of allegations that the engagement in the Shindand district of Herat Province, Friday, may have resulted in civilian casualties apart from those already reported."

On August 28, the U.S. military "investigation" released its results, confirming that only thirty Afghans had died. On August 29, however, General David D. McKiernan, American commander of NATO forces, raised the number, suggesting that "up to 40" Afghans might have died, though still insisting that only five of them had been civilians, the rest being "men of military age." These revised numbers were still being touted on September 2, when, according to the *Washington Post*, "U.S. military officials flatly rejected" the Afghan and UN figures. On September 4, the *Los Angeles Times* reported that the U.S. military was now "acknowledging" thirty-five militants and seven civilians—forty-two Afghans—had died in the attack. Over a span of two weeks, the Americans slowly gave way on those previously definitive figures, moving modestly closer to the ones offered by the Karzai and UN teams, without ever giving way on their version of what had happened.

The investigations: The first investigation, according to U.S. military spokespeople, occurred the morning after the attack, when investigators from the attacking force supposedly went house to house "assessing damage and casualties" and "taking photos." Combat photographers were said to have "documented the scene." According to Gall, the U.S. military claimed its forces had made a "thorough sweep of this small western hamlet, a building-by-building search a few hours after the air strikes, and a return visit on Aug. 26, which villagers insist never occurred."

As claims of civilian deaths mounted and Karzai denounced the attacks, Major General Jeffrey J. Schloesser, then commander of coalition forces in Afghanistan, ordered an "investigation" into the episode. ("All allegations of civilian casualties are taken very seriously. Coalition forces make every effort to prevent the injury or loss of innocent lives. An investigation has been directed.")

On August 29, the conclusions of the investigation, completed in near-record time, were released. The casualty count—only thirty Afghans, twenty-five of them Taliban militants—had been definitively confirmed. A future "joint investigation" with the Afghan government was, however, proposed. That same day, General McKiernan suggested that the UN, too, should be part of the joint investigation. On September 3, the Afghans accepted the U.S. proposal for what was now a "tripartite investigation." On September 7, "emerging evidence"—a grainy video taken on a cell phone by a doctor in Azizabad, "showing dozens of civilian bodies, including those of numerous children, prepared for burial"—led General McKiernan to ask that the U.S. investigation be reopened. Normally, such investigations, whose results usually remain classified, are no more than sops, meant to quiet matters until attention dies away. In this case, the minimalist military investigation, which merely backed up the initial cover-up about the assault on Azizabad, was forced into the open and, as protest in Afghanistan widened, was essentially consigned to the trash heap of history.

The rhetoric: Initially, according to the *Washington Post*, "a U.S. military spokeswoman dismissed as 'outrageous' the Afghan government's assertions that scores of civilians had been killed in the attack.... A U.S. official in Washington, speaking on the condition of anonymity, said the Taliban has become adept at spreading false intelligence to draw U.S. strikes on civilians." In not-for-attribution comments, U.S. military officials would later suggest "that the villagers fabricated such evidence as grave sites." Lieutenant Colonel Rumi Nielson-Green, a spokesperson for the U.S. military, insisted: "We're confident that we struck the right compound." On August 24, as protests over the deaths at Azizabad mounted in Afghanistan, White House spokesperson Tony Fratto said at a press gaggle: "We regret the loss of life among the innocent Afghanis who we are committed to protect.... Coalition forces take precautions to prevent the loss of civilians, unlike the Taliban and militants who target civilians and place civilians in harm's way."

On August 25, Fratto added: "We believe from what we've heard from officials at the Department of Defense that they believe it was a good strike.... I should tell you, though, first of all, we obviously mourn the loss of any innocent civilians that may lose their lives in these attacks in— whether they're in Afghanistan or in Iraq, in any of these conflict areas." On that same day, Pentagon spokesperson Bryan Whitman said: "We continue at this point to believe that this was a legitimate strike against the Taliban. Unfortunately there were some civilian casualties, although that figure is in dispute, I would say. But this is why it is being investigated."

On August 27, at a Pentagon press conference, Commandant of the Marine Corps General James Conway said:

> [I]f the reports of the Afghan civilian casualties are accurate—and sometimes that is a big "if" because I think we all understand the Taliban capabilities with regard to information operations—but if that proves out, that will be truly an unfortunate incident. And we need to avoid that, certainly, at every cost....
>
> You know, air power is the premiere asymmetric advantage that we hold over both the Taliban and, for that matter, the al Qaeda in Iraq.... And when we find that you're up against hardened people in a hardened type of compound, before we throw our Marines or soldiers against that, we're going to take advantage of our asymmetric advantage....
>
> You don't always know what's in that compound, unfortunately.
>
> And sometimes we think there's been overt efforts on the part of the Taliban, in particular, to surround themselves with civilians so as to, at a minimum, reap an IO [information operations] advantage if civilians are killed.

On August 29, General McKiernan reiterated the American position, while expressing regrets for any loss of civilian life: "This was a legitimate insurgent target. We regret the loss of civilian life, but the numbers that we find on this target area are nowhere near the number reported in the media, and that we believe there was a very deliberate information operation orchestrated by the insurgency, by the Taliban." He also complained about the UN investigation, saying, "I am very disappointed in the United Nations because they have not talked to this headquarters before they made that release," and he suggested that President Karzai had been the victim of bad information.

On September 3, with pressure growing, U.S. ambassador to the UN Zalmay Khalilzad put the disparities in numbers down to the "fog of war," while urging a new joint investigation: "I believe that there is a bit of a fog of war involved in some of these initial reports. Sometimes initial reports can be wrong. And the best way to deal with it is to have the kind of investigation that we have proposed, which is U.S., coalition, plus the Afghan government, plus the United Nations." On the same day, Karzai's office issued a statement indicating that President Bush had phoned the Afghan president: "The President of America has expressed his regret and sympathy for the occurrence of Shindand incident." They quoted him as saying, "I am a partner in your loss and that of the Afghan people." Also that same day, General McKiernan said: "Every death of a civilian in wartime is a terrible tragedy. Even one death is too many.... I wish to again express my sincere condolences and apologies to the families whose loved ones were inadvertently killed in the cross fire with the insurgents in Azizabad." Though the Afghans seem to have largely died due to U.S. air strikes, not in a crossfire, this was as close to an apology as anyone related to the U.S. government or military has come.

Under fire for its account of the raid, the U.S. military was quick to point out that its now discredited findings at Azizabad "were corroborated by an independent journalist embedded with the U.S. force." That man turned out to be none other than Oliver North, working for FOX News. North had not only gained notoriety as an official of, a defender of, and a shredder of papers for the Reagan administration in the Iran-Contra scandal, but had earlier fought in Vietnam. He actually appeared as a witness for the defense in the case of one of the marines accused of carrying out a massacre of Vietnamese at Son Thang in February 1970.

As now, so in Vietnam, were "hearts and minds" being hunted both from the air and on the ground; so, too, civilians were repeatedly blown away there; and so, too, as in the case of the infamous My Lai massacre, cover stories were fabricated to explain how civilians—Vietnamese peasants—had died and those stories were publicized by the U.S. military, even though they bore little or no relation to what had actually happened.

Today, "hearts and minds" are being similarly hunted across large stretches of the planet, and people in surprising numbers continue to die while simply trying to lead their lives.

This sort of "collateral damage" is an ongoing modern nightmare, which, unlike dead Amish girls or school shootings, does not fascinate either our media or, evidently, Americans generally. It seems we largely don't want to know what happened, and generally speaking, that's lucky because the media isn't particularly interested in telling us. This is one reason the often absurd accounts sometimes offered by the U.S. military go relatively unchallenged—as, fortunately, they did not in the case of the incident at Azizabad.

Of course, it matters what you value and what you dismiss as valueless. When you overvalue yourself and undervalue others, you naturally over-estimate your own power and are remarkably blind to the potential power of others.

In this way, not just Vice President Cheney but President Bush and his top officials remained self-protectively embunkered throughout their years in office. The sixty or so children slaughtered in Azizabad, each of whom belonged to some family, did not matter to them. But those children do matter. And when you kill them, and so many others like them, you surely play with fire.

Launching the Drone Wars

In 1984, Skynet, the supercomputer that rules a future Earth, sent a cyborg assassin, a "terminator," back to our time. His job was to liquidate the woman who would give birth to John Connor, the leader of the un-derground human resistance of Skynet's time. You with me so far?

That, of course, was the plot of the first *Terminator* movie, and for the multimillions who saw it, the images of future machine war—of hunter-killer drones flying above a wasted landscape—are unforgettable. Since then, as Hollywood's special effects took off, there have been three sequels, during which the original terminator somehow morphed into a friendlier figure on-screen, and even more miraculously, off-screen, into the humanoid governor of California.

Meanwhile, hunter-killer drones haven't waited for Hollywood. Actual unmanned aerial vehicles (UAVs), pilotless surveillance and assassination drones armed with Hellfire missiles, are now patrolling our expanding global battlefields, hunting down human beings. And in the Pentagon and the labs of defense contractors, UAV supporters are already talking about and working on next-generation machines. Post-2020, according to these dreamers, drones will be able to fly *and* fight, discern enemies *and* incinerate them without human decision-making. They're even discussing just how to program human ethics—or, rather, American ethics—into them.

It may never happen, but it should still give us pause that there are people eager to bring the fifth iteration of *Terminator* not to local multiplexes, but to the skies of our perfectly real world—and that the Pentagon is already funding them to do so.

As futuristic weapons planning went, UAVs started out pretty low-tech in the 1990s. Even in 2009, the most commonplace of the two American armed drones, the Predator, cost only $4.5 million a pop, while the most advanced model, the Reaper—both are produced by General Atomics Aeronautical Systems of San Diego—came in at $15 million. (Compare that to $350 million for a single F-22 Raptor, which proved essentially useless in America's recent counterinsurgency wars.) It's lucky UAVs are cheap, since they are also prone to crashing.

UAVs came to life as surveillance tools during the wars over the former Yugoslavia, were armed by February 2001, were hastily pressed into operation in Afghanistan after 9/11, and like many weapons systems, began to evolve generationally. As they did, they developed from surveillance eyes in the sky into something far more sinister and previously restricted to terra firma: assassins. One of the earliest armed acts of a CIA-piloted Predator, back in November 2002, was an assassination mission over Yemen in which a jeep, reputedly transporting six suspected al-Qaeda operatives, was incinerated.

Today, the advanced UAV, the Reaper, housing up to four Hellfire missiles and two 500-pound bombs, packs the sort of punch once reserved for a jet fighter. Dispatched to the skies over the farthest reaches of the American empire, powered by a 1,000-horsepower turbo prop engine at its rear, the Reaper can fly at up to 21,000 feet for up to twenty-two hours (until fuel runs short), streaming back live footage from three cameras (or sending it to troops on the ground)—16,000 hours of video a month. There is no need to worry about a pilot dozing off during those twenty-two hours. The human crews "piloting" the drones, often from thousands of miles away, just change shifts when tired. So the planes are left to endlessly cruise Iraqi, Afghan, and Pakistani skies relentlessly seeking out, like so many terminators, specific enemies whose identities can, under certain circumstances (or so the claims go) be determined even through the walls of houses. When a "target" is found and agreed upon—in Pakistan, the permission of Pakistani officials to fire is no longer considered necessary—and a missile or bomb is unleashed, the cameras are so powerful that "pilots" can watch the facial expressions of those being liquidated on their computer monitors "as the bomb hits."

Approximately 5,500 UAVs, mostly unarmed—less than 250 of them are Predators and Reapers —operated in 2009 over Iraq and the so-called Af-Pak (Afghanistan-Pakistan) theater of operations. Part of the more than century-long development of war in the air, drones have become favorites of U.S. military planners.

And yet, keep in mind that the UAV still remains in its (frightening) infancy. Such machines are not, of course, advanced cyborgs. They are in some ways not even all that advanced. Because someone wants publicity for the drone-war program, reporters from the United States and elsewhere have been given "rare behind-the-scenes" looks at how it works. As a result, and also because the "covert war" in the skies over Pakistan makes Washington's secret warriors proud enough to regularly leak news of its "successes," we know something more about how our drone wars work.

We know, for instance, that at least part of the air force's Afghan UAV program runs out of Kandahar Air Base in southern Afghanistan. It turns out that, pilotless as the planes may be, a pilot does have to be nearby to guide them into the air and handle landings. As soon as the drone is up, a two-man team, a pilot and a "sensor monitor," backed by intelligence experts and meteorologists, takes over the controls either at Davis-Monthan Air Force Base in Tucson, Arizona, or at Creech Air Force Base northwest of Las Vegas, Nevada, some 7,000-odd miles away. (Other U.S. bases may be involved, as well, including Al-Udeid Air Base, a billion-dollar facility in the Persian Gulf nation of Qatar from which the air force evidently oversees its drone wars.)

According to Christopher Drew of the *New York Times*, who visited Davis-Monthan, where Air National Guard members handle the controls, the pilots sit unglamorously "at 1990s-style computer banks filled with screens, inside dimly lit trailers." Depending on the needs of the moment, they can find themselves "over" either Afghanistan or Iraq, or even both on the same work shift. All of this is remarkably mundane—pilot complaints generally run to problems "transitioning" back to wife and children after a day at the joystick over battle zones—and at the same time, right out of Ali Baba's *One Thousand and One Nights*.

In those dimly lit trailers, the UAV teams have taken on an almost god-like power. Their job is to survey a place thousands of miles distant (and completely alien to their lives and experiences), assess what they see, and spot "targets" to eliminate—even if on their somewhat antiquated computer systems it "takes up to 17 steps—including entering data into pull-down windows—to fire a missile" and incinerate those below. They only face danger when they leave the job: a sign at Creech warns a pilot to "drive carefully" because this is "the most dangerous part of your day." Those involved claim that the fear and thrill of battle do not completely escape them, but the descriptions we now have of their world sound discomfortingly like a cross between the far frontiers of sci-fi and a call center in India.

The most intense of our various drone wars, the one on the other side of the Afghan border in Pakistan, is also the most mysterious. We know that some or all of the drones engaged in it take off from Pakistani airfields; that this "covert war" (which regularly makes front-page news) is run by the CIA out of its headquarters in Langley, Virginia; that its pilots are also located somewhere in the United States; and that at least some of them are hired private contractors.

William Saletan of *Slate* has described our drones as engaged in "a bloodless, all-seeing airborne hunting party." Of course, in the twenty-first century what was once an elite activity performed in person has been transformed into a 24/7 industrial activity fit for human drones.

Our drone wars also represent a new chapter in the history of assassination. Once upon a time, to be an assassin for a government was a furtive, shameful thing. In those days, of course, an assassin, if successful, took down a single person, not the targeted individual and anyone in the vicinity (or simply, if targeting intelligence proves wrong, anyone in the vicinity). No more poison-dart-tipped umbrellas, as in past KGB operations, or toxic cigars, as in CIA ones. Assassination has taken to the skies as an everyday, year-round activity. Today, we increasingly display our assassination wares with pride. To us, at least, it seems perfectly normal for aerial assassination operations to be a part of an open discussion in Washington and in the media. Consider this a new definition of "progress" in our world.

Proliferation and Sovereignty

One of the truths of our time is that no weapons system, no matter where first created, can be kept as private property for long. Today, we talk not of arms races, but of "proliferation," which is what you have once a global arms race of one takes hold. But don't for a minute imagine that those hunter-killer skies dominated by Predators and Reapers won't someday fill with the drones of other nations. The Chinese, the Russians, the Israelis, the Pakistanis, the Georgians, and the Iranians, among others, already have drones. In 2006, Hezbollah flew drones over Israel. In fact, if you have the skills, you can create your own drone, more or less in your living room (as do-it-yourself drone websites make clear).

Undoubtedly, the future holds unnerving possibilities not just for states, but for small groups intent on assassination from the air. Already the skies are growing more crowded. In March 2009, not long after coming into office, President Barack Obama issued what Reuters termed "an unprecedented videotaped appeal to Iran…offering a 'new beginning' of diplomatic engagement to turn the page on decades of U.S. policy toward America's longtime foe." It was in the form of a Persian New Year's greeting. But, as the New York Times also reported, the U.S. military beat the president to the punch. They sent their own "greetings" to the Iranians a couple of days earlier. The U.S. military sent out Colonel James Hutton to meet the press and "confirm" that "allied aircraft" had shot down an "Iranian unmanned aerial vehicle" over Iraq on February 25, more than three weeks earlier. Between that day and mid-March, the relevant Iraqi military and civilian officials were, the *Times* tells us, not informed. The reason? That drone was intruding on our (borrowed) airspace, not theirs. You probably didn't know it, but according to an Iraqi Defense Ministry spokesperson, "protection of Iraqi airspace remains an American responsibility for the next three years." And naturally enough, we don't want other countries' drones in "our" airspace, though that's hardly likely to stop them. The Iranians, for instance, have already announced the development of "a new generation of 'spy drones' that provide real-time surveillance over enemy terrain."

Of course, when you openly control squads of assassination drones patrolling airspace over other countries, you've already made a mockery of whatever national sovereignty might once have meant. It's a precedent that might someday even make us distinctly uncomfortable. But not right now.

If you doubt this, check out the stream of self-congratulatory comments being leaked by Washington officials about our drone assassins. These often lead off news pieces about America's "covert war" over Pakistan ("An intense, six-month campaign of Predator strikes in Pakistan has taken such a toll on Al Qaeda that militants have begun turning violently on one another out of confusion and distrust, U.S. intelligence and counter-terrorism officials say"). But be sure to read to the end of such pieces. Somewhere in them, after the successes have been touted and toted up, you get the real news: "In fact, the stepped-up strikes have coincided with a deterioration in the security situation in Pakistan."

In Pakistan, a war of machine assassins is visibly provoking terror—and terrorism—as well as anger and hatred among people who are by no means fundamentalists. It is part of a larger destabilization of the country.

The Future Awaits Us

If you want to read the single most chilling line yet uttered about drone warfare American-style, it comes at the end of Christopher Drew's piece. He quotes Brookings Institution analyst Peter Singer saying of our Predators and Reapers, "these systems today are very much Model T

Fords. These things will only get more advanced." In other words, our drone wars are being fought with the airborne equivalent of cars with cranks, but the "race" to the horizon is already under way. Soon, some Reapers will have a far more sophisticated sensor system with twelve cameras capable of filming a two-and-a-half mile round area from twelve different angles. That program has been dubbed "Gorgon Stare," but it doesn't compare to the future 92-camera Argus program whose initial development is being funded by the Pentagon's blue-skies outfit, the Defense Advanced Research Projects Agency.

Soon enough, a single pilot may be capable of handling not one but perhaps three drones, and drone armaments will undoubtedly grow progressively more powerful and "precise." In the meantime, BAE Systems already has a drone four years into development, the Taranis, that should someday be "completely autonomous," meaning it theoretically will operate without human pilots. Initial trials of a prototype were scheduled for 2010. By 2020, so claim UAV enthusiasts, drones could be engaging in aerial battle and choosing their victims themselves. As Robert S. Boyd of *McClatchy* reported, "The Defense Department is financing studies of autonomous, or self-governing, armed robots that could find and destroy targets on their own. On-board computer programs, not flesh-and-blood people, would decide whether to fire their weapons."

It's a particular sadness of our world that, in Washington, only the military can dream about the future in this way, and then fund the "arms race" of 2018 or 2035. Rest assured that no one with a governmental red cent is researching the health care system of 2018 or 2035, or the public education system of those years.

In the meantime, the skies of our world are filling with round-the-clock assassins. They will only evolve and proliferate. Of course, when we check ourselves out in the movies, we like to identify with John Connor, the human resister, the good guy of this planet, against the evil machines. Elsewhere, however, as we fight our drone wars ever more openly, as we field mechanical techno-terminators with all-seeing eyes and loose our missiles from thousands of miles away ("*Hasta la vista*, baby!"), we undoubtedly look like something other than a nation of John Connors to those living under the Predators.

True, we can't send our drones into the past to wipe out the young Ayman al-Zawahiri in Cairo or the teenage Osama bin Laden speeding down some Saudi road in his gray Mercedes sedan. True, the UAV enthusiasts, who are already imagining all-drone wars run by "ethical" machines, may never see anything like their fantasies come to pass. Still, the fact that without the help of a single advanced cyborg we are already in the process of creating a Terminator planet should give us pause for thought...or not.

FOUR

The Language of War, American-Style

Which War Is This Anyway?

Consider this description:

The "rebels" or "freedom fighters" are part of a nationwide "resistance
movement." While many of them are local, even tribal, and fight simply because they are outraged by the occupation of their country, hundreds of others among the "resistance fighters"—young Arabs—are
arriving from as far away as "Lebanon, Syria, Egypt and Jordan," not
to speak of Saudi Arabia and Algeria, to engage in *jihad*, ready as one
of them puts it, to stay in the war "until I am martyred." Fighting for
their "Islamic ideals," "they are inspired by a sense of moral outrage
and a religious devotion heightened by frequent accounts of divine
miracles in the war." They slip across the country's borders to fight the
"invader" and the "puppet government" its officials have set up in the
capital in their "own image." The invader's sway, however, "extends
little beyond the major cities, and even there the…freedom fighters
often hold sway by night and sometimes even by day."

Sympathetic as they may be, the rebels are badly overwhelmed by
the firepower of the occupying superpower and are especially at risk
in their daring raids because the enemy is "able to operate with virtual
impunity in the air." The superpower's soldiers are sent out from their
bases and the capital to "make sweeps, but chiefly to search and destroy,

not to clear and hold." Its soldiers, known for their massive human rights abuses and the cruelty of their atrocities, have in some cases been reported to press "on the throats of prisoners to force them to open their mouths while the guards urinate into them, [as well as] setting police dogs on detainees, raping women in front of family members and other vile acts."

On their part, the "guerrillas," armed largely with Russian and Chinese rifles and rocket propelled grenade launchers, have responded with the warfare of the weak. They have formed car-bombing squads and use a variety of cleverly constructed wheelbarrow, bicycle, suitcase, and roadside bombs as well as suicide operations performed by volunteers chosen from among the foreign jihadists. They engage in assassinations of, for example, university intellectuals and other sabotage activities in the capital and elsewhere aimed at killing the occupying troops and their sympathizers. They behead hostages to instill fear in the other side. Funding for the resistance comes, in part, from supporters in sympathetic Islamic countries, including Saudi Arabia. However, "if the mujaheddin are ever to realize their goal of forcing [the occupiers] out, they will need more than better arms and training, more than their common faith. They will need to develop a genuinely unified resistance.... Above all, the analysts say, they will need to make the war...even costlier and more difficult for the [occupiers] than it is now."

It's easy enough to identify this composite description, right? Our recent wars in Iraq or Afghanistan, as portrayed perhaps in the Arab press and on Arab websites. As it happens, actually not. With the exception of the material on bombs, which comes from Steve Coll's book *Ghost Wars*, and on the beheading of hostages, which comes from an Amnesty International report, all of the above is taken from either the statements of U.S. officials or coverage in either the *Washington Post* or the *New York Times* of the Afghan anti-Soviet jihad of the 1980s, fostered, armed, and funded to the tune of billions of dollars by the Central Intelligence Agency with the help of the Saudi and Pakistani intelligence services.

Well, then try this one:

Thousands of troops of the occupying power make a second, carefully planned "*brutal* advance" into a large city to root out Islamic "rebels."

The first attack on the city failed, though it all but destroyed neighborhoods in a "*ferocious* bombardment." The soldiers advance behind "*relentless* air and artillery strikes." This second attempt to take the city, the capital of a "rebellious province," defended by a determined "rebel force" of perhaps five hundred to three thousand, succeeds, though the fighting never quite ends. The result? A "razed" city, "where virtually every building has been bombed, burned, shelled beyond recognition or simply obliterated by war"; a place where occupying "soldiers fire at anything that moves" and their checkpoints are surrounded by "endless ruins of former homes and gutted, upended automobiles." The city has been reduced to "rubble" and, for the survivors, "rebel" fighters and civilians alike, it and surrounding areas are now a "killing field." The city lacks electricity, water, or much in the way of food, and yet the rebels hold out in its ruins, and though amusements are few, "on one occasion, a...singer came and gave an impromptu guitar concert of patriotic and folk tunes [for them]."

In the carnage involved in the taking of the city, the resistance showed great fortitude. "'See you in paradise,' [one] volunteer said. 'God is great.'" Hair-raising news reports from the occupied city and from refugee camps describe the "traumatized" and maimed. ("Here in the remains of Hospital Number Nine—[the city's] only hospital with electricity—she sees a ceaseless stream of mangled bodies, victims of gunfire and shellings"); press reports also acknowledge the distance between official promises of reconstruction and life in the gutted but still resistant city, suggesting "the contrast between the symbolic peace and security declared by [occupation] officials and the city's mine-ridden, bullet-flying reality." Headlines don't hesitate to highlight claims made by those who fled and survived—"Refugees Describe Atrocities by Occupation Troops"—and reports bluntly use the label given the acts of the occupiers by human rights organizations—"war crimes." Such organizations are quoted to devastating effect on the subject. The rebels may be called "bandits" by the occupiers, but it's clear in news reports that they are the ones to be admired.

No question of the sources here at least. Obviously the above is a composite account of the 2004 American assault on the Sunni city of Falluja taken from Arab press reports or sympathetic Arab websites. As it happens, if you believed that, you'd be zero for two. In fact, all of the above is taken from contemporary accounts of the January 2000 Russian assault on Grozny, the capital of Chechnya, that appeared in the *Washington Post*, the *New York Times*, or the *Boston Globe*.

How to Spot a Terrorist

I put together these descriptions from American reports on the Afghan anti-Soviet jihad of the 1980s, written in the midst of the Cold War, and on the second battle for Grozny ten years after the Cold War ended, because both seemed to have certain eerie similarities to events in Iraq after Baghdad fell to American troops in March 2003, though obviously neither presents an exact analogy. Both earlier moments of reportage do, however, highlight certain limitations in our press coverage of the war in Iraq (and also Afghanistan).

After all, in the case of Afghanistan in the 1980s, there was also a fractured and fractious rebellion against an invading imperial superpower intent on controlling the country and setting up its own regime in the capital. The anti-Soviet rebellion was (like the present one in Iraq) conducted in part by Islamic rebels, many of whom were extremist Sunni jihadists (and some of whose names, from Osama bin Laden to Gulbuddin Hekmatyar, remain significant today). The Afghan guerrilla war was backed by that other superpower, the United States, for a decade through its spy agency, the CIA, which promoted methods that, in the Iraq context, would be called "terrorism."

In the case of the Russian assault on Grozny, the capital of the breakaway region of Chechnya, you also have an imperial power, if no longer exactly a superpower, intent on wresting a city—and a "safe haven"—from a fractious, largely Islamist insurgency and ready to make an example of a major city to do so. The Russian rubblizing of Grozny may have been more extreme than the American destruction of Falluja (or so it seems), but the events remain comparable. In the case of Grozny, the U.S. government did not actively back the rebels as they had in Afghanistan, but the Bush administration, made up of former Cold Warriors who had imbibed the idea of "rolling back" the Soviet Union in their younger years, was certainly sympathetic to the rebels.

What, then, are some of the key differences I noticed in reading through examples of this reportage and comparing it to the products of our present embedded state? Let me list four differences—and suggest a question: To what degree are American reporters as a group destined to follow, with only modest variation, the paths opened for them by our government's positions on its wars of choice?

Language: Those in rebellion in Iraq today are, according to our military, "anti-Iraqi forces" (a phrase that, in quotes, often makes it into news pieces and is just about never commented upon by reporters). Other terms, most of them also first issuing from the mouths of U.S. officials, have been "dead-enders," "bitter enders," "Baathist remnants," "terrorists," and most regularly (and neutrally), "insurgents" who are fighting in an "insurgency"—but rarely "guerrillas."

The Afghans in the 1980s, on the other hand, were almost invariably in "rebellion" and so "rebels" as headlines at the time made clear ("Officials Say U.S. Plans to Double Supply of Arms to Afghan Rebels," *New York Times*). They were part of a "resistance movement" and as their representatives could write op-eds for our papers, the *Washington Post*, for instance, had no hesitation about headlining Matthew D. Erulkar's op-ed of January 13, 1987, "Why America Should Recognize the Afghan Resistance" or identifying its author as working "for the Afghan resistance."

But the phrase "Afghan resistance" or "the resistance" was no less likely to appear in news pieces, as in an October 22, 1983, report by *Post* reporter William Branigin, "Feuding Guerrilla Groups Rely on Uneasy Pakistan." Nor, as in James Rupert's "Dreams of Martyrdom Draw Islamic Arabs to Join Afghan Rebels" (*Washington Post*, July 21, 1986), was there any problem calling an Islamic "fundamentalist party" that was part of the "Afghan Jihad" a "resistance party." President Ronald Reagan at the time regularly referred to fundamentalist Afghans and their Arab supporters as "freedom fighters" (while the CIA, through the ISI, the Pakistani intelligence service, shuttled vast sums of money and stores of weaponry to the most extreme of the Afghan jihadist parties). "Freedom fighter" was commonly used in the press, sometimes interchangeably with "the Afghan resistance," as in a March 12, 1981, piece by *Post* columnist Joseph Kraft, "The Afghan Chaos" ("Six different organizations claiming to represent Afghan freedom fighters").

Similarly, the Chechens in Grozny in 2000 were normally referred to in U.S. news accounts as "rebels": "separatist rebels," "rebel ambushes," "a rebel counterattack," and so on. ("Rebel," as anyone knows who remembers American rock 'n' roll or movies of the 1950s and 1960s, is a positive term in our lexicon.) Official Russian terms for the Chechen rebels, who were fighting grimly like any group of outgunned urban guerrillas in a manner similar to the Sunni guerrillas in Iraq today— "bandits" or "armed criminals in camouflage and masks"—were quoted, but then (as "anti-Iraqi forces" and other Bush administration terms are not) put in context or contrasted with Chechen versions of reality.

In a typical piece from CNN, you could find the following quote: "'The [Russians] aren't killing any bandits,' one refugee said after reaching Ingushetia. 'They're killing old men, women and children. And they keep on bombing—day and night.'" In a Daniel Williams piece in the *Washington Post*, the Russian government's announcements about the fighting in Grozny have become a "daily chant," a phrase that certainly suggests how the reporter feels about their accuracy.

Here's a quote from a discussion in a *Washington Post* editorial of an Associated Press photo of the destruction in Grozny. The photo was described elsewhere as "a pastel from hell" and was evidently of a sort we've seen far too little of in our press from either Falluja or the Old City of Najaf:

> Russian leaders announced with pride Sunday that their armed forces had captured Grozny, the capital of Chechnya, five months into their war to subdue that rebellious province. Reports from the battle zone suggested that the Russians had not so much liberated the city as destroyed it.... Grozny resembles nothing so much as Stalingrad, reduced to rubble by Hitler's troops before the Red Army inflicted a key defeat that Russian schoolchildren still celebrate.... All in all, this is not likely to be a victory that Russian schoolchildren will celebrate generations hence.

Similar writing certainly certainly wasn't found on American editorial pages when it came to the "razing" of Falluja, nor were those strong adjectives like "brutal," once wielded in the Grozny accounts, much to be found either.

Testimony: Perhaps the most striking difference between news stories about the Afghan revolt, the destruction of Grozny, and the destruction of Falluja may be that in the cases of the first two, American reporters were willing, even eager, to seek out refugee accounts, even if the refugees were supporters of the rebels or rebels themselves. Such testimony was, for instance, regularly offered as evidence of what was happening in Grozny and more generally in Chechnya (even when the accounts couldn't necessarily be individually confirmed). So the *Post*'s Daniel Williams, for instance, in "Brutal Retreat from Grozny Led to a Killing Field" (February 12, 2000) begins by following Heda Yusupova, mother of two "and a cook for a group of Chechen rebels" as she flees the city: "[She] froze in her tracks when she heard the first land mine explode. It was night, and she and a long file of rebels were making a dangerous retreat from Grozny, the Chechen capital, during the final hours of a brutal Russian advance. Another explosion. Her children, ages 9 and 10, screamed." It's a piece that certainly puts the Russian assault on Grozny in a striking perspective.

Post reporter Sharon LaFraniere wrote a piece on June 29, 2000, bluntly entitled "Chechen Refugees Describe Atrocities by Russian Troops," in which she reported on "atrocities" in what the Russians labeled a "pro-bandit village": "'I have never imagined such tortures, such cruelty,' [the villager] said, sitting at a small table in the dim room that has housed her family here for nearly three years. 'There were a lot of men who were left only half alive.'" And when Russian operations against individual Chechens were described, it was possible to see them through Chechen eyes: "Three times last month, Algayeva said, Russian soldiers broke in, threatening to shoot the school's guard. They smashed doors, locks and desks. The last time, May 20, they took sugar, plates and a brass bell that was rung at school ceremonies."

As in a February 29, 2000, *Boston Globe* piece ("Chechen Horror"), it was also possible for newspapers to discuss editorially both "the suffering of the Chechens" and the way "the United States and the rest of the international community can no longer ignore their humanitarian obligation to alleviate—and end—[that suffering]."

The equivalent pieces for Iraq are largely missing, though every now and then—as with an Edward Wong piece in the *New York Times* on life in resistant Sadr City, Baghdad's huge Shiite slum—there have been exceptions. Given the dangers Western reporters face in Iraq and the constricting system of "embedding" that generally prevails, when you read of Americans breaking into Iraqi homes, you're ordinarily going to see the event from the point of view of the troops. Iraqi refugees have not been much valued in our press for their testimony. (There is a deep irony in this, since the Bush administration launched its war citing mainly exile—that is, refugee—testimony.)

We know, of course, that it's difficult for U.S. reporters to go in search of such testimony in Iraq, but not impossible. For instance, Dahr Jamail, a determined freelance journalist, managed to interview refugees from Falluja, and their testimony sounds remarkably like the Grozny testimony from major American newspapers in 2000: "The American warplanes came continuously through the night and bombed everywhere in Fallujah! It did not stop even for a moment! If the American forces did not find a target to bomb, they used sound bombs just to terrorize the people and children. The city stayed in fear; I cannot give a picture of how panicked everyone was."

For the "suffering of the Iraqis," you had to turn to the periodic "testimony" of Iraqi bloggers like the pseudonymous Riverbend of Baghdad Burning or perhaps Al Jazeera. The suffering we actually hear most about in our press is American suffering, in part because it's the American troops with whom our reporters are embedded, with whom they bond, and fighters on battlefields anywhere almost invariably find themselves in grim and suffering circumstances.

Human rights evidence: The reports from Grozny in particular often made extensive use of the investigations of human rights groups of various sorts (including Russian ones), and reporters then were willing to put the acts of the Russians in Grozny (as in Afghanistan) in the context of "war crimes," as indeed they were. In Iraq, on the other hand, while pieces on human rights reports about our occupation can sometimes be found deep in our papers, the evidence supplied by human rights groups is seldom deployed by American reporters as an evidentiary part of war pieces.

"Terrorism": Finally, it's interesting to see how, in different reporting contexts and different moments, the term "terrorism" is or is not brought to bear. In Grozny, for instance, the "rebels" used "radio controlled land mines" and assassinated Chechens who worked for the Russians (just as Iraqi insurgents and terrorists explode roadside IEDs and assassinate those who work for the Americans) and yet the Chechens remained "rebels."

On this topic, though, Afghanistan in the 1980s is of special interest. There, as Steve Coll tells us in his riveting book *Ghost Wars*, the CIA organized terror on a major scale in conjunction with the Pakistani ISI, which trained "freedom fighters" in how to mount car-bomb and even camel-bomb attacks on Soviet officers and soldiers in Russian-occupied cities (techniques personally "endorsed," according to Coll, by CIA director William Casey). The CIA also supplied the Afghan rebels with long-range sniper rifles (meant for assassinations) and delayed-timing devices for plastic explosives. "The rebels fashioned booby-trapped bombs from gooey black contact explosives, supplied to Pakistani intelligence by the CIA, that could be molded into ordinary shapes or poured into innocent utensils." Kabul cinemas and cultural shows were bombed, and suicide operations mounted using Arab jihadis. "Many tons of C-4 plastic explosives for sabotage operations" were shipped in, and the CIA took to supplying so-called dual-use weapons systems that could be used against military targets, "but also in terror attacks and assassinations." Much of this was known, at least to some degree at the time (and some of it reported in press accounts), and yet the Afghans remained "freedom fighters" and a resistance movement, even after the Afghan jihad began to slip across the other Pakistani border into Indian Kashmir.

What changed? What made such people, according to our press, "terrorists"? The answer is, of course, that we became their prime enemy and target. Coll offers this observation:

> Ten years later the vast training infrastructure that [the Pakistani ISI] built with the enormous budgets endorsed by NSDD-166 [the official American plan for the Afghan jihad]—the specialized camps, the sabotage training manuals, the electronic bomb detonators, and so on—would be referred to routinely in America as "terrorist infrastructure."

At the time of its construction, however, it served a jihadist army that operated openly on the battlefield, attempted to seize and hold territory, and exercised sovereignty over civilian populations

—in Soviet Afghanistan, that is.

In the Afghan anti-Soviet war, the CIA looked favorably indeed upon the recruitment of thousands of Arab jihadists and eagerly supported a particularly unsavory and murderous Afghan extremist warlord, Gulbuddin Hekmatyar, who refused at the time to travel to Washington and shake the hand of our "infidel" president, Ronald Reagan. (Today, Hekmatyar fights U.S. troops in Afghanistan.) As it turned out, the "freedom fighters" fell on each other's throats even as Kabul was being taken, and then, within years, some of them turned on their former American patrons with murderous intent. No figure tells the story better, I think, than this one: "In 1971 there had been only nine hundred madrassas [Islamic schools] in all of Pakistan. By the summer of 1988 there were about 8,000 official religious schools and an estimated 25,000 unregistered ones, many of them clustered along the Pakistan-Afghanistan frontier and funded by wealthy patrons from Saudi Arabia and other Gulf states."

The Russians in Afghanistan and Chechnya were indeed brutes and committed war crimes of almost every imaginable sort. The language of the American press, watching the invading army of a former superpower turn the capital city of a small border state into utter rubble, was appropriate indeed, given what was going on. In both Afghanistan and in Iraq, on the other hand, where the American government is actively involved, reporters generally—and yes, there are always exceptions—have followed the government's lead with the terminology—"freedom fighter" versus "terrorist"—falling into place as befit the moment, even though many of the acts being described remained the same.

The press is always seen as a weapon of war by officials, and so it has been seen by the Pentagon and official Washington. Reporters and editors obviously feel that and the pressures that flow from it in all sorts of complex ways. Whether consciously or not, it's striking how such perceptions shade and limit even individual stories, alter small language choices, and the nature of what passes for evidence as well as news.

The Imperial Unconscious

Sometimes, it's the everyday things, the ones that fly below the radar, that matter.

Here is an excerpt from a news story about Secretary of Defense Robert Gates's testimony on the Afghan War before the Senate Armed Services Committee in January 2009: "U.S. goals in Afghanistan must be 'modest, realistic,' and 'above all, *there must be an Afghan face on this war*,' Gates said. 'The Afghan people must believe this is their war and we are there to help them. If they think we are there for our own purposes, then we will go the way of every other foreign army that has been in Afghanistan.'"

Now, in our world, a statement like this seems so obvious, so reasonable as to be beyond comment. And yet, stop a moment and think about this part of it: "there must be an Afghan face on this war." U.S. military and civilian officials used an equivalent phrase in 2005 and 2006, when things were going really wrong in Iraq. It was then commonplace—and no less unremarked upon—for them to urgently suggest that an "Iraqi face" be put on events there.

The phrase is revelatory—and oddly blunt. As an image, there's really only one way to understand it (not that anyone here stops to do so). After all, what does it mean to "put a face" on something that assumedly already has a face? In this case, it has to mean putting an Afghan *mask* over what we know to be the actual "face" of the Afghan War—ours—a foreign face that men like Gates recognize, quite correctly, is not the one most Afghans want to see. It's hardly surprising that the secretary of defense would pick up such a phrase, part of Washington's everyday arsenal of words and images when it comes to geopolitics, power, and war. And yet, make no mistake, this is Empire-speak, American-style. It's the language (behind which lies a deeper structure of argument and thought) that is essential to Washington's vision of itself as a planet-straddling Goliath. It is part of the flotsam and jetsam that regularly bubbles up from the American imperial unconscious.

Of course, words create realities even though such language, in all its strangeness, essentially passes unnoticed here. Largely uncommented upon, it helps normalize American practices in the world, comfortably shielding us from certain global realities. It also has the potential to blind us to those realities, which can be dangerous indeed. So let's consider just a few entries in what might be thought of as *The Dictionary of American Empire-Speak*.

War hidden in plain sight: There has recently been much reporting on, and even some debate about, the efficacy of the Obama administration's decision to increase the intensity of CIA missile attacks from drone aircraft in what Washington, in a newly coined neologism reflecting a widening war, calls "Af-Pak"—the Pashtun tribal borderlands of Afghanistan and Pakistan. The pace of such attacks has risen since Barack Obama entered the Oval Office, as have casualties from the missile strikes, as well as popular outrage in Pakistan over the attacks.

Thanks to Senator Dianne Feinstein, we also know that, despite strong official Pakistani government protests, someone official in that country is doing more than looking the other way while they occur. As the senator revealed, at least some of the CIA's unmanned aerial vehicles (UAVs) cruising the skies over Af-Pak are evidently stationed at Pakistani bases. We also learned that American special operations units are now regularly making forays inside Pakistan "primarily to gather intelligence"; that a unit of seventy American Special Forces advisers, a "secret task force, overseen by the United States Central Command and Special Operations Command," is aiding and training Pakistani Army and Frontier Corps paramilitary troops, again inside Pakistan; and that, despite (or perhaps, in part, because of) these American efforts, the influence of the Pakistani Taliban is actually expanding, even as Pakistan threatens to melt down.

Mystifyingly enough, however, this Pakistani part of the American war in Afghanistan is still referred to in major U.S. papers as a "covert war." As news about it pours out, who it's being hidden from is one of those questions no one bothers to ask.

On February 20, 2009, Mark Mazzetti and David E. Sanger of the *New York Times* typically wrote: "With two missile strikes over the past week, the Obama administration has expanded the covert war run by the Central Intelligence Agency inside Pakistan, attacking a militant network seeking to topple the Pakistani government.... Under standard policy for covert operations, the C.I.A. strikes inside Pakistan have not been publicly acknowledged either by the Obama administration or the Bush administration."

On February 25, 2009, Mazzetti and Helene Cooper reported that new CIA head Leon Panetta essentially bragged to reporters that "the agency's campaign against militants in Pakistan's tribal areas was the 'most effective weapon' the Obama administration had to combat Al Qaeda's top leadership.... Mr. Panetta stopped short of directly acknowledging the missile strikes, but he said that 'operational efforts' focusing on Qaeda leaders had been successful." Siobhan Gorman of the *Wall Street Journal* reported the next day that Panetta said the attacks are "probably the most effective weapon we have to try to disrupt al Qaeda right now." She added, "Mr. Obama and National Security Adviser James Jones have strongly endorsed their use, [Panetta] said."

"Covert" war? These "operational efforts" have been front-page news in the Pakistani press for months, they were part of the U.S. presidential campaign debates, and they certainly can't be a secret for the Pashtuns in those border areas who must see drone aircraft overhead relatively regularly, or experience the missiles arriving in their neighborhoods.

In the United States, "covert war" has long been a term for wars that were openly discussed, debated, and often lauded in this country, such as the U.S.-backed Contra War against the Sandinistas in Nicaragua in the 1980s. To a large extent, when aspects of these wars have actually been "covert"—that is, purposely hidden from anyone—it has been from the U.S. public, not the targets of our intervention. Such language, however threadbare, may also offer official Washington a kind of "plausible deniability" when it comes to thinking about what kind of an "American face" we present to the world.

Imperial naming practices: In our press, anonymous U.S. officials routinely point with pride to the increasing "precision" and "accuracy" of drone missile attacks in taking out Taliban or al-Qaeda figures without (supposedly) taking out the tribespeople who live in the same villages or neighboring compounds. Such pieces lend our air war an almost sterile quality. They tend to emphasize the extraordinary lengths to which planners go to avoid "collateral damage." To many Americans, it must then seem strange, even irrational, that perfectly non-fundamentalist Pakistanis should be so outraged about attacks aimed at the world's worst terrorists.

On the other hand, consider for a moment the names of those drones now regularly in the skies over "Pashtunistan." These are no less regularly published in our press to no comment at all. The most basic of the armed drones goes by the name of Predator, a moniker that might as well have come directly from those nightmarish sci-fi movies about an alien that feasts on humans. Undoubtedly, however, it was used in the way Colonel Michael Steele of the 101st Airborne Division meant it when he exhorted his brigade deploying to Iraq (according to Thomas E. Ricks' book *The Gamble*) to remember: "You're the predator."

The Predator drone is armed with two missiles. The more advanced drone, originally called the Predator B, now being deployed to the skies over Af-Pak, has been dubbed the Reaper—as in the Grim Reaper. Now, there's only one thing such a "hunter-killer UAV" could be reaping, and you know just what that is: lives. It can be armed with up to fourteen missiles (or four missiles and two 500-pound bombs), which means it packs quite a deadly wallop. Those missiles are named as well. They're Hellfire missiles. So, if you want to consider the nature of this covert war in terms of names alone: Predators and Reapers are bringing down the fire from some satanic hell upon the peasants, fundamentalist guerrillas, and terrorists of the Af-Pak border regions.

In Washington, when the Af-Pak war is discussed, it's in the bloodless, bureaucratic language of "global counterinsurgency" or "irregular warfare," of "soft power," "hard power," and "smart power." But flying over the Pashtun wildlands is the blunt-edged face of predation and death, ready at a moment's notice to deliver hellfire to those below.

Imperial arguments: Faced with rising numbers of civilian casualties from U.S. and NATO air strikes in Afghanistan and an increasingly outraged Afghan public, American officials tend to place the blame for most skyborne "collateral damage" squarely on the Taliban. As Joint Chiefs Chairman Michael Mullen bluntly explained, "[T]he enemy hides behind civilians." Hence, so this Empire-speak argument goes, dead civilians are actually the Taliban's doing.

U.S. military and civilian spokespeople have long accused Taliban guerrillas of using civilians as "shields," or even of purposely luring devastating air strikes down on Afghan wedding parties to create civilian casualties and inflame the sensibilities of rural Afghans. This commonplace argument has two key features: a claim that *they* made *us* do it (kill civilians) and the implication that the Taliban fighters "hiding" among innocent villagers or wedding revelers are so many cowards, willing to put their fellow Pashtuns at risk rather than come out and fight like men—and, of course, given the firepower arrayed against them, die.

The U.S. media regularly records this argument without reflecting on it. In this country, in fact, the evil of combatants "hiding" among civilians seems so self-evident, especially given the larger evil of the Taliban and al-Qaeda, that no one thinks twice about it. And yet like so much of Empire-speak, this argument is distinctly unidirectional. What's good for the guerrilla goose, so to speak, is inapplicable to the imperial gander. To illustrate, consider the American "pilots" flying those unmanned Predators and Reapers. We don't know exactly where all of them are (other than not in the drones), but some are certainly at Nellis Air Force Base just outside Las Vegas.

In other words, were the Taliban guerrillas to leave the protection of those civilians and come out into the open, there would be no enemy to fight in the usual sense, not even a predatory one. The pilot firing that Hellfire missile into some Pakistani border village or compound is, after all, using the UAV's cameras, including by next year a new system hair-raisingly dubbed "Gorgon Stare," to locate his target and then, via console, as in a single-shooter video game, firing the missile, possibly from many thousands of miles away.

And yet nowhere in our world will you find anyone making the argument that those pilots are in "hiding" like so many cowards. Such a thought seems absurd to us, as it would if it were applied to the F-18 pilots taking off from aircraft carriers near the Afghan coast or the B-1 pilots flying out of unnamed Middle Eastern bases or the Indian Ocean island base of Diego Garcia. And yet, whatever those pilots may do in Afghan skies, unless they experience a mechanical malfunction, they are in no more danger than if they, too, were somewhere outside Las Vegas. In the last seven years, some helicopters, but no planes, have gone down in Afghanistan.

When the Afghan mujahedeen fought the Soviets in the 1980s, the CIA supplied them with handheld Stinger missiles, and they did indeed start knocking Soviet helicopters and planes out of the skies (which proved the beginning of the end for the Russians). The Afghan or Pakistani Taliban or al-Qaeda terrorists have no such capability today, which means, if you think about it, that what we here imagine as an "air war" involves none of the dangers we would normally associate with war. Looked at in another light, those missile strikes and bombings are really one-way acts of slaughter.

The Taliban's tactics are, of course, the essence of guerrilla warfare, which always involves an asymmetrical battle against more powerful armies and weaponry, and which, if successful, always depends on the ability of the guerrilla to blend into the environment, natural and human, or, as Chinese Communist leader Mao Zedong so famously put it, to "swim" in the "sea of the people." If you imagine your enemy simply using the villagers of Afghanistan as "shields" or "hiding" like so many cowards among them, you are speaking the language of imperial power but also blinding yourself (or the American public) to the actual realities of the war you're fighting.

Imperial thought: To justify those missile attacks in Pakistan, U.S. officials have been leaking details on the program's "successes" to reporters. Anonymous officials have offered the "possibly wishful estimate" that the CIA "covert war" has led to the deaths (or capture) of eleven of al-Qaeda's top twenty commanders, including, according to a *Wall Street Journal* report, "Abu Layth al-Libi, whom U.S. officials described as 'a rising star' in the group." "Rising star" is such an American phrase, melding as it does imagined terror hierarchies with the lingo of celebrity tabloids. In fact, one problem with Empire-speak, and imperial thought more generally, is the way it prevents imperial officials from imagining a world not in their own image. So it's not surprising that, despite their best efforts, they regularly conjure up their enemies as a warped version of themselves—hierarchical, overly reliant on leaders, and top heavy.

In the Vietnam era, U.S. officials spent a remarkable amount of effort sending troops to search for, and planes to bomb, the border sanctuaries of Cambodia and Laos on a fruitless hunt for COSVN (the so-called Cen-

56643

tral Office for South Vietnam), the supposed nerve center of the communist enemy, aka "the bamboo Pentagon." Of course, it wasn't there to be found. It only existed in Washington's imperial imagination. In the Af-Pak "theater," we may be seeing a similar phenomenon. Underpinning the CIA killer-drone program is a belief that the key to combating al-Qaeda (and possibly the Taliban) is destroying its leadership one by one. As key Pakistani officials have tried to explain, the missile attacks, which have indeed killed some al-Qaeda and Pakistani Taliban figures, as well as whoever was in their vicinity, are distinctly counterproductive. The deaths of those figures in no way compensate for the outrage, the destabilization, the radicalization that the attacks engender in the region. They may, in fact, be functionally strengthening each of those movements.

What is hard for Washington to grasp is this: "Decapitation," to use another American imperial term, is not a particularly effective strategy with a decentralized guerrilla or terror organization. The fact is a headless guerrilla movement is nowhere near as brainless or helpless as a headless Washington would be.

Imperial dreams and nightmares: Americans have rarely liked to think of themselves as "imperial," so what is it about Rome in these last years? First, the neocons, in the flush of seeming victory in 2002 and 2003, began to imagine the United States as a "new Rome" (or new British Empire). As Charles Krauthammer wrote as early as February 2001 in *Time*, "America is no mere international citizen. It is the dominant power in the world, more dominant than any since Rome."

All roads on this planet, they were then convinced, led ineluctably to Washington. Now, of course, they visibly don't, and the imperial bragging about surpassing the Roman or British empires has long since faded away. When it comes to the Afghan War, in fact, those (resupply) "roads" seem to lead, embarrassingly enough, through Pakistan, Kyrgyzstan, Uzbekistan, Russia, and Iran. But the comparison to conquering Rome evidently remains on the brain.

When, for instance, Joint Chiefs Chairman Mike Mullen wrote an op-ed for the *Washington Post*, drumming up support for the revised, age-of-Obama mission in Afghanistan, he just couldn't help starting off with an inspiring tale about the Romans and a small Italian city-state, Locri, that they conquered. As he told it, the ruler the Romans installed in Locri, a rapacious fellow named Pleminius, proved a looter and a tyrant. And yet, Mullen assured us, the Locrians so believed in "the reputation for equanimity and fairness that Rome had built" that they sent a delegation to the Roman Senate, knowing they could get a hearing, and demanded restitution. And indeed, the tyrant was removed. Admittedly, this may seem like a far-fetched analogy for the United States in Afghanistan (and don't for a second mix up Pleminius, that rogue, with Afghan president Hamid Karzai, even though the Obama-ites have come to consider him corrupt and replaceable). Still, as Mullen saw it, the point was: "We don't always get it right. But like the early Romans, we strive in the end to make it right. We strive to earn trust. And that makes all the difference." Mullen is, it seems, the Aesop of the joint chiefs of staff and, in his somewhat overheated brain, we evidently remain the conquering (but just) "early" Romans—before, of course, the fatal rot set in.

And then there's the *Washington Post*'s Thomas Ricks. Reflecting on Iraq, where he believes we could still be fighting in 2015, Ricks writes:

> In October 2008, as I was finishing my latest book on the Iraq war, I visited the Roman Forum during a stop in Italy. I sat on a stone wall on the south side of the Capitoline Hill and studied the two triumphal arches at either end of the Forum, both commemorating Roman wars in the Middle East....
>
> ...The structures brought home a sad realization: It's simply un-realistic to believe that the U.S. military will be able to pull out of the Middle East.
>
> It was a week when U.S. forces had engaged in combat in Syria, Iraq, Afghanistan and Pakistan—a string of countries stretching from the Mediterranean Sea to the Indian Ocean—following in the footsteps of Alexander the Great, the Romans and the British.

With the waning of British power, Ricks continued, it "has been the United States' turn to take the lead there." And our turn, as it happens, just isn't over yet. Evidently that, at least, is the view from our imperial capital and from our military viceroys out on the peripheries.

Honestly, Freud would have loved these guys. They seem to channel the imperial unconscious. Take CentCom commander General David

Petraeus. For him, too, the duties and dangers of empire evidently weigh heavily on the brain. Like a number of key figures, civilian and military, he has begun to issue warnings about Afghanistan's dangers. As the *Washington Post* reported, "[Petraeus] suggested that the odds of success were low, given that foreign military powers have historically met with defeat in Afghanistan. 'Afghanistan has been known over the years as the graveyard of empires,' he said. 'We cannot take that history lightly.'"

Of course, he's worrying about the graveyard aspect of this, but what I find curious—exactly because no one thinks it odd enough to comment on here—is the functional admission in the use of this old adage about Afghanistan that we fall into the category of empires, whether or not in search of a graveyard in which to die. And he's not alone in this. Secretary of Defense Gates put the matter similarly, according to Bloomberg News: "Without the support of the Afghan people, Gates said, the U.S. would simply 'go the way of every other foreign army that's ever been in Afghanistan.'"

Imperial blindness: Think of the above as just a few prospective entries in *The Dictionary of American Empire-Speak* that will, of course, never be compiled. We're so used to such language, so inured to it and to the thinking behind it, so used, in fact, to living on a one-way planet in which all roads lead to and from Washington, that it doesn't seem like a language at all. It's just part of the unexamined warp and woof of everyday life in a country that still believes it normal to garrison the planet, regularly fight wars halfway across the globe, and produce military manuals on counterinsurgency warfare the way a do-it-yourself furniture maker would produce instructions for constructing a cabinet from a kit. We don't find it strange to have seventeen intelligence agencies, some devoted to listening in on, and spying on, the planet, or capable of running "covert wars" in tribal borderlands thousands of miles distant, or of flying unmanned drones over those same borderlands destroying those who come into camera view. We're inured to the bizarreness of it all and of the language and pretensions that go with it.

If *The Dictionary of American Empire-Speak* were ever produced, who here would buy it? Who would feel the need to check out what seems like the only reasonable and self-evident language for describing the world? How else, after all, would we operate? How else would any American in a position of authority talk in Washington or Baghdad or Islamabad or Rome?

So it undoubtedly seemed to the Romans, too. And we know what finally happened to their empire and the language that went with it. Such a language plays its role in normalizing the running of an empire. It allows officials (and in our case the media as well) not to see what would be inconvenient to the smooth functioning of such an enormous undertaking. In the good times, its uses are obvious. On the other hand, when the normal ways of empire cease to function well, that same language can suddenly blind the imperial custodians—which is, after all, what the foreign policy "team" of the Obama era is—to necessary realities. At a moment when it might be important to grasp what the "American face" in the mirror actually looks like, they can't see it, and sometimes what you can't bring yourself to see can hurt you.

Fixing What's Wrong in Washington... in Afghanistan

Explain something to me.

In the first months of 2010, unless you were insensate, you couldn't help running across someone talking, writing, speaking, or pontificating about how busted government is in the United States. State governments are increasingly broke and getting broker. The federal government, while running up the red ink, is, as just about everyone declares, "paralyzed" and so incapable of acting intelligently on just about anything.

No less a personage than Vice President Biden assured the co-anchor of the CBS *Early Show*, "Washington, right now, is broken." Indiana senator Evan Bayh used the very same word, *broken*, when he announced that he would not run for reelection and, in response to his decision, *Washington Post* media critic Howard Kurtz typically commented, "The system has been largely dysfunctional for nearly two decades, and everybody knows it." Voters seem to agree. Two words, "polarization" and "gridlock"—or hyperbolic cousins like "paralyzing hyperpartisanship"—dominated the news when the media described that dysfunctionalism. Foreign observers were similarly struck, hence a spate of pieces like the one in the British magazine the *Economist* headlined, "America's Democracy, a Study in Paralysis."

Washington's incapacity to govern now evidently seems to ever more Americans at the root of many looming problems. As the *New York Times* summed up one of them in a recent headline: "Party Gridlock in Washington Feeds Fear of a Debt Crisis." When President Obama leaves the confines of Washington for the campaign trail, he promptly attacks congressional "gridlock" and the "slash and burn politics" that have left the nation's capital tied in knots.

The Republicans, who ran us into this ditch in the Bush years, are now perfectly happy to be the party of "no"—and polls seem to indicate that it may be a fruitful strategy for the 2010 election. Meanwhile, special interests rule Washington and lobbying is king. As if to catch the spirit of this new reality, the president recently offered his vote of support to the sort of Wall Street CEOs who took Americans to the cleaners in the great economic meltdown of 2008 and are once again raking in the millions, while few have faith that change or improvement of any kind is in our future. Good governance, in other words, no longer seems part of the American tool kit and way of life.

Meanwhile, on the other side of the planet, to the tune of billions of taxpayer dollars, the U.S. military is promoting "good governance" with all its might. In a major campaign in the modest-sized city of Marja (a place next to no one had heard of) in Taliban-controlled Helmand Province, Afghanistan, it placed a bet on its ability to "restore the credibility" of President Hamid Karzai's government. In the process, it announced plans to unfurl a functioning city administration where none existed. According to its commanding general, Stanley McChrystal, as soon as the U.S. Army and the marines, along with British troops and Afghan forces, drove the Taliban out of town, he was prepared to roll out an Afghan "government in a box," including police, courts, and local services.

The U.S. military was intent, according to the *Wall Street Journal*, on "delivering a new administration and millions of dollars in aid to a place where government employees didn't dare set foot a week ago." Slated to be the future "mayor" of Marja, Haji Zahir, a businessman who spent fifteen years in Germany, was, according to press reports, living on a U.S. Marine base in the province until, one day soon, the American military could install him in an "abandoned government building" or simply "a clump of ruins" in that city.

He was, we were told, to arrive with four U.S. civilian advisers, two from the State Department and two from the U.S. Agency for International Development, described (in the typically patronizing language of American press reports) as his "mentors." They were to help him govern, and especially dole out the millions of dollars that the U.S. military has available to "reconstruct" Marja. Road-building projects were to be launched, schools refurbished, and a new clinic built, all to win Pashtun "hearts and minds." As soon as the fighting abated, White House press secretary Robert Gibbs suggested, the post-military emphasis would be on "economic development," with an influx of "military and civilian workers" who would "show a better way of life" to the town's inhabitants.

So explain something to me: Why does the military of a country convinced it's becoming ungovernable think itself so capable of making another ungovernable country governable? What's the military's skill set here? What lore, what body of political knowledge, are they drawing on? Who do they think they represent, the Philadelphia of 1776 or the Washington of 2010, and if the latter, why should Americans be considered the globe's leading experts in good government anymore? And while we're at it, fill me in on one other thing: Just what has convinced American officials in Afghanistan and the nation's capital that they have the special ability to teach, prod, wheedle, bribe, or force Afghans to embark on good governance in their country if we can't do it in Washington or Sacramento?

Explain something else to me: Why are our military and civilian leaders so confident that, after nine years of occupying the world's leading narco-state, nine years of reconstruction boondoggles and military failure, they suddenly have *the* key, *the* formula, to solve the Afghan mess? Why do leading officials suddenly believe *they* can make Afghan president Hamid Karzai into "a Winston Churchill who can rally his people," as one unnamed official told Matthew Rosenberg and Peter Spiegel of the *Wall Street Journal*—and all of this only months after Karzai, returned to office in a wildly fraudulent presidential election, overseeing a government riddled with corruption and drug money, and honeycombed with warlords sporting derelict reputations, was considered a discredited figure in Washington? And why do they think they can turn a man known mockingly as the "mayor" or "president" of Kabul (because his government has so little influence outside the capital) into a political force in southern Afghanistan?

And someone tell me: Just who picked the name Operation Moshtarak for the campaign in Marja? Why am I not convinced that it was an Afghan? Though news accounts say that the word means "togetherness" in Dari, why do I think that a better translation might be "crushing embrace"? What could "togetherness" really mean when, according to the *Wall Street Journal*, to make the final decision to launch the operation, already long announced, General McChrystal "stepped into his armored car for the short drive…to the presidential palace," and reportedly roused President Karzai from a nap for "a novel moment." Karzai agreed, of course, supposedly adding, "No one has ever asked me to decide before."

This is a black comedy of "governance." So is the fact that, from the highest administration officials and military men to those in the field, everyone speaks, evidently without the slightest self-consciousness, about putting an "Afghan face" on the (American) Marja campaign. National Security Adviser James Jones, for instance, spoke of the campaign having "'a much bigger Afghan face,' with two Afghans for every one U.S. soldier involved." And this way of thinking is so common that news reports regularly used the phrase, as in a recent Associated Press story: "Military officials say they are learning from past mistakes. The offensive is designed with an 'Afghan face.'"

And here's something else I'd like explained to me: Why does the U.S. press, at present so fierce about the lack of both "togetherness" and decent governance in Washington, report this sort of thing without comment, even though it reflects the deepest American contempt for putative "allies"? Why, for instance, can those same *Wall Street Journal* reporters write without blinking: "Western officials also are bringing Afghan cabinet members into strategy discussions, allowing them to select the officials who will run Marjah once it is cleared of Taliban, and pushing them before the cameras to emphasize the participation of Afghan troops in the offensive"? Allow? Push? Is this what we mean by "togetherness"?

Try to imagine all this in reverse—an Afghan general motoring over to the White House to wake up the president and ask whether an operation, already announced and ready to roll, can leave the starting gate? But why go on?

Just explain this to me: Why are the representatives of Washington, civilian and military, always so tone deaf when it comes to other peoples and other cultures? Why is it so hard for them to imagine what it might be like to be in someone else's shoes (or boots or sandals)? Why do they always arrive not just convinced that they have identified the right problems and are asking the right questions, but that they, and only they, have the right answers, when at home they seem to have none at all?

Thinking about this, I wonder what kind of "face" should be put on global governance in Washington?

FIVE

The Bush Legacy: What They Did (Wrong)

Ponzi Scheme Presidency

From the ninth to the seventh centuries BCE, the palace walls of the kings who ruled the Assyrian Empire were decorated with vast stone friezes, filled with enough dead bodies to sate any video-game maker and often depicting—in almost comic-strip style—various bloody royal victories and conquests. At least one of them shows Assyrian soldiers lopping off the heads of defeated enemies and piling them into pyramids for an early version of what, in the VCE (Vietnam Common Era) of the 1960s, Americans came to know as the "body count." So I learned by wandering through a traveling exhibit of ancient Assyrian art from the British Museum. On the audio tour accompanying the show, one expert pointed out that Assyrian scribes, part of an impressive imperial bureaucracy, carefully counted those heads and recorded the numbers for the greater glory of the king (as, in earlier centuries, Egyptian scribes had recorded counts of severed hands for victorious pharaohs).

Give credit to art museums. Is there anything stranger than wandering through one and locking eyes with a Rembrandt burgher staring out at you across the centuries? What a reminder of the common humanity we share with the distant past. In a darker sense, it's no less a reminder of our kinship across time to spot a little pyramid of heads on a frieze, imagine an Assyrian scribe making his count, and—eerily enough—feel at home. What a measure of just how few miles "the march of civilization" (as my parents' generation once called it) has actually covered.

Prejudiced Toward War

If you need an epitaph for the Bush administration, here's one to test out: *They tried. They really tried. But they couldn't help it. They just had to count.*

In a sense, George W. Bush did the Assyrians proud. With his secret prisons, his outsourced torture chambers, his officially approved kidnappings, the murders committed by his interrogators, the massacres committed by his troops and mercenaries, and the shock-and-awe slaughter he ordered from the air, it's easy enough to imagine what those Assyrian scribes would have counted. True, his White House didn't have friezes of his victories (one problem being that there were none to glorify). All it had was Saddam Hussein's captured pistol proudly stored in a small study off the Oval Office.

Almost three thousand years later, however, Bush's "scribes," still traveling with the imperial forces, continued to count the bodies as they piled ever higher in Iraq, Afghanistan, the Pakistani borderlands, and elsewhere. Many of those body counts were duly made public. This record of American "success" was visible to anyone who visited the Pentagon's website and viewed its upbeat news articles complete with enumerations of "Taliban fighters" (or, in Iraq, "terrorists"), the air force's news feed listing the number of sorties against "anti-Afghan forces," or the U.S. Central Command's stories of killing "Taliban militants."

On the other hand, history, as we know, doesn't repeat itself and—unlike the Assyrians—the Bush administration would have preferred *not* to count, or at least not to make its body counts public. One of its small but tellingly unsuccessful struggles, a sign of the depth of its failure on its own terms, was to avoid the release of those counts. This aversion to the body count made some sense. After all, since the 1950s, body counting for the U.S. military has invariably signaled not impending victory, but disaster, and even defeat.

One of the strangest things about the American empire has been this: Between 1945 and George W. Bush's second term, the U.S. economy, American corporations, and the dollar have held remarkable sway over much of the rest of the world. New York City has been the planet's financial capital and Washington its war capital. (Moscow, even at the height of the cold war, always came in a provincial second.) In the same period, the U.S. military effectively garrisoned much of the globe from the Horn of Africa to Greenland, from South Korea to Qatar, while its navy controlled the seven seas, its air force dominated the global skies, its nuclear command stood ready to unleash the powers of planetary death, and its space command watched the heavens. In the wake of the cold war, its various military commands (including Northcom, set up by the Bush administration in 2002, and Africom, set up in 2007) divided the greater part of the planet into what were essentially military satrapies. And yet, the U.S. military, post-1945, simply could not win the wars that mattered.

Because the neocons of the Bush administration brushed aside this counterintuitive fact, they believed themselves faced with an unparalleled opportunity triggered by the attacks of 9/11. With the highest-tech military on the planet, funded at levels no other set of nations could cumulatively match, the United States, they were convinced, was uniquely situated to give the phrase "sole superpower" historically unprecedented meaning. Even the Assyrians at their height, the Romans in their Pax Romana centuries, the British in the endless decades when the sun could never set on their empire, would prove amateurs by comparison.

In this sense, President Bush, Vice President Dick Cheney, Secretary of Defense Donald Rumsfeld, National Security Adviser Condoleezza Rice, and the various neocons in the administration were fundamentalist idolaters—and what they worshipped was the staggering power of the U.S. military. They were believers in a church whose main tenet was the efficacy of force above all else. Though few of them had the slightest military experience, they gave real meaning to the word "bellicose." They were prejudiced toward war. With awesome military power at their command, they were convinced that they could go it alone as the dominating force on the planet. As with true believers everywhere, they had only contempt for those they couldn't convert to their worldview. That contempt made "unilateralism" their strategy of choice, and a global Pax Americana their goal (along with, of course, a Pax Republicana at home).

The Return of the Body Count

It was in this context that they were not about to count the enemy dead. In their wars, as these fervent, inside-the-Beltway utopians saw it, there would be no need to do so. With the "shock and awe" forces at their command, they would refocus American attention on the real metric of victory, the taking of territory and of enemy capitals. At the same time, they were preparing to disarm the only enemy that truly scared them, the American people, by making none of the mistakes of the Vietnam era, including—as the president later admitted—counting bodies.

Of course, both the Pax Americana and the Pax Republicana would prove will-o'-the-wisps. As it turned out, the Bush administration, blind to the actual world it faced, disastrously miscalculated the nature of American power—especially military power—and what it was capable of doing. And yet, had they taken a clear-eyed look at what U.S. military power actually achieved in action since 1945, they might have been sobered. In the major wars (and even some minor actions) the military fought in those decades, it had been massively destructive but never victorious, nor even particularly successful. In many ways, in the classic phrase of Chinese Communist leader Mao Zedong, it had been a "paper tiger."

Yes, it had "won" largely meaningless victories—in Operation Urgent Fury, the invasion of the tiny Caribbean island of Grenada in 1983; against the toothless Panamanian regime of Manuel Noriega in Operation Just Cause in 1989; in Operation Desert Storm, largely an air campaign against Saddam Hussein's helpless military in 1990 (in a war that settled nothing); in NATO's Operation Deliberate Force, an air war against the essentially defenseless Serbian military in 1995. On the other hand, in Korea in the early 1950s and in Vietnam, Laos, and Cambodia from the 1960s into the early 1970s, it had committed its forces all but atomically, and yet had met nothing but stalemate, disaster, and defeat against enemies who, on paper at least, should not have been able to stand up to American power, while also, in more minor operations, running afoul of Iran in 1980 and Somalia in 1993.

It was in the context of defeat and then frustration in Korea that the counting of enemy bodies began. Once Chinese Communist armies had entered that war in massive numbers in late 1950, and inflicted a terrible series of defeats on American forces without being able to sweep them off the peninsula, that conflict settled into a "meat grinder" of a stalemate in which the hope of taking significant territory faded. Yet some measure of success was needed as public frustration mounted in the United States. In this way began the infamous body count of enemy dead.

The body count reappeared quite early in the Vietnam War, again as a shorthand way of measuring success in a conflict in which the taking of territory was almost meaningless, the countryside a hostile place, the enemy hard to distinguish from the general population, and our own in-country allies weak and largely unable to strengthen themselves. Those tallies of dead bodies, announced daily by military spokesmen to increasingly dubious reporters in Saigon, were the public face of American "success" in the Vietnam era. Each body was to be further evidence of what General William Westmoreland called "the light at the end of the tunnel." When those dead bodies and any sense of success began to part ways, however, when, in the terminology of the times, a "credibility gap" opened between the metrics of victory and reality, the body count morphed into a symbol of barbarism as well as of defeat, helping to stoke an antiwar movement.

This was why, in choosing to take on Saddam Hussein's shattered military in 2003—the administration expected a "cakewalk" campaign that would "shock and awe" enemies throughout the Middle East—they officially chose not to release any counts of enemy dead. General Tommy Franks, commander of the administration's Afghan operation in 2001 and the 2003 invasion of Iraq, put the party line succinctly: "We don't do body counts." As the president finally admitted in some frustration to a group of conservative columnists in October 2006, his administration had "made a conscious effort not to be a body-count team." Not intending to repeat the 1960s experience, he and his advisers had planned out an opposites war on the home front (anything done in Vietnam would not be done this time around), and that meant not offering official counts of the dead that might stoke an antiwar movement—until, that is, frustration truly set in, as in Korea and Vietnam.

When the taking of Baghdad in April 2003 proved no more a capstone on American victory than the taking of Kabul in November 2001, when everything began to go disastrously wrong and the carefully enumerated count of the U.S. military dead in Iraq rose precipitously, when "victory" (a word that the president still invoked fifteen times in a single speech in November 2005) adamantly refused to make an appearance, the moment for the body count had arrived. Despite all the planning, they just couldn't stop themselves. A frustrated President Bush expressed it this way: "We don't get to say that—a thousand of the enemy killed, or whatever the number was. It's happening. You just don't know it."

Soon enough the Pentagon was regularly releasing such figures in reports on its operations, and, in December 2006, the president, too, first slipped such a tally into a press briefing: "Our commanders report that the enemy has also suffered. Offensive operations by Iraqi and coalition forces against terrorists and insurgents and death squad leaders have yielded positive results. In the months of October, November, and the first week of December, we have killed or captured nearly 5,900 of the enemy."

It wasn't, of course, that no one had been counting. The president, as we know from *Washington Post* reporter Bob Woodward, kept "his own personal scorecard for the [global] war [on terror]"—photographs with "brief biographies and personality sketches" of the "Most Wanted Terrorists" ready to be crossed off when U.S. forces took them out. The military had been counting bodies as well, but as the possibility of victory disappeared into the charnel houses of Iraq and Afghanistan, the Pentagon and the president finally gave in. While this did not stoke an antiwar movement, it did represent a kind of surrender. It was as close as an administration that never owned up to error could come to admitting that two more disastrous wars had been added to a string of military failures in the truncated American Century.

That implicit admission, however, took years to arrive, and, in the meantime, Iraqis and Afghans—civilians, insurgents, terrorists, police, and military men—were dying in prodigious numbers.

The Charnel House of History

As it happened, others were also counting. Among the earliest of them, Iraq Body Count carefully added up Iraqi civilian deaths as documented in reputable media outlets. (Their estimate has over the years reached about 100,000—and, circumscribed by those words "documented" and "civilian," doesn't begin to get at the full scope of Iraqi deaths.) Various groups of scholars and pollsters also took up the task, using sophisticated sampling techniques, including door-to-door interviews under exceedingly dangerous conditions, to arrive at reasonable approximations of the Iraqi dead. They have come up with figures ranging from the low hundreds of thousands to a million or more in a country with a prewar population of perhaps twenty-six million. UN representatives have similarly attempted, under difficult circumstances, to keep a count of Iraqis fleeing into exile—exile being, after a fashion, a form of living death—and have estimated that more than 2 million Iraqis fled their country, while another 2.7 million, having fled their homes, were "internally displaced."

Similar attempts have been made for Afghanistan. Human Rights Watch has, for instance, done its best to tally civilian deaths from air strikes in that country. But, of course, the real body count in either country will never be known. One thing is certain, however: it is an obscenity of the present moment that Iraq, still a charnel house, still in a state of near total disrepair, still on the edge of a whole host of potential conflicts, should routinely be portrayed as a success, thanks to the Bush administration's "surge" policy in 2007–08. Only a country—or a punditry or a military—incapable of facing the depths of destruction let loose could reach such a conclusion.

If all roads once led to Rome, all acts of the Bush administration have led to destruction, and remarkably regularly to piles of dead or tortured bodies, counted or not. In fact, it's reasonable to say that every Bush administration foreign policy dream, including its first-term fantasy about a pacified "Greater Middle East" and its late second-term vision of a facilitated "peace process" between the Israelis and Palestinians, has ended in piles of bodies and in failure. The Bush administration's Global War on Terror and its subsidiary wars in Afghanistan and Iraq have, in effect, been a giant Ponzi scheme. At a cost of one trillion taxpayer dollars (but sure to be in the multitrillions when all is said and done), Bush's mad "global war" simply sucked needed money out of our world at levels that made Bernie Madoff seem like a street-corner hustler. Madoff, by his own accounting, squandered perhaps $50 billion of other people's money. The Bush administration took a trillion dollars of ours and handed it out to its crony corporate buddies and to the Pentagon as down payments on disaster. The laid off, the pensionless, the foreclosed, the suicides—imagine what that trillion dollars might have meant to them. And the price tag continues to soar.

Bernie Madoff ended up behind bars, but Bush administration officials will face no such accountability. Eight years of bodies, dead, broken, mutilated, abused; eight years of ruined lives down countless drains; eight years of massive destruction to places from Baghdad to New Orleans where nothing of significance was ever rebuilt. All this was brought to us by a president who said the following in his first inaugural address: "I will live and lead by these principles: to advance my convictions with civility...to call for responsibility and try to live it as well."

Bush ruled, we know, by quite a different code. Perhaps, in the future, historians will call him a Caesar—of destruction.

Veni, vidi, vastavi...I came, I saw, I devastated.

With Us or Against Us?

On September 11, 2001, in his first post-attack address to the nation, George W. Bush was already using the phrase "the war on terror." On September 13, Deputy Secretary of Defense Paul Wolfowitz announced that the administration was planning to do a lot more than just take out those who had attacked the United States. It was going to go about "removing the sanctuaries, removing the support systems, ending states who sponsor terrorism." We were, Bush said that day, in a state of "war." In fact, we were already in "the first war of the twenty-first century." As R. W. Apple Jr. of the *New York Times* reported, "[T]he Bush administration today gave the nations of the world a stark choice: stand with us against terrorism...or face the certain prospect of death and destruction." *Stand with us against terrorism*—or else. That would be the measure by which everything was assessed in the years to come. That very day, Secretary of State Colin Powell suggested that the United States would "rip [the bin Laden] network up" and "when we're through with that network, we will continue with a global assault on terrorism."

A global assault on terrorism. How quickly the president's Global War on Terror was on the scene. And no nation was immune. On September 14, the news was leaked that "a senior State Department official" had met with "15 Arab representatives" and delivered a stiff "with us or against us" message: Join "an international coalition against terrorism" or pay the price. There would be no safe havens. The choice—as Deputy Secretary of State Richard Armitage would reportedly inform Pakistan's intelligence director after the 9/11 attacks—was simple: Join the fight against al-Qaeda or "be prepared to be bombed. Be prepared to go back to the Stone Age."

From that day to this, the Global War on Terror would be the organizing principle for the Bush administration as it shook off "the constraints," loosed the CIA, and sent the U.S. military into action—as it went, in short, for the Stone Age jugular. The phrase "Global War on Terror," while never quite catching on with the public, would become so familiar in the corridors of Washington that it would soon morph into one of the least elegant acronyms around (GWOT), sometimes known among neocons as "World War IV"—they considered the cold war as World War III—or by military men and administration officials, after Iraq devolved from fantasy blitzkrieg into disaster, as "the Long War."

In the administration's eyes, the GWOT was to be the key to the magic kingdom, the lever with which the planet could be pried open for American dominion. It gave us an interest everywhere. After all, as Pentagon spokesperson Victoria Clarke would say in January 2002, "The estimates are anywhere from 50 or 60 to 70 countries that have al Qaeda cells in them. The scope extends far beyond Afghanistan." Administration officials, in other words, were already talking about a significant portion of existing states as potential targets. This was not surprising, since the GWOT was meant to create planetary free-fire zones. These al-Qaeda targets or breeding grounds, after all, had to be emptied. We were, as De-

fense Secretary Donald Rumsfeld and other top officials were saying almost immediately after 9/11, going to "drain" the global "swamp" of terrorists. And any countries that got in the way had better watch out.

With us or against us, that was the sum of it, and terror was its measure. If any connection could be made—even, as in the case of Saddam
Hussein and al-Qaeda, a thoroughly bogus one—it immediately offered
a compelling home-front explanation for possible intervention. The
safety and security of Americans was, after all, at stake in every single
place where those terrorist mosquitoes might be breeding. If you had the
oil lands of the planet on your mind (as was true with Dick Cheney's infamous Energy Task Force), then the threat of terrorism, especially nuclear terrorism, was a safe bet. If you wanted to fortify your position in
new oil lands, then the ticket was to have the Pentagon move in, as in
Africa, to help weak, possibly even failing, states prepare themselves
against the forces of terror.

At home, too, you were for us or against us. Those few who opposed
the Patriot Act, for instance, were obviously not patriots. The minority
who claimed that you couldn't be at "war" with "terror," that what was
needed in response to 9/11 was firm, ramped-up police action were simply laughed out of the room. In the kindliest light, they were wusses; in
the worst light, essentially traitors. They lacked not only American red-
bloodedness, but a willingness to be bloody-minded. End of story.

In the wake of those endlessly replayed, apocalyptic-looking scenes
of huge towers crumbling and near-mushroom-clouds of ash billowing
upwards, a chill of end-time fear swept through the nation. War, whatever
name you gave it, was quickly accepted as the obvious, commensurate
answer. In a nation in the grips of the politics of fear, it seemed reasonable
enough that a restoration of "security"—American security—should be
the be-all and end-all globally. Everything, then, was to be calibrated
against the successes of the GWOT.

From Seattle to Tampa, Toledo to Dallas, fear of terrorism became
a ruling passion, as well as a pure moneymaker for the mini homeland-
industrial complex that grew up around the new Department of Homeland Security. A thriving industry of private security firms, surveillance
outfits, and terror consultants proliferated. With their help, the United

States would be locked down in an unprecedented way—and to do that, we would also have to lock down the planet by any means necessary. We would fight "them" everywhere else, as the president would say again and again, so as not to fight them here.

A Nation of Cowards?

Most of the things that needed to be done to make us safer after 9/11 undoubtedly could have been done without much fuss, without a new, more bureaucratic, less efficient Department of Homeland Security, without a new, larger U.S. "intelligence community," without pumping ever more money into the Pentagon, and certainly without invading and occupying Iraq. Most societies that have dealt with terror, often far worse campaigns than what we have experienced, despite 9/11, have faced the dangers involved without becoming obsessive over their safety and security, without locking down their countries, and then attempting to do the same with the planet, as the Bush administration did. In the process, we may have turned ourselves into the functional equivalent of a nation of cowards, ready to sacrifice so much of value on the altar of the god of "security."

Think of it: Nineteen fanatics with hijacked planes, backed and funded by a relatively small movement based in one of the most impoverished places on the planet, did all this. Or, put more accurately, faced with the look of the apocalypse and the dominating urges of the Bush administration, we did what al-Qaeda's crew never could have done. Blinding ourselves via the GWOT, we released American hubris and fear upon the world, in the process making almost every situation we touched progressively worse for this country.

The fact is that those who run empires *can* sometimes turn the right levers in societies far away. Historically, they have sometimes been quite capable of seeing the world and actual power relations as they are, clearly enough to conquer, occupy, and pacify other lands. Sometimes, they were quite capable of dividing and ruling local peoples for long periods, or hiring native troops to do their dirty work. But here's the dirty miracle of the Bush administration: thinking GWOT all the way, its every move seemed to do more damage than the last, not just to the world, but to the fabric of the country they claimed they were protecting.

Opinion polls indicate that terrorism is no longer at the top of the American agenda of worries. Nonetheless, don't for a second think that the subject isn't lodged deep in national consciousness. When asked "How worried are you that you or someone in your family will become a victim of terrorism," a striking 39 percent of Americans were either "very worried" or "somewhat worried," and another 33 percent registered as "not too worried," according to the pollsters of CNN/Opinion Research Corporation.

The obsession with terrorism has also been built into our institutions, from Guantánamo to the Department of Homeland Security. It's had the time to sink its roots into fertile soil. It now has its own industries, lobbying groups, profit centers. Unbuilding it will be a formidable task indeed. It is a Bush legacy that no president is likely to reverse soon, if at all.

Ask yourself honestly: Can you imagine a future America without a Department of Homeland Security? Can you imagine a new administration ending the global lockdown that has become synonymous with Americanism?

Yet here's the irony. Essential power relations in the world turn out to have next to nothing to do with the War on Terror (which may someday be seen as the last great ideological gasp of American globalism). In this sense, terrorism, no matter how frightening, is an ephemeral phenomenon. The fact is, non-state groups wielding terror as their weapon of choice can cause terrible pain, harm, and localized mayhem, but they simply don't take down societies like ours. To think that possible is to misunderstand power on this planet. In that sense, the Global War on Terror's greatest achievement—for American rulers and ruled alike—may simply have been to block out the world as it was, to block out, that is, reality.

Hold Onto Your Underwear, This Is Not a National Emergency

Let me put American life in the Age of Terror into context, and then tell me you're not ready to get on the nearest plane heading anywhere, even toward Yemen.

In 2008, 14,180 Americans were murdered, according to the FBI. In that year, there were 34,017 fatal vehicle crashes in the United States and, so the U.S. Fire Administration tells us, 3,320 deaths by fire. More than 11,000 Americans died of the swine flu between April and mid-December 2009, according to the Centers for Disease Control and Prevention; on average, a staggering 443,600 Americans die yearly of illnesses related to tobacco use, reports the American Cancer Society; 5,000 Americans die annually from food-borne diseases; an estimated 1,760 children died from abuse or neglect in 2007; and the next year, 560 Americans died of weather-related conditions, according to the National Weather Service, including 126 from tornadoes, 67 from riptides, 58 from flash floods, 27 from lightning, 27 from avalanches, and 1 from a dust devil.

As for airplane fatalities, no American died in a crash of a U.S. carrier in either 2007 or 2008, despite 1.5 billion passengers transported. In 2009, planes certainly went down and people died. In June, for instance, a French flight on its way from Rio de Janeiro to Paris disappeared in bad weather over the Atlantic, killing 226. Continental Connection Flight 3407, a regional commuter flight, crashed into a house near Buffalo, New York, that February, killing 50, the first fatal crash of a U.S. commercial flight since August 2006. And in January 2009, US Airways Flight 1549, assaulted by a flock of birds, managed a brilliant landing in New York's Hudson River when disaster might have ensued. In none of these years did an airplane go down anywhere due to terrorism, though in 2007 two terrorists smashed a Jeep Cherokee loaded with propane tanks into the terminal of Glasgow International Airport. (No one was killed.)

The now-infamous Northwest Airlines Flight 253, carrying Umar Farouk Abdulmutallab and his bomb-laden underwear toward Detroit on Christmas Day 2009, had 290 passengers and crew, all of whom survived. Had the inept Abdulmutallab actually succeeded, the death toll would not have equaled the 324 traffic fatalities in Nevada in 2008; while the destruction of four Flight 253s from terrorism would not have equaled New York State's 2008 traffic death toll of 1,231 (341 of whom, or 51 more than those on Flight 253, were classified as "alcohol-impaired fatalities").

Had the twenty-three-year-old Nigerian set off his bomb, it would have been a nightmare for the people on board, and if it actually succeeded in taking the plane down, a tragedy for those who knew them. It would certainly have represented a safety and security issue, but it would not have been a national emergency, nor a national-security crisis.

And yet here's the strange thing: thanks to what didn't happen on Flight 253, the media essentially went mad, 24/7. Newspaper coverage of the failed plot and its ramifications actually grew for two full weeks after the incident until it had achieved something like full-spectrum dominance, according to the Pew Research Center's Project for Excellence in Journalism. In the days after Christmas, more than half the news links in blogs related to Flight 253. At the same time, the Republican criticism machine (and the media universe that goes with it) ramped up on the subject of the Obama administration's terror wimpiness; the global air transport system plunked down millions of dollars on new technology that evidently will *not* find underwear bombs; the homeland security–industrial complex had a field day; and fear, that adrenaline rush from hell, was further embedded in the American way of life.

Under the circumstances, you would never know that Americans living in the United States were in vanishingly little danger from terrorism, but in significant danger driving to the mall; or that alcohol, tobacco, *E. coli* bacteria, fire, domestic abuse, murder, and the weather present the sort of potentially fatal problems that might be worth worrying about, or even changing your behavior over, or perhaps investing some money in. Terrorism, not so much.

The few Americans who, since 2001, have died from anything that could be called a terror attack in the United States—whether the thirteen killed at Fort Hood or the soldier murdered outside an army recruiting office in Little Rock, Arkansas—were far outnumbered by the thirty-two dead in a 2007 mass killing at Virginia Tech, not to speak of the relatively regular moments when workers or former workers "go postal." Since September 11, terror in the United States has rated above fatalities from shark attacks and not much else. Since the economic meltdown of 2008, it has, in fact, been left in the shade by violent deaths that stem from reactions to job loss, foreclosure, inability to pay the rent, and so on.

This is seldom highlighted in a country perversely convulsed by, and that can't seem to get enough of, fantasies about being besieged by terrorists.

Institutionalizing Fear Inc.

The attacks of September 11, 2001, brought the fear of terrorism into the American bedroom via the TV screen. That fear was used with remarkable effectiveness by the Bush administration, which color-coded terror for its own ends.

Today, any possible or actual terror attack, any threat no matter how far-fetched, amateurish, poorly executed, or ineffective, raises a national alarm, always seeming to add to the power of the imperial presidency and threatening to open new "fronts" in the now-unnamed global war. The latest is in Yemen, thanks in part to that young Nigerian who was evidently armed with explosives by a home-grown organization of a few hundred men that goes by the name al-Qaeda in the Arabian Peninsula.

The fear of terrorism has, by now, been institutionalized in our society—quite literally so—even if the thing we're afraid of has, on the scale of human problems, something of the will-o'-the-wisp about it. For those who remember their cold war fiction, it's more specter than SPECTRE.

That fear has been embedded in what once was an un-American word, more easily associated with Soviet Russia or Nazi Germany: "homeland." It has replaced "country," "land," and "nation" in the language of the terror-mongers. "The homeland" is the place that terrorism, and nothing but terrorism, can violate. In 2002, that terror-embedded word got its own official government agency: the Department of Homeland Security, our second "defense" department, which has a 2010 budget of $39.4 billion (while overall "homeland security" spending in the 2010 budget reached $70.2 billion). Around it has grown up a little-attended-to homeland-security complex with its own interests, businesses, associations, and lobbyists (including jostling crowds of ex-politicians and ex-government bureaucrats).

As a result, more than eight years after 9/11, an amorphous state of mind has manifested itself in the actual state as a kind of Fear Inc. A number of factors have clearly gone into the creation of Fear Inc. and now ensure that fear is the drug constantly shot into the American body politic. These would include:

The imperial presidency: The Bush administration used fear not only to promote its wars and its Global War on Terror, but also to unchain the commander in chief of an already imperial presidency from a host of re-straints. The dangers of terror and of al-Qaeda, which became the global bogeyman, and the various proposed responses to it, including kidnapping ("extraordinary rendition"), secret imprisonment, and torture, turned out to be the royal road to the American unconscious and so to a presidency determined, as Secretary of Defense Donald Rumsfeld and others liked to say, to take the gloves off. It remains so and, as a result, under Barack Obama, the imperial presidency only seems to gain ground. Under the pressure of the Flight 253 incident, for instance, the Obama administration has adopted the Bush administration's position that a president, under certain circumstances, has the authority to order the assassination of an American citizen abroad. In this case, New Mexico–born Islamic cleric Anwar Aulaqi, who has been linked to the 9/11 plotters, the Fort Hood killer, and Abdulmutallab. The Bush administration opened the door to this possibility and now a Democratic president may be stepping through.

The 24/7 media moment: 24/7 blitz coverage was once reserved for the deaths of presidents (as in the assassination of John F. Kennedy) and public events of agreed-upon import. In 1994, however, it became the coin of the media realm for any event bizarre enough, sensational enough, celebrity-based enough to glue eyeballs. That June, O. J. Simpson engaged in his infamous low-speed car "chase" through Orange County followed by more than twenty news helicopters while ninety-five million viewers tuned in and thousands more gathered at highway overpasses to watch. No one's ever looked back. Of course, in a traditional media world that's shedding foreign and domestic bureaus and axing hordes of reporters, radically downsizing newsrooms and shrinking papers to next to nothing, the advantages of focusing reportorial energies on just one thing at a time are obvious. Those 24/7 energies are now regularly focused on the fear of terrorism and events that contribute to it, like the plot to down Flight 253.

The Republican criticism machine and the media that go with it: Once upon a time, even successful Republican administrations didn't have their own megaphone. That's why, in the Vietnam era, the Nixon admin-istration battled the *New York Times* so fiercely (and—my own guess—that played a part in forcing the creation of the first "op-ed" page in 1970, which allowed administration figures like Vice President Spiro Agnew and ex-Nixon speechwriter William Safire to gain a voice at the paper). By the George W. Bush era, the struggle had abated. The *Times* and papers like it only had to be pacified or cut out of the loop, since from TV to talk radio, publishing to publicity, the Republicans had their own megaphone ready at hand. This is, by now, a machine chockablock full of politicians and ex-politicians, publishers, pundits, military "experts," journalists, shock jocks, and the like (categories that have a tendency to blend into each other). It adds up to a seamless web of promotion, publicity, and din. It's capable of gearing up on no notice and going on until a subject—none more popular than terrorism and Democratic spinelessness in the face of it—is temporarily flogged to death. It ensures that any failed terror attack, no matter how hopeless or pathetic, will be in the headlines and in public consciousness. It circulates constant fantasies about possible future apocalyptic terror attacks with atomic weaponry or other weapons of mass destruction. (And in all of the above, of course, it is helped by a host of tagalong pundits and experts, news shows, and news reports from the more liberal side of the aisle.)

The Democrats who don't dare: It's remarkable that the sharpest president we've had in a while didn't dare get up in front of the American people after Flight 253 landed and tell everyone to calm down. He didn't, in fact, have a single intelligent thing to say about the event. He certainly didn't remind Americans that, whatever happened to Flight 253, they stood in far more danger heading out of their driveways behind the wheel or pulling into a bar on the way home for a beer or two. Instead, the Obama administration essentially abjectly apologized, insisted it would focus yet more effort and money on making America safe from air terrorism, widened a new front in the Global War on Terror in Yemen (speeding extra money and U.S. advisers that way), and when the din from its critics didn't end, "pushed back," as Peter Baker of the *New York Times* wrote, by claiming "that they were handling terror suspects much as the previous administration did." It's striking when a Democratic administration finds safety in the claim that it's acting like a Republican one, that it's following the path to the imperial presidency already cleared by George W. Bush. Fear does that to you, and the fear of terror has been institutionalized at the top as well as the bottom of society.

9/11 Never Ends

Fear has a way of reordering human worlds. That only a relatively small number of determined fanatics with extraordinarily limited access to American soil keep Fear Inc. afloat should, by now, be obvious. What the fear machine produces is the dark underside of the charming Saul Steinberg *New Yorker* cover, "A View of the World from 9th Avenue," in which Manhattan looms vast as the rest of the planet fades into near nothingness.

When you see the world "from 9th Avenue," or from an all-al-Qaeda-all-the-time "news" channel, you see it phantasmagorically. It's out of all realistic shape and proportion, which means you naturally make stupid decisions. You become incapable of sorting out what matters and what doesn't, what's primary and what's secondary. You become, in short, manipulable.

This is our situation today.

People always wonder: What would the impact of a second 9/11-style attack be on this country? Seldom noticed, however, is that all the pinprick terror events blown up to apocalyptic proportions add up to a second, third, fourth, fifth 9/11 when it comes to American consciousness.

So the next time a Flight 253 occurs and the Republicans go postal, the media morphs into its 24/7 national security disaster mode, the pundits register red on the terror-news scale, the president defends himself by reaffirming that he is doing just what the Bush administration would have done, the homeland security lobbyists begin calling for yet more funds for yet more machinery, and nothing much happens, remember those drunken drivers, arsonists, and tobacco merchants, even that single dust devil and say:

Hold onto your underpants, this is *not* a national emergency.

SIX

Obama's War

How Safe Do You Want to Be?

Almost like clockwork, the reports float up to us from thousands of miles away, as if from another universe. Every couple of days they seem to arrive from Afghan villages that few Americans will ever see without weapon in hand. Every few days, they appear from a world almost beyond our imagining, and always they concern death—so many lives snuffed out so regularly for years now. Unfortunately, those news stories are so unimportant in our world that they seldom make it onto, no less off of, the inside pages of our papers. They're so repetitive that, once you've started reading them, you could write them in your sleep from thousands of miles away.

Like obituaries, they follow a simple pattern. Often the news initially arrives buried in summary war reports based on U.S. military (or NATO) announcements of small triumphs—so many "insurgents," or "terrorists," or "foreign militants," or "anti-Afghan forces" killed in an air strike or a raid on a house or a village. And these days, often remarkably quickly, even in the same piece, come the challenges. Some local official or provincial governor or police chief in the area insists that those dead "terrorists" or "militants" were actually so many women, children, old men, innocent civilians, members of a wedding party or a funeral. (A recent study of the death-dealing weapons of the Iraq war, published in the *New England*

Journal of Medicine, indicates that air strikes are notoriously good at taking out civilians. Eighty-five percent of the deaths from air strikes in Iraq were, the study estimated, women and children, and of all methods, including suicide and car bombs, airpower "killed the most civilians per event.")

Then come the standard-issue denials from U.S. military officials or coalition spokespeople: those killed were insurgents, and the intelligence information on which the strike or raid had been based was accurate. In these years, American spokespeople have generally retreated from their initial claims only step by begrudging step. Admittedly, there's been some change in the assertion/repeated denial/investigation pattern instituted by American forces. Now, assertion and denial are sometimes followed relatively quickly by acknowledgment, apology, and payment. Now, when the irrefutable meets the unchallengeable, American spokespeople tend to own up to it. This new tactic has been a response to rising Afghan outrage over the repeated killing of civilians in U.S. raids and air strikes. But like the denials and the investigations, this, too, is intended to make everything go away, while our war itself—those missiles loosed, those doors kicked down in the middle of the night—continues.

Consider just one incident that went almost uncovered in the U.S. media. According to an Agence France-Presse account, in a raid in the eastern Afghan province of Khost, the U.S. military first reported a small success: four "armed militants" killed. It took next to no time, however, for those four militants to morph into the family of an Afghan National Army artillery commander named Awal Khan. As it happened, Khan himself was on duty in another province at the time. According to the report, the tally of the slain, some of whom may have gone to the roof of their house to defend themselves against armed men they evidently believed to be robbers or bandits, included Awal Khan's "schoolteacher wife, a 17-year-old daughter named Nadia, a 15-year-old son, Aimal, and his brother, who worked for a government department. Another daughter was wounded." The report continues, "After the shooting, the pregnant wife of Khan's cousin, who lived next door, went outside her home and was shot five times in the abdomen." She survived, but her fetus, "hit by bullets," didn't. Khan's wife worked at a school supported by the international aid organization CARE, which issued a statement strongly condemning the raid and demanding that "international military forces operating in Afghanistan are held accountable for their actions and avoid all attacks on innocent civilians in the country."

In accordance with its new policy, the United States issued an apology:

> Further inquiries into the Coalition and [Afghan National Security Forces] ANSF operation in Khost earlier today suggest that the people killed and wounded were not enemy combatants as previously reported.... Coalition and Afghan forces do not believe that this family was involved with militant activities and that they were defending their home against an unknown threat.... "We deeply regret the tragic loss of life in this precious family. Words alone cannot begin to express our regret and sympathy and we will ensure the surviving family members are properly cared for," said Brig. Gen. Michael A. Ryan, U.S. Forces–Afghanistan.

A U.S. military spokesman added, "There will undoubtedly be some financial assistance and other types of assistance [to the survivors]."

But the family quite reasonably wanted more than a press-release apology. The grieving husband, father, and brother said, "I want the coalition leaders to expose those behind this and punish them," adding, "[T]he Afghan government should resign if it could not protect its people." Afghan president Hamid Karzai, as he has done many times during past incidents, repeatedly demanded an explanation for the deaths and asked that such raids and air strikes be drastically curtailed.

What Your Safety Is Worth

All of this, however, is little more than a shadow play against which the ongoing war continues to be relentlessly prosecuted. In Afghanistan, and increasingly in Pakistan, civilian deaths are inseparable from this war. Though they may be referred to as "collateral damage," increasingly in all wars, and certainly in counterinsurgency campaigns involving air power, the killing of civilians lies at the heart of the matter, while the killing of soldiers might be thought of as the true collateral activity.

Pretending that these "mistakes" will cease or be ameliorated as long as the war is being prosecuted is little short of folly. After all, "mistake" after "mistake" continues to be made. The first Afghan wedding party was obliterated in late December 2001, when an American air strike killed up to 110 Afghan revelers with only 2 survivors. At least 4 more have been blown away since then. And count on it, there will be others.

A UN survey tallied up 2,118 civilians killed in Afghanistan in 2008, a striking rise over the previous year's figure, of which 828 were ascribed to U.S., NATO, and Afghan Army actions rather than to suicide bombers or Taliban guerrillas. Given the difficulty of counting the dead in wartime, any figures like these are likely to be significant undercounts.

By now, we've filled up endless "towers" with dead Afghan civilians. And that's clearly not going to change, apologies or not, especially when U.S. forces are "surging" into the southern and eastern parts of the country, while the CIA's drone war on the Pakistani border expands.

And how exactly do we explain this ever-rising pile of civilian dead to ourselves? It's being done, so we've been told, for our safety and security here in the United States. The former vice president has made clear that among the great achievements of the Bush administration was the prevention of a second 9/11. And President Obama continues to play the 9/11 card heavily. As he reportedly put it, he is not "'naive about how dangerous this world is' and...wakes up every day and goes to bed every night thinking and worrying 'about how to keep the American people safe.'"

Personally, I always thought that we could have locked our plane doors and gone home long ago. We were never in mortal danger from al-Qaeda in the backlands of Afghanistan, despite the perfervid imagination of the previous administration and the riotous fears of so many Americans. The rag-tag group that attacked us in September 2001 was then capable of committing acts of terror on a spectacular scale (two U.S. embassy buildings in Africa, a destroyer in a Yemeni harbor, and of course those towers in New York and the Pentagon), but only every couple of years. In other words, al-Qaeda was capable of stunning this country and of killing Americans, but was never a threat to the nation itself.

All this, of course, was compounded by the fact that the Bush administration couldn't have cared less about al-Qaeda before the 9/11 attacks, that the "Defense Department" imagined its job to be "power projection" abroad, not protecting American shores (or air space), and that our intelligence agencies were in chaos. So those towers came down and rather than simply going after the group that had acted against us, we invaded Afghanistan ("no safe havens for terrorists") and began plans for "regime change" in Iraq and beyond. In the process, the Bush administration went to extreme efforts to fetishize our own safety and security, and simultaneously turned "security" into a lucrative endeavor.

Of course, elsewhere people have lived through remarkable paroxysms of violence and terror without the sort of fuss and fear this nation exhibited, or the money-making that went with it. If you want to be reminded of just how fetishistic our focus on our own safety was, consider a 2005 news article written for a Florida newspaper, "Weeki Wachee Mermaids in Terrorists' Cross Hairs?" It began:

> Who on earth would ever want to harm the Weeki Wachee mermaids?
>
> It staggers the imagination.
>
> Still, the U.S. Department of Homeland Security has named Weeki Wachee Springs as the potential terror target of Hernando County, according to a theme park official.
>
> The Weeki Wachee staff is teaming up with the Hernando County Sheriff's Office to "harden the target" by keeping the mermaid theater and the rest of the park safe from a potential terror attack, said marketing and promotion manager John Athanason....
>
> Terror-prevention plans for Weeki Wachee may include adding surveillance cameras, installing lights in the parking lot and securing areas in the roadside attraction where there may be "security breaches," he said.
>
> But Athanason is also realistic. He said Walt Disney World is a bigger attraction and is likely to receive more counterterrorism funds.

This was how, in deepest Florida, distant Utah, or on the Texas border, all places about as likely to be hit by an al-Qaeda attack as by a meteor, Americans were obsessing about keeping everything near and dear to them safe and secure. At the same time, of course, the Bush administration was breaking the bank at the Pentagon and in its Global War on Terror, while preparing the way for an America that would be plunged into startling economic insecurity.

Let's for a moment assume, however, that our safety really was, and remains, at stake in a war halfway across the planet. If so, let me ask you a question: What's your "safety" really worth? Are you truly willing to trade the lives of Awal Khan's family for a blanket guarantee of your safety, and not just his family, but all those Afghan one-year-olds, all those wedding parties that are—yes, they really are—going to be blown away in the years to come for you?

If, in 1979, as the Carter presidency was ending and our Afghan wars were beginning, you had told any group of Americans that we would be ever more disastrously involved in Afghanistan for thirty years, that, even then, no end would be in sight, and that we would twice declare victory (in 1989 after the Soviets withdrew, and again in 2001 when the Afghan capital Kabul was taken from the Taliban) only to discover that disaster followed, they undoubtedly would have thought you mad. Afghanistan? Please. You might as well have said Mars. Now, three decades later, it's possible to see that every step taken from the earliest support for Afghan jihadis in their anti-Soviet war has only made things worse for us, and ever so much worse for the Afghans.

Maybe it's time to put less value on the idea of absolute American safety, since in many ways the Bush administration definition of our safety and security, which did not go into retirement with George and Dick, is now in the process of breaking us. Even if Dick Cheney and his minions prevented another 9/11 (and there's no evidence they did), in doing so, look what they brought down around our ears—and all in the name of our safety, and ours alone.

Ask yourself these questions, then, in the dead of night: Do we really want stories like Awal Khan's to float up out of the villages of Afghanistan, Pakistan, and who knows where else for years, even decades, to come? Does that seem right? Is your supposed safety worth that?

General "Manhunter"

Stanley McChrystal is the general from the dark side (and proud of it). So his appointment by President Obama to run the Afghan War seems to signal an administration going for broke. It's heading straight into what, in the Vietnam era, was known as "the big muddy," doubling down on the bad decisions of his predecessor.

General McChrystal comes from a world where killing by any means is the norm and a blanket of secrecy provides the necessary protection. For five years he commanded the Pentagon's super-secret Joint Special Operations Command (JSOC), which, among other things, ran what Seymour Hersh has described as an "executive assassination wing" out of Vice President Cheney's office. Cheney returned the favor by giving McChrystal a ringing endorsement for the position of Afghan War commander: "I think you'd be hard put to find anyone better than Stan."

McChrystal gained a certain renown when President Bush touted him as the man responsible for tracking down and eliminating al-Qaeda-in-Mesopotamia leader Abu Musab al-Zarqawi. The secret force of "man-hunters" he commanded in Iraq had its own secret detention and interrogation center near Baghdad, Camp Nama, where bad things happened regularly, and the unit there, Task Force 6-26, had its own slogan: "If you don't make them bleed, they can't prosecute for it." (Since some of the task force's members were, in the end, prosecuted, the bleeding evidently wasn't avoided.) In the Bush years, McChrystal was extremely close to Secretary of Defense Donald Rumsfeld. The super-secret force he commanded was, in fact, part of Rumsfeld's effort to seize control of, and Pentagonize, the covert, on-the-ground activities that were once the purview of the CIA.

Behind McChrystal lies a string of targeted executions that may run into the hundreds, as well as accusations of torture and abuse by troops under his command, not to speak of a role in the cover-up of the circumstances surrounding the death of army ranger and former National Football League player Pat Tillman. The general has reportedly long thought of Afghanistan and Pakistan as a single battlefield, which means that he was a premature adherent to the idea of an Af-Pak—that is, expanded—war. While in Afghanistan in 2008, the New York Times reported, he was a "key advocate…of a plan, ultimately approved by President George W. Bush, to use American commandos to strike at Taliban sanctuaries in Pakistan." This end-of-term Bush program provoked such anger and blowback in Pakistan that it was reportedly halted after two cross-border raids, one of which killed civilians.

All of this offers more than a hint of the sort of "new thinking and new approaches"—to use Secretary of Defense Robert Gates's words—that the Obama administration expects General McChrystal to bring to the devolving Af-Pak battlefield. He is, in a sense, both a legacy figure from the worst days of the Bush-Cheney-Rumsfeld era and the firstborn child of Obama-era Washington's growing desperation and hysteria over the wars it inherited.

But none of this matters to what remains of mainstream news analysis. The press establishment has had a long-term love affair with McChrystal. Back in 2006, when Bush first touted him, *Newsweek* reporters Michael Hirsh and John Barry dubbed him "a rising star" in the army and one of the "Jedi Knights who are fighting in what Cheney calls 'the shadows.'" More recently, in that mix of sports lingo, Hollywood-ese, and just plain hyperbole that makes armchair war strategizing just so much fun, *Washington Post* columnist David Ignatius claimed that CentCom commander General David Petraeus, who picked McChrystal as his man in Afghanistan, is "assembling an all-star team" and that McChrystal himself is "a rising superstar who, like Petraeus, has helped reinvent the U.S. Army." Is that all?

When it comes to pure hagiography, however, the prize goes to Elisabeth Bumiller and Mark Mazzetti of the *New York Times*, who wrote a front-pager, "A General Steps from the Shadows," that painted a picture of McChrystal as a mutant cross between Superman and a saint. Among other things, it described the general as "an ascetic who...usually eats just one meal a day, in the evening, to avoid sluggishness. He is known for operating on a few hours' sleep and for running to and from work while listening to audio books on an iPod.... [He has] an encyclopedic, even obsessive, knowledge about the lives of terrorists.... [He is] a warrior-scholar, comfortable with diplomats, politicians." The quotes Bumiller and Mazzetti dug up from others were no less spectacular: "He's got all the Special Ops attributes, plus an intellect." "If you asked me the first thing that comes to mind about General McChrystal...I think of no body fat."

Above all, General McChrystal was praised for being "more aggressive" than his stick-in-the-mud predecessor. He would, as Bumiller and Thom Shanker reported in another piece, bring "a more aggressive and innovative approach to a worsening seven-year war." The general, we were assured, liked operations without body fat, but with plenty of punch. And though no one quite said this, given his closeness to Rumsfeld and possibly Cheney, his mentality was undoubtedly a GWOT one, which translates into no respect for boundaries, restraints, or the sovereignty of others. After all, as journalist Gareth Porter pointed out in a thoughtful *Asia Times* portrait of the new Afghan War commander, Secretary of Defense Donald Rumsfeld granted the parent of JSOC, the Special Operations Command (SOCOM), "the authority to carry out actions unilaterally anywhere on the globe."

McChrystal's appointment, then, represented a decision by Washington to dispatch the bull directly to the china shop. The *Post*'s Ignatius even compared McChrystal's boss Petraeus and Obama's special envoy to the region, Richard Holbrooke, to "two headstrong bulls in a small paddock." He then concluded his paean to all of them with this passage: "Obama knows the immense difficulty of trying to fix a broken Afghanistan and make it a functioning, modern country. But with his two bulls, Petraeus and Holbrooke, he's marching his presidency into the 'graveyard of empires' anyway." McChrystal is evidently the third bull, the one slated to start knocking over the tombstones.

Of course, there were now so many bulls in this particular china shop that smashing was increasingly the name of the game. The early moves of the Obama administration, when combined with the momentum of the situation it inherited, resulted in a surprisingly sweeping expansion of the Af-Pak War. President Obama has, in fact, opted for a down-and-dirty war strategy in search of some at least minimalist form of success. For this, McChrystal was the poster boy. Former Afghan commander General David McKiernan believed that, "as a NATO commander, my mandate stops at the [Afghan] border. So unless there is a clear case of self-protection to fire across the border, we don't consider any operations across the border in the tribal areas." Not so Stan McChrystal. The idea that the "responsibilities" of U.S. generals fighting the Afghan War "ended at the border with Pakistan," Mark Mazzetti and Eric Schmitt of the *Times* reported, was now considered part of an "old mind-set." McChrystal represented those "fresh eyes" that Secretary of Defense Robert Gates talked about in the press conference announcing the general's appointment. As Mazzetti and Schmitt pointed out, "Among [McChrystal's] last projects as the head of the Joint Special Operations Command was to better coordinate Pentagon and Central Intelligence Agency efforts on both sides of the porous border."

For those old enough to remember, we've been here before. Administrations that start down a path of expansion in such a war find themselves strangely locked in if things don't work out as expected and the situation continues to deteriorate. In Vietnam, the result was escalation after escalation. President Obama and his foreign policy team now seem locked into an expanding war. Despite the fact that the application of force has not only failed for years, but actually fed that expansion, they also seem to be locked into a policy of applying ever greater force, leading to further expansions of what is already "Obama's war."

Obama and the Imperial Presidency

Let's face it. Barack Obama did not win an election to be president of Goodwill Industries, or the YMCA, or the Ford Foundation. He may be remarkable in many ways, but he is also president of the United States, which means that he is head honcho for the globe's single great garrison state that now, to a significant extent, lives off war and the preparations for future war. He is today the proprietor of U.S. bases, or facilities, or prepositioned military material (or all of the above) in Djibouti in the Horn of Africa, in Bahrain, Oman, the United Arab Emirates, Qatar, Kuwait, Iraq (and Iraqi Kurdistan), Turkey, Afghanistan, Pakistan (where the U.S. military and the CIA share Pakistani military facilities), and a major air force facility on the British-controlled Indian Ocean island of Diego Garcia, to speak only of the region extending from North Africa to the Chinese border that the Bush loyalists used to call "the Greater Middle East." Some U.S. bases in these countries are microscopic and solitary, but others, like Camp Victory or Balad Air Base, both in Iraq, are gigantic installations in a web of embedded bases.

When he entered the Oval Office, Barack Obama also inherited the largest embassy on Earth, built in Baghdad by the Bush administration to imperial proportions as a regional command center. It now houses what are politely referred to as a thousand "diplomats." As it happens, this project wasn't just an aberration of the Bush era. Another embassy, just as gigantic, expected to house "a large military and intelligence contingent," will be constructed by the Obama administration in its new war capital, Islamabad, Pakistan. Once the usual cost overruns are added in, it may turn out be the first billion-dollar embassy. Each of these command centers will, assumedly, anchor the U.S. presence in the Greater Middle East.

Barack Obama is also now the commander in chief of eleven aircraft carrier strike groups, which regularly patrol the planet's sea-lanes. He sits atop a U.S. Intelligence Community (yes, that's what our intelligence crew like to call themselves) of at least sixteen squabbling, overlapping agencies, heavily Pentagonized, and often at each other's throats. They have a cumulative hush-hush budget of perhaps $50 billion or more. (Imagine a power so obsessively consumed by the idea of "intelligence" that it is willing to support sixteen sizeable separate outfits doing such work, and that's not even counting various smaller offices dedicated to intelligence activities.)

The new president will preside over a country that now ponies up almost half the world's total military expenditures. His 2010 estimated Pentagon budget will be marginally higher than the last staggering one from the Bush years.

He now inhabits a Washington in which deep thinking consists of a pundit like Michael O'Hanlon of the Brookings Institution whining that these bloated sums are, in fact, too little to "maintain" U.S. forces (a budgetary increase of 7 to 8 percent per year for the next decade would, he claims, be just adequate); in which forward looking means Secretary of Defense Robert Gates reorienting military spending toward preparations for fighting one, two, many Afghanistans; and in which out-of-the-box, futuristic thinking means letting the blue-skies crew at DARPA (the Defense Advanced Research Projects Agency) loose on far-out problems like how to turn "programmable matter" into future Transformer-like weapons of war.

While Obama enthusiasts can take pride in the appointment of some out-of-the-box thinkers in domestic areas, including energy, health, and the science of the environment, in two crucial areas his appointments are pure old-line Washington and have been so from the first post-election transitional moments. His key economic players and advisers are largely a crew of former Clintonistas, or Clintonista wannabes or protégés like

Secretary of the Treasury Tim Geithner. They are distinctly inside-the-boxers, some of them responsible for the thinking that, in the 1990s, led directly to global economic catastrophe.

As for foreign policy, had the November election results been different, Obama's top team of today could just as easily have been appointed by Senator John McCain. National Security Adviser James Jones was actually a McCain friend, Gates is someone he admired, and Hillary Clinton is a figure he could well have picked for a top post after a narrow election victory, had he decided to reach out to the Democrats. As a group, Obama's key foreign policy figures and advisers are traditional players in the national security state and pre-Bush-style Washington guardians of American power, thinking globally in familiar ways.

The Dream Team in Afghanistan

Barack Obama didn't just inherit the presidency. He went for it. And he isn't just sitting atop it. He's actively using it. He's wielding power. In foreign policy terms, Obama is settling in—and doing so in largely predictable ways. He may, for example, have declared a sunshine policy when it comes to transparency in government, but in his war policies in Afghanistan and Pakistan, his imperial avatar is already plunging deep into the dark, distinctly opaque valley of death. He chose to appoint as his Afghan commander General Stanley A. McChrystal, who from 2003 to 2008 ran a special operations outfit in Iraq (and then Afghanistan) so secret that the Pentagon avoided mention of it. In those years, its operatives were torturing, abusing, and killing Iraqis as part of a systematic targeted assassination program on a large scale. It was, for those who remember the Vietnam era, a mini–Phoenix program in which possibly hundreds of enemies were assassinated: al-Qaeda-in-Iraq types, but also Sunni insurgents, and Sadrists (not to speak of others, since informers always settle scores and turn over their own personal enemies as well). Although he's being touted in the press as the man to bring the real deal in counterinsurgency to Afghanistan (and "protect" the Afghan population in the bargain), his actual field is "counterterrorism."

The team McChrystal assembled to lead his operations in Afghanistan and Pakistan tells you what you really need to know. It's filled with special operations types. The expertise of his chosen key lieutenants is, above all, in special ops work. At the same time, reports Rowan Scarborough at Fox News, an extra thousand special operations troops are being "quietly" dispatched to Afghanistan, bringing the total number there to about five thousand. The special operations forces, with their kick-down-the-door night raids and air strikes, have been involved in the most notorious incidents of civilian slaughter, which continue to enrage Afghans.

Note, by the way, that while the president is surging into Afghanistan twenty-one thousand troops and advisers (as well as those special ops forces), ever more civilian diplomats and advisers, and ever larger infusions of money, there is now to be a command surge as well. General McChrystal, according to the *New York Times*,

> has been given carte blanche to handpick a dream team of subordinates, including many special operations veterans....
>
> [He] is assembling a corps of 400 officers and soldiers who will rotate between the United States and Afghanistan for a minimum of three years. That kind of commitment to one theater of combat is unknown in the military today outside special operations, but reflects an approach being imported by General McChrystal, who spent five years in charge of secret commando teams in Iraq and Afghanistan.

Like the new mega-embassy in Pakistan, this figure tells us a great deal about the top-heavy manner in which the planet's super-garrison state fights its wars.

That team of Spartans, according to the *New York Times*, is being formed with, minimally, a three-year time horizon (though the actual Spartans needed only three hundred warriors in total at the battle of Thermopylae). This in itself is striking. After all, the Afghan War started in November 2001. So when the shortest possible Afghan tour of duty of the four hundred is over, the war will have been going on for more than ten and a half years—and no one dares to predict that, three years from now, the war will actually be at an end. If we are more honest, the figure cited should be not one decade, but three. After all, our Afghan adventure really began in 1980, when, in the jihad against the Soviets, we were supporting some of the very same fundamentalist figures now allied with the Taliban and fighting against us in Afghanistan—just as, once upon a time, we looked positively upon the Taliban; just as, once, we looked positively upon Saddam Hussein, who was for a while seen as our potential bulwark in the Middle East against the fundamentalist Islamic Republic of Iran. (Remarkably enough, only Iran has steadily retained its position as our regional enemy over these decades.)

What a record, then, of blood and war, of great power politics and imperial hubris, of support for the heinous (including various fundamentalist groups and grim, authoritarian Middle Eastern regimes who remain our allies to this day). What a tale of imperial power frittered away and treasure squandered. Truly, Rudyard Kipling would have been able to do something with this.

As for me, I find myself in awe of these decades of folly. I'm no Kipling, but I am aware that this sorry tale has taken up almost half of my lifetime with no end in sight.

In the meantime, our new president has loosed the manhunters. *His* manhunters. This is where charisma disappears into the charnel house of history.

A War That No Longer Needs a Justification

The Bush administration invaded Iraq in March 2003 with a force of approximately 130,000 troops. Top White House and Pentagon officials like Deputy Secretary of Defense Paul Wolfowitz were convinced that, by August, those troops, welcomed with open arms by the oppressed Iraqis, would be drawn down to 30,000 or 40,000 and housed in newly built, permanent military bases largely away from the country's urban areas. This was to be part of what now is called a "strategic partnership" in the Middle East. Almost five and a half years later, the United States still has approximately 130,000 troops in Iraq. Top administration officials are now talking about "modestly accelerated" rates of troop withdrawal, if all goes well. This is what passes for progress in Iraq today.

To understand the real prospects for withdrawal, we would do well to consider some interlocking histories in Iraq.

A history of the bicycle in Iraq: In imagistic terms, the Bush administration biked into Iraq. Top Washington officials loved the idea that they were training the eager Iraqi kid in how to ride the bike of democracy. President George W. Bush talked regularly about the moment when we might take the "training wheels" off the Iraqi bike and let the little fella ride into the democratic sunset on his own. His secretary of defense, Donald Rumsfeld, spoke about the difficult moment when a parent has to decide whether to take that steadying hand off the bike seat and let the tyke pedal on his own. "You're running down the street," as he put it in 2004, "holding onto the back of the seat. You know that if you take your hand off, they could fall, so you take a finger off and then two fingers, and pretty soon you're just barely touching it."

Some years later, after kid and parent had made it around one of those "corners" they were always turning—on the way to various "tipping points"—and found themselves instead at the "precipice," after Rumsfeld had, in fact, been asked to resign by his president, he wrote a final memo to the White House, the last of his famed "snowflakes," on "new options" in Iraq. In it, he suggested, "Begin modest withdrawals of U.S. and Coalition forces (start 'taking our hand off the bicycle seat'), so Iraqis know they have to pull up their socks, step up and take responsibility for their country."

Rumsfeld's tenure could qualify as the longest biking lesson in history and still, it seemed, the Iraqis couldn't do without that hand on the seat. Even when his president followed him two years later, their imagery of choice remained behind. In March 2009, for instance, the chief American military spokesperson in Iraq, Major General David G. Perkins, discussing a possible drawdown of American forces, said, "We need to take our hands off the handlebars, or the training wheels, at some point."

Colonel Timothy R. Reese, an American adviser to the Iraqi military's Baghdad command, created a stir in summer 2009 in a memorandum leaked to the *New York Times* in which he also used the metaphor. While the official Obama-era target for an American withdrawal remained then (as in the last months of the Bush era) the end of 2011, Reese urged that all U.S. forces be pulled out on an expedited schedule by August 2010. In this, he resurrected a Vietnam-era suggestion of Vermont Republican senator George Aiken by headlining his memo: "It's Time for the US to Declare Victory and Go Home."

And there, in the midst of a generally scathing assessment of the deficiencies of the Iraqi military (and the Iraqi government), was that bicycle again:

> The SA [Bush-era Security Agreement between the U.S. and Iraq] outlines a series of gradual steps towards military withdrawal, analogous to a father teaching his kid to ride a bike without training wheels.... We now have an Iraqi government that has gained its balance and thinks it knows how to ride the bike in the race. And in fact they probably do know how to ride, at least well enough for the road they are on against their current competitors. Our hand on the back of the seat is holding them back and causing resentment. We need to let go before we both tumble to the ground.

It just goes to show. Under the pressure of war, images that won't go away, like people, have the capacity to change. The Iraqi child with the training wheels was now, according to Reese, old enough to enter an actual bike race.

Who exactly will bike out of Iraq under the Obama withdrawal plan, however, still remains to be defined. After all, at the end of his memo, the most urgent call for withdrawal from Iraq yet to emerge from the higher levels of the U.S. military, Colonel Reese offered his version of a full-scale American withdrawal. "During the withdrawal period," he wrote, "the USG [United States government] and GOI [government of Iraq] should develop a new strategic framework agreement that would include some lasting military presence at 1-3 large training bases, airbases, or key headquarters locations. But it should not include the presence of any combat forces save those for force protection needs or the occasional exercise." Moreover, his proposal was, with rare exceptions, rejected out of hand by all and sundry, in and out of the military high command and in Washington. In other words, even the most Xtreme American biker of this moment still imagines us in Iraq forever and a day.

A history of experts on Iraq: Once upon a time, the playing field, the stadium, and sports events were regularly compared to war, even considered suitable preparation for actual battle. Ever since the First Gulf War, this has been reversed. Now, war—or at least its coverage—is based on sports. And just as, sooner or later, the smoothest players and savviest coaches depart the "field of battle" for the press box and the TV spotlight, for pre-game, game, and post-game commentary, so the commanders of the last war now leave the battlefield for the TV booth and offer us their expertise on the next war. As former Houston Rockets coach Jeff Van Gundy has been paid to discuss the decisions of his brother Stan, coach of the Orlando Magic, in ESPN playoff commentary, so the commanders of our previous wars cover our next wars and their commanders, possibly even officers once under their own command.

We now live with the ESPN version of war, including slo-mo replays, and the logos, interactive charts, and fabulous graphics of the sports world. And once anointed as experts, our John Maddens of war, like their sports counterparts, never go away. In April 2008, for instance, *New York Times* journalist David Barstow wrote a front-page exposé focused on the many retired military officers who had been hired as media consultants for the Iraq War. As a group, they made up, he suggested, a "kind of media Trojan horse," because most of them were marching to a carefully organized Pentagon campaign of disinformation on the war. In addition, most of them had ties, not acknowledged on the air, "to military contractors vested in the very war policies they are asked to assess."

Barstow's piece concluded:

> To the public, these men are members of a familiar fraternity, presented tens of thousands of times on television and radio as "military analysts" whose long service has equipped them to give authoritative and unfettered judgments about the most pressing issues of the post–Sept. 11 world.
>
> Hidden behind that appearance of objectivity, though, is a Pentagon information apparatus that has used those analysts in a campaign to generate favorable news coverage of the administration's wartime performance.

Barstow named names and made connections. Those names included, for example, retired air force general and Fox News senior military analyst Thomas G. McInerney, retired army general and NBC/MSNBC military analyst Montgomery Meigs, and retired army general and NBC/MSNBC military analyst Barry R. McCaffrey. After the exposé appeared, though, they seem to have just carried right on with their media duties.

Much of the print media has similarly adhered to the principle of once-an-expert-always-an-expert. For instance, on the fifth anniversary of Bush's disastrous invasion of Iraq, the *New York Times* decided to ask a range of "experts on military and foreign affairs" to look back on that fiasco—and then rounded up the usual suspects. Of the nine experts it came up with, six were intimately involved in that catastrophe either as drumbeaters for the invasion, instigators of it, or facilitators of the occupation that followed—Kenneth Pollack, Danielle Pletka, and Frederick Kagan (enthusiasts all), Richard Perle (aka "the prince of darkness"), L. Paul Bremer (the administration's first viceroy in Baghdad), and General Paul D. Eaton (who trained Iraqi troops in the early years of the occupation). Notably absent was anyone who had seriously opposed the invasion. The closest was Anne-Marie Slaughter, a "liberal hawk" who wrote a supportive *New York Times* op-ed on March 18, 2003, two days before the invasion began, headlined, "Good Reasons for Going Around the U.N."

The *Times* anniversary spread appeared in March 2008. Jump ahead a year-plus and the *Times* once again launched what undoubtedly was a mighty search for experts who might consider Colonel Reese's suggestion that we take our hand off that Iraqi bike—and came up with a typical crew of seven: One, retired Lieutenant Colonel John Nagl, president of the Center for a New American Security, was an adviser to General David Petraeus, former top U.S. commander in Iraq, now Centcom commander overseeing the wars in Iraq and Afghanistan. A second, Stephen Biddle, senior fellow for defense policy at the Council on Foreign Relations, was also an adviser to Petraeus and had most recently been on the "team" that advised General Stanley A. McChrystal in his review of Afghan War strategy. A third, Anthony Cordesman, Arleigh A. Burke Chair in Strategy at the Center for Strategic and International Studies, was on the same McChrystal team. A fourth, Thomas Ricks, former *Washington Post* military reporter and now senior fellow at Nagl's center, was the author of the bestselling book *The Gamble*, a highly complimentary account of Petraeus's role in Iraq in which Nagl is, of course, a figure. (Ricks, by the way, has long made it clear that he believes we will be in that country for years to come.) A fifth, Kori Schake, now at the Hoover Institution, was a former national security adviser on defense issues to President George W. Bush. A sixth, Jonathan

Morgenstein, was a senior national security policy fellow at Third Way, another Washington think tank, and "was a military transition team adviser to the Iraqi Army." Not surprisingly, all six of these experts, with the most modest of caveats, dismissed Reese's suggestion out of hand, agreeing that it was in no one's interest to expedite an American departure. ("The pace of progress in Iraq will be slow, but we can't throw up our hands and walk away," as one of them commented.) Only a seventh expert, author and retired colonel Douglas Macgregor, agreed with Reese.

Consider that a little history of expertise about our recent wars. There's a corollary. If you're not anointed an expert, you're never likely to be one. Among those automatically disqualified for expertise on Iraq: just about anyone who bluntly rejected the idea of invading Iraq or predicted any version of the catastrophe that ensued before it happened. Disqualified above all were any of those antiwar types who actually took to the streets of cities across the United States by the hundreds of thousands before the invasion to raise homemade placards to its un-wisdom. They obviously knew nothing. Their very stance indicated a bias that evidently disqualified them on the spot.

Someone—I can't claim to remember who—once made the point that within any administration you could afford to be a hawk and be wrong, just not a dove and right. When it comes to TV war commentators, that seems to hold true as well.

It would, of course, be easy enough to imagine the antiwar equivalent of those generals-as-analysts. In our world of expertise, though, it's unthinkable.

A history of the Iraqi Air Force: For all the talk of "taking the training wheels off," here is an interesting fact: Iraqis will not be able to defend their own airspace for the foreseeable future. The Iraqi Air Force will remain the U.S. Air Force for some time to come, which undoubtedly means the United States will be running the giant airbase it built at Balad, as well. The Iraqis have said they want American F-16s. Unfortunately, according to *New York Times* reporter Elisabeth Bumiller, General Odierno, the top American commander in that country, has claimed that "it would be impossible to build and deliver them by the end of 2011, even if the Iraqis were able to afford them." And even in that unlikely event, Iraq has no trained pilots to fly them. In other words, years of work still remain on the horizon for the U.S.A.F. in Iraq.

Fortunately, *Aviation Week* reported that the Iraqis have a plan to overcome their problem. It's a "three-phase, 11-year improvement plan" that will move their air force from T-6 trainers to a few dozen F-16s by "the middle of the next decade" (in case you were wondering just how long the U.S.A.F. is likely to be filling in).

Here, then, is the true tragedy of our moment. We want to leave Iraq. Maybe not as quickly as Colonel Reese would like, but really we do. President Obama has made that clear. Unfortunately, the Iraqis just won't let us. Imagine! They weren't even thinking about an air force until recently—and what would a country in the Middle East be if, as Bumiller points out, it had "no way to intercept another jet that invades the country's airspace." Just who might invade Iraqi airspace remains a subject for speculation.

Since it's so easy to obliterate the past, it's helpful to remind ourselves of the history of the Iraqi Air Force. Now that Iraq essentially has no air force, who remembers that Saddam Hussein's Iraq once had a very large and active one? Baghdad had 950 planes in the 1980s. In 1990, according to the website GlobalSecurity.org, it still had the sixth-largest air force in the world and plenty of trained pilots to go with it. During the First Gulf War, nearly half of that air force fled to neighboring Iran, on which Iraqi planes had dropped more than their share of bombs and even poison gas in the 1980s. Those planes were never returned. Of the relatively small force that remained, many were destroyed in the First Gulf War and some of the rest, at Saddam Hussein's orders, were buried in the desert as the invasion of 2003 began.

The history that's really been forgotten, though, is even more recent. The fact is, the Iraqis don't have an air force because Washington didn't want them to. Much attention has been paid to the Bush administration's lack of planning for the occupation of Iraq, but relatively little to what it did plan. In May 2003, L. Paul Bremer's Coalition Provisional Authority disbanded the Iraqi Army. Pentagon plans for rebuilding it called for a future, border-patrolling Iraqi military-lite of perhaps forty thousand men with minimal armaments and no air force to speak of. In the Middle

East, this had only one meaning: from a series of mega-bases already on Pentagon drawing boards as American troops crossed the Kuwaiti border in 2003, the U.S. Army and Air Force would fill in as the real Iraqi military for eons to come. Under the pressure of a fierce Sunni insurgency, the army part of that plan was soon jettisoned. But "standing up" the Iraqi military—"As Iraqis stand up, we will stand down," was long President Bush's mantra—has meant just that: two feet on the ground.

Until relatively recently, the Iraqis were essentially not permitted to take to the skies. Now, the lack of that air force will surely come to the fore as an excuse for why any U.S. "withdrawal" will have to have caveats and qualifications—and why, if ours proves to be a non-withdrawal withdrawal, it will be Iraq's fault.

A history of devastation in Iraq: Until the United States arrived in Baghdad, things seemed bad enough. There was Saddam Hussein, the megalomanic dictator of the endless Disneyesque palaces, with his secret prisons, torture chambers, and helicopter gunships. There were the international sanctions strangling the country. There were the mass graves in the north and the south. There was an oil industry held together by duct tape and ingenuity. It was a gruesome enough mess.

That was before the invasion to "liberate" the country. Since then, Saddam Hussein's killing fields have been dwarfed by a fierce set of destructive U.S. military operations, as well as insurgencies-cum-civil-wars-cum-terrorist-acts: major cities have been largely or partially destroyed, or ethnically cleansed; millions of Iraqis have been forced from their homes, becoming internal refugees or going into exile; untold numbers of Iraqis have been imprisoned, assassinated, tortured, or abused; and the country's cultural heritage has been ransacked. Basic services—electricity, water, food—were terribly impaired and the economy was simply wrecked. Health services were crippled. Oil production, upon which Iraq now depends for up to 90 percent of its government funds, has only relatively recently barely surpassed the worst levels of the pre-invasion era.

Iraq, in other words, has been devastated. The U.S. invasion and the occupation that followed acted like whirlwinds of destruction, unraveling a land already bursting with problems and potential animosities.

In what once was the breadbasket of civilization, Iraqi agriculture, ignored by the occupiers, is withering and the country is desertifying at a frightening pace under the pressure of a several-year-old drought. Rivers are drying up, wells are disappearing, and desperate Iraqi farmers are deserting the land for the city (where unemployment rates remain high). Everywhere dust gathers, awaiting the winds that create the monstrous dust storms that carry the precious soil of Iraq into the fragile lungs of urban Iraqis. "Now," writes Liz Sly of the *Los Angeles Times*, "the Agriculture Ministry estimates that 90 percent of [Iraq's] land is either desert or suffering from severe desertification, and that the remaining arable land is being eroded at the rate of 5 percent a year." Expecting the worst harvest in a decade and with the wheat crop at 40 percent of normal, the government has been forced to buy enormous amounts of grain abroad at a time when oil prices, dropping precipitously from 2008 highs, left it with far less money available. However overused the image may be, the Bush administration created the perfect storm in Iraq, a "mission accomplished" version of hell on earth. And it's because Iraq is in such desperate shape that, of course, we, as the protectors of its fragile "stability," can't leave.

A history of justifications: When we invaded Iraq, serial justifications were offered. There was the grim dictator who threatened the world. There were his killing fields. (Never again!) There was 9/11 and his "support for terrorism." (Top Bush administration officials long claimed a link between Saddam Hussein and al-Qaeda, despite convincing evidence to the contrary.) There was liberation for the Shiites and the ending of what Deputy Secretary of Defense Paul Wolfowitz called "criminal treatment of the Iraqi people." There was the reestablishment of an American version of order in the region. There were those heavily emphasized, if nonexistent, weapons of mass destruction the dictator supposedly had squirreled away, as well as his (also nonexistent) program to get his hands on a nuclear weapon.

Later, when things began to take a turn for the worse and another reason was needed, there was the propagation of democracy (a great guiding principle to which the Bush administration arrived rather late in Iraq and only under pressure from Grand Ayatollah Ali Sistani). Even later, when things were going far worse, there was the idea that it was far better to fight the terrorists over there than here. And, as the president liked to confide to foreign leaders, there was God himself commanding him to strike Saddam Hussein and so thwart Gog and Magog.

Among the cognoscenti, of course, there were other expectations and justifications, caught best perhaps in the neoconservative quip of 2003, "Everyone wants to go to Baghdad. Real men want to go to Tehran." After all, the neocons in and around the Bush administration truly did believe that a Middle Eastern Pax Americana was within their shock-and-awe grasp. As for oil—or what President Bush referred to, on the rare occasions when he mentioned it, as Iraq's "patrimony"—mum was the word, even though that country had the world's third-largest proven petroleum reserves and sat strategically at the heart of the energy heartlands of the planet.

Now, with almost 100,000 troops still there, not to speak of the scads of rent-a-guns and private contractors, with that overstuffed, overstaffed embassy the size of the Vatican, with a series of major military bases still well occupied, with significant numbers of Iraqis and small numbers of Americans dying each month, with millions of Iraqis still internal or external refugees, with the land devastated and basic services hardly restored, with ethnic tensions still running high and a government quietly allied to Iran in place in Baghdad backed by a 250,000-man military, with the nature of an American withdrawal still a matter of definition, no one even bothers to offer the slightest justification for being in Iraq. After all, why would explanations be necessary when we're getting ready to leave?

If you go hunting for an official explanation today, you'll be disappointed. Why are we in Iraq? Because we're there. Because the Iraqis need us. Because something terrible would happen if we left precipitously. So we still occupy Iraq and no one even asks why.

A history of withdrawal from Iraq: There is none.

How the Pentagon Counts Coups in Washington

Sometimes it pays to read a news story to the last paragraph where a reporter can slip in that little gem for the news jockeys, or maybe just for the hell of it. You know, the irresistible bit that doesn't fit comfortably into the larger news frame, but that can be packed away in the place most of your readers will never get near, where your editor is likely to give you a free pass. So it was, undoubtedly, with *New York Times* reporter Elisabeth Bumiller, who accompanied Secretary of Defense Robert Gates as he stumbled through a challenge-filled, error-prone, two-day trip to Pakistan in January 2010. Gates must have felt a little like a punching bag by the time he boarded his plane for home, having, as Juan Cole pointed out, managed to signal "that the U.S. is now increasingly tilting to India and wants to put it in charge of Afghanistan security; that Pakistan is isolated…and that Pakistani conspiracy theories about Blackwater were perfectly correct and he had admitted it. In baseball terms, Gates struck out."

In any case, here are the last two paragraphs of Bumiller's parting January 23 piece on the trip:

> Mr. Gates, who repeatedly told the Pakistanis that he regretted their country's "trust deficit" with the United States and that Americans had made a grave mistake in abandoning Pakistan after the Russians left Afghanistan, promised the military officers that the United States would do better.
>
> His final message delivered, he relaxed on the 14-hour trip home by watching "Seven Days in May," the cold war-era film about an attempted military coup in the United States.

Three major cautionary political films came out in the anxiety-ridden year of 1964, not so long after the Cuban missile crisis. All three concerned nuclear politics, "oops" moments, and Washington. The first, and best remembered, was *Dr. Strangelove*, Stanley Kubrick's classic vision of the end of the world, American-style. ("I'm not saying we wouldn't get our hair mussed, but I do say no more than ten to twenty million people killed, tops," General "Buck" Turgidson notes in the film.) The second was *Fail-Safe*, in which a computerized nuclear response system too fast for human intervention malfunctions and fails to stop an erroneous nuclear attack on Moscow, forcing a U.S. president to save the world by nuking New York City. It was basically *Dr. Strangelove* done straight. (It's worth pointing out that Americans loved to stomp New York City in their fantasies long before 9/11.) The third was the secretary of defense's top pick, *Seven Days in May,* which came with this tagline: "You are soon to be shaken by the most awe-

some seven days in your life!" In it, a right-wing four-star general linked
to an incipient fascist movement attempts to carry out a coup d'état
against a dovish president who has just signed a nuclear disarmament pact
with the Soviet Union. The plot is uncovered and defused by a marine
colonel played by Kirk Douglas. ("I'm suggesting, Mr. President," says
Colonel Martin "Jiggs" Casey, "there's a military plot to take over the government. This may occur sometime this coming Sunday.")

These were, of course, the liberal worries of a long-gone time. Now,
one of the films is iconic and the other two half-forgotten. All three would
make a perfect film festival for a secretary of defense with fourteen hours
to spare. Just the sort of retro fantasy stuff you could kick back and enjoy
after a couple of rocky days on the road, especially if you were headed
for a "homeland" where no one had a bad, or even a challenging, thing
to say about you. After all, in the last two decades our fantasies about nuclear apocalypse have shrunk to a far more localized scale, and a military
plot to take over the government is entertainingly outré exactly because,
in the Washington of today, such a thought is ludicrous. After all, every
week in Washington is now the twenty-first-century equivalent of *Seven
Days in May* come true.

Think of the week after the secretary of defense flew home, for instance, as *Seven Days in January*.

After all, if Gates was blindsided in Pakistan, he already knew that a
$626 billion Pentagon budget, including more than $128 billion in war
funds, had passed Congress in December and that his next budget for
fiscal year 2011 would likely cross the $700 billion mark. He probably
also knew that, in the upcoming State of the Union Address, President
Obama was going to announce a three-year freeze on discretionary domestic spending starting in 2011, but leave national security expenditures
of any sort unfrozen. He undoubtedly knew as well that, in the week after
his return, news would come out about the president's plans to ask Congress for $14.2 billion extra, most for 2011, to train and massively bulk
up the Afghan security forces, more than doubling the 2010 funds already
approved by Congress for that task.

Or consider that only days after his plane landed, the nonpartisan
Congressional Budget Office released its latest "budget outlook" indicating

that the Iraq and Afghan Wars had already cost the American taxpayer more than one trillion congressionally approved dollars, with no end in sight. Just as the non-freeze on defense spending in the State of the Union Address caused next to no mainstream comment, so there would be no significant media response to these budget figures. And bear in mind that these costs don't even include the massive projected societal price of the two wars, including future care for wounded soldiers and the replacement of worn-out or destroyed equipment, which will run so much higher.

Each of these announcements could be considered another little coup for the Pentagon and the U.S. military to count. Each was part of Pentagon blank-check-ism in Washington. Each represented a national security establishment ascendant in a way that the makers of *Seven Days in May* might have found hard to grasp.

To put just the president's domestic cost-cutting plan in a Pentagon context: If his freeze on domestic programs goes through Congress intact (an unlikely possibility), it would still be chicken feed in the cost-cutting sweepstakes. The president's team estimates savings of $250 billion over ten years. On the other hand, the National Priorities Project has done some sober figuring, based on projections from the Office of Management and Budget, and finds that, over the same decade, the total increase in the Pentagon budget should come to $522 billion. (And keep in mind that this figure doesn't include possible increases in the budgets of the Department of Homeland Security, non-military intelligence agencies, or even any future war supplemental funds appropriated by Congress.) That $250 billion in cuts, then, would be but a small brake on the guaranteed further rise of national security spending. American life, in other words, is being sacrificed to the very infrastructure meant to provide this country's citizens with "safety."

Or consider that $14.2 billion meant for the Afghan military and police. Forget, for a moment, all obvious doubts about training, by 2014, up to 400,000 Afghans for a force bleeding deserters and evidently whipping future Taliban fighters into shape, or the fact that impoverished Afghanistan will never be able to afford such a vast security apparatus (which means it's ours to fund into the distant future), or even that many of those training dollars may go to Xe/Blackwater or other mercenary private contracting companies. Just think for a minute, instead, about the fact that the State of the Union Address offered not a hint that a single further dollar would go to train an adult American, especially an out-of-work one, in anything whatsoever.

Hollywood loves remakes, but a word of advice to those who admire the secretary of defense's movie tastes: Do as he did and get the old *Seven Days in May* from Netflix. Unlike *Star Trek*, the James Bond films, *Bewitched*, and other sixties "classics," *Seven Days* isn't likely to come back, not even if Matt Damon were available to play the marine colonel who saves the country from a military takeover, because these days there's little left to save—and every week is the Pentagon's week in Washington.

SEVEN

Living in the Shadow of War

G.I. Joe, Post-American Hero

In my childhood, I played endlessly with toy soldiers—a crew of cowboys and bluecoats to defeat the Indians and win the West, a bag or two of tiny olive-green plastic marines to storm the beaches of Iwo Jima. Alternately, I grabbed my toy six-guns, or simply picked up a suitable stick in the park, and with friends replayed scenes from the movies of World War II, my father's war. It was second nature to do so. No instruction was necessary. After all, a script involving a heady version of American triumphalism was already firmly in place, as it had been long before my grandfather made it to this land in steerage in the 1890s.

My sunny fantasies of war play were intimately connected to the wars Americans had fought by an elaborate mythology of American goodness and ultimate victory. If my father tended to be silent about the war he had taken part in, it made no difference. I already knew what he had done. I had seen it at the movies, in comic books, and sooner or later in shows like *Victory at Sea* on that new entertainment medium, television.

And when, in the 1960s, countless demonstrators from my generation went into opposition to a brutal American war in Vietnam, they did so still garbed in cast-off "Good War" paraphernalia—secondhand army jackets and bombardier coats—or they formed themselves into "tribes" and turned goodness and victory over to the former enemies in their childhood war stories. They transformed the "V for Victory" into a peace sign and made themselves into beings recognizable from thousands of Westerns. They wore the Pancho Villa mustache, sombrero, and serape, or the Native American headband and moccasins. They painted their faces and grew long hair in the manner of the formerly "savage" foe, and smoked the peace (now, hash) pipe.

American mytho-history, even when turned upside down, was deeply embedded in their lives. How could they have known that they would be its undertakers, that their six-shooters would become eBayable relics?

You can bet on one thing today: in those streets, fields, parks, or rooms, children in significant numbers are not playing G.I. versus Sunni insurgent, or special ops soldier versus Taliban fighter; and if those kids are wielding toy guns, they're not replicas from the current arsenal, but flashingly neon weaponry from some fantasy future.

As it happens, G.I. Joe—then dubbed a "real American hero"—proved to be my introduction to this new world of child's war play. I had, of course, grown up years too early for the original G.I. Joe (b. 1964), but one spring in the mid-1980s, during his second heyday, I paid a journalistic visit to the Toy Fair, a yearly industry bash for toy-store buyers held in New York City. Hasbro, which produced the popular G.I. Joe action figures, was one of the Big Two in the toy business. Mattel, the maker of Joe's original inspiration and big sister, Barbie, was the other. Hasbro had its own building and, on arriving, I soon found myself being led by a company minder through a labyrinthine exhibit hall in the deeply gender-segregated world of toys. Featured were blond models dressed in white holding baby dolls and fashion dolls of every imaginable sort, set against an environment done up in nothing but pink and robin's egg blue.

Here, the hum of the world seemed to lower to a selling hush, a baby-doll whisper, but somewhere off in the distance, you could faintly hear the high-pitched whistle of an incoming mortar round amid brief bursts of machine-gun fire. And then, suddenly, you stepped across a threshold and out of a world of pastels into a kingdom of darkness, of netting and camouflage, of blasting music and a soundtrack of destruction, as well-muscled male models in camo performed battle routines

while displaying the upcoming line of little G.I. Joe action figures or
their evil Cobra counterparts.

It was energizing. It was electric. If you were a toy buyer, you wanted
in. You wanted Joe, then the rage in the boy's world of war play, as well as
on children's TV where an animated series of syndicated half-hour shows
was nothing but a toy commercial. I was as riveted as any buyer, and yet
the world I had just been plunged into seemed alien. These figures bore no
relation to my toy soldiers. On first sight, it was hard even to tell the good
guys from the bad guys or to figure out who was fighting whom, where,
and for what reason. And that, it turned out, was just the beginning.

In summer 2009, G.I. Joe returned, this time to the big screen in *G.I.
Joe: The Rise of Cobra*. Nobody mentioned it then, but the most impressive thing about the movie came during the eight minutes or so of credits,
which made it clear that to produce a twenty-first-century shoot-'em-
up, you needed to mobilize a veritable army of experts. There may have
been more "compositors" than actors and more movie units (Prague
Unit, Prague Second Unit, Paris Unit) than units of Joes. After the last
shot, those credits still scrolled inexorably onward, like a beachhead in
eternity, the very eternity in American cultural life that G.I. Joe already
seems to inhabit. The credits did, of course, finally end, and on a note of
gratitude that, almost uniquely in the film, evoked an actual history. "The
producers also wish to thank the following," and the list that followed
was headed by the Department of Defense, which has been "advising"
Hollywood on how to make war movies, with generous loans of equipment, troops, consultants, and weaponry in return for script "supervision," since the silent era.

I caught *G.I. Joe: The Rise of Cobra* one sunny afternoon in a multi-
plex theater empty of customers except for a few clusters of teenage boys.
So where to start? How about with the Joes' futuristic military base, all
flashing screens, hi-tech weaponry, and next-generation surveillance
equipment, built under the Egyptian desert. (How this most postmod-
ern of bases got under pharaonic sands or what kind of Status of Forces
Agreement the Joes have with the government of Egypt are not questions
this film considers.) But here's the thing: well-protected as the base is,
spectacularly armed and trained as the Joes are, it turns out to be a snap

to break into—if you happen to be a dame in the black catsuit of a dominatrix and a ninja dressed in white. And then there's that even spiffier ultra-evil base under the Arctic ice (a location only slightly less busy than Times Square in movies like this). It's the sort of setup that would have made Captain Nemo salivate. Oh, and don't forget the introductory scene about a Scottish arms dealer in seventeenth-century France condemned to having a molten mask fitted over his face for selling weapons to all sides or his great-great-great-something-or-other who's doing the same thing in our world. Then there are those weaponized exoskeletons lifted from *Iron Man* (which also had its own two-faced arms dealer), the X-wing-fighter-style space battle from *Star Wars* but transposed under the ocean (à la James Bond in *Thunderball*), not to speak of the Bond-like scene in which the evildoer, having captured the hero, introduces him to a fate so much worse than death and so time-consuming it can't possibly work.

And then there is the requisite scene in which a famous landmark (in this case, the Eiffel Tower) is destroyed by the forces of evil, collapsing on panicked crowds below, as in *Independence Day* or just about any disaster movie you'd care to mention. Throw in the sort of car chase introduced a zillion years ago in *Bullitt*, but now pumped up beyond all recognition, and, oh yes, there's someone who wants to control the world and who will do anything, including killing millions, to achieve his purpose (ha-ha-ha!).

Movies like this are Hollywood's version of recombinant DNA. They can be written in the dark or, as in the case of *G.I. Joe*, in a terrible hurry because of an impending writers' strike. All that matters is that they deliver the chases and explosions, the fake blood and weird experiments, the wild weaponry and futuristic sets, the madmen and heroes at such a pace and decibel level that your nervous system is brought fully to life jangling like a fire alarm. Their sole justification is to deliver boys and young men—and so the franchise—to studios like Paramount (and, in cases like *G.I. Joe,* to the Department of Defense as well): the Batman franchise, the Bond franchise, the Terminator franchise, the X-Men franchise, the Bourne franchise, the Iron Man franchise, the Transformers franchise. And now—if it works—the G.I. Joe franchise.

After all, the first word that appears on screen without explanation in this latest junior epic is, appropriately enough, Hasbro. We're talking about the toy company that *is* G.I. Joe and, in a synergistic fury, was then releasing an endless range of toys, action figures, video games, board games, Burger King giveaways, and who knows what else as synergistic accompaniments to this elaborate "advertainment."

Barbie's Little Brother

Hasbro first brought Joe to market in 1964. He was then twelve inches tall and essentially a Barbie for boys, a soldier doll you could dress in that "Ike" jacket with the red scarf or a "beachhead assault fatigue shirt," then undress, and take into that pup tent with you for the night. Of course, nobody could say such a thing. Officially, the doll was declared to be a "poseable action figure for boys," and that phrase, "action figure," for a new boy toy, like Joe himself, never went away. He had no "backstory" (a word still to be invented), and no name. G.I.—for "Government Issue"—Joe was a generic term for an American foot soldier, redolent of the last American war in which total victory had been possible. Nor did he have an enemy, in part because young boys still knew a version of American history, of World War II and the cold war. They still knew who the enemy was without a backstory or a guidebook.

Though born on the cusp of the Vietnam War, Joe prospered for almost a decade until antiwar sentiment began to turn war toys into the personae non gratae of the toy world, and, in 1973, the first oil crunch hit, making the twelve-inch Joe far more expensive to produce. First, he shrank, and then, like so many of his warring kin, he was (as Hasbro put it) "furloughed." He left the scene, in part a casualty, like much of war play then, of Vietnam distaste and of an American victory that never came.

Despite being in his grave for a number of years, as the undead of the toy world he would rise again. In 1977, paving the way for his return, George Lucas brought the war flick and war play back into the child's world via the surprise hit *Star Wars* and its accompanying three-and-three-quarter-inch-high action figures that landed on Earth with an enormous commercial bang. Between them, they introduced the child to a self-enclosed world of play (in a galaxy "far, far away") shorn of Vietnam's defeat.

In 1982, seeing an opening, Hasbro's planners tagged Joe "a real American hero," and reintroduced him as part of a set of *Star Wars*–sized small action figures, each with its own little backstory. Hundreds of millions of these would subsequently be sold. The Joe team now had an enemy as well—another team, of course. In this case, though the cold war was still going full blast in those early years of Ronald Reagan's presidency, it wasn't the Russians. As it happened, Hasbro's toymakers did a better job of predicting the direction of the cold war than the CIA or the rest of our government. They sensed that the Russians wouldn't last and so chose a vaguer, potentially more long-lasting enemy, a bogeyman called "terrorism" embodied in Cobra, an organization of super-bad guys who lived not in Moscow, but in—gasp—Springfield, U.S.A. (Hasbro researchers had discovered that a Springfield existed in every state except Rhode Island, where the company was located.)

In story and style, the Joes and their enemies now left history and the battlefields of this planet behind for some alternate Earth. There, they disported themselves with bulked-up weaponry and a look that befitted not so much "real American heroes" as a set of superheroes and supervillains in any futuristic space epic. And so, catching the zeitgeist of their moment, at a child's level, the crew at Hasbro created the most successful boy's toy of that era by divorcing war play from war American-style.

The Next War, On-Screen and Off

Twenty-seven years later, Joe, who lost his luster a second time in the 1990s but never quite left the toy scene, returned yet again with his new movie and assorted products. Whether the latest iteration proves to be another lucrative round for the franchise depends not just on whether enough American boys turn out to see him, but on whether his version of explosive action, special effects, and futuristic conflict is beloved by Saudis, Poles, Indians, and Japanese. Today, for Hollywood, when it comes to shoot-'em-ups, the international market means everything.

Abroad, *G.I. Joe: The Rise of Cobra* opened smashingly in South Korea, and, in its first week, hit number one in China and Russia, as well. It took in nearly $100 million overseas in its first twelve days, putting its U.S. take in the shade.

Whatever his fate, Joe, we know, can't die. On the other hand, that once supreme all-American tale of battle triumph shows little sign of revival. Admittedly, the new G.I. Joe movie does mention NATO in passing, and one member of Joe's force is said, also in passing, to have been stationed in Afghanistan. In addition, the evil arms maker's company produces its superweapons in the obscure but perfectly real former Soviet republic of Kyrgyzstan, where the United States now rents out a base to support its Afghan operations. Otherwise, the film's only link with real-world battlefields comes from the Pentagon-loaned Apache helicopters and Humvees, and the fact that some of the military extras lent by the Pentagon were unable to see the film when it opened because they were then stationed in Iraq or Afghanistan.

Soon after the film begins, a caption announces, *Star Wars*–style, that we're "in the not too distant future," and immediately you know that you're in Hollywood's comfort zone, a recognizable battle landscape that is no part of what once would have been the war movie. Also recognizable is that loaned Pentagon equipment and the fantasy weaponry mixed so seamlessly in with it—"That's a Night Raven!"—make the film an "advertainment" for the techno-coolness of the U.S. military. The Pentagon, you might say, is perfectly willing to make do with post-historical battle space. It may be ever less all-American, but it's where the recruitable young are heading.

For Hollywood, deserting actual American battlefields isn't the liberal thing to do, it's the business thing to do. In fact, those planning out the film for Hasbro and Paramount reportedly wanted to transform the Joes into an international special ops force based in Belgium, where NATO is headquartered. However, fan grumbling at the early teasers Paramount released (and evidently a Pentagon reluctance to help a less-than-American force) caused them to pull back somewhat.

Still, one thing is certain: if the American car has gone to hell, Hollywood's products still rule the globe. And yet, in that international arena, American-style war, as in Iraq or Afghanistan, is a complete turnoff and real-world all-American triumph just doesn't fly anymore. That's certainly part of what's happened to the American war film, but far from all of it. After all, how long has it been since all-American mythology and imagery—the bluecoats' charge, the marines' advance—has brought a mass audience to a movie screen. The last such film, in 1998, was *Saving Private Ryan*, and it was already an anomaly. Today, as close as it gets is the parallel universe that passes for World War II in Quentin Tarantino's *Inglourious Basterds*.

It seems that American audiences are largely in accord with the international crowd. They may not want their Joe force stationed in Belgium, but they don't want to see real war American-style on a recognizable planet Earth either. They voted with their feet most recently on a bevy of Iraq films. Given the couple of hundred years that made triumphalism a kind of American sacrament, it's nothing short of remarkable that the young are no longer willing to troop to movie theaters to see such films. If you think of Hollywood as a kind of crude commercial democracy, this can be seen as a popular measure of imperial overstretch or the decline of the globe's sole superpower.

Only recently has a mainstream discussion of U.S. decline begun in Washington and among the pundits. But at the movies it's been going on for a long, long time. It's as if the grim reality of our seemingly never-ending wars seeped into the pores of a nation that no longer really believes victory is our due, or that American soldiers will triumph forever and a day. There may even be an unacknowledged element of shame in all this. At least there is now a consensus that we fight wars not fit for entertainment.

As a result, war as entertainment has been sent offshore—like imprisonment and punishment. Hollywood has launched it into a netherworld of aliens, superheroes, and robots. Something indelibly American, close to a national religion, has gone through the wormhole and is unlikely to return.

Joe lives. So does war, American-style, the brutal, real thing in Afghanistan and Iraq, at Guantánamo and Bagram, in the Predator- and Reaper-filled skies over the Pakistani tribal borderlands, among the Blackwater (now Xe) mercenaries and the tens of thousands of other private military contractors who outnumber U.S. troops in Afghanistan. But the two of them no longer have much to do with each other.

If the Chinese, and South Koreans, and Saudis, and enough American young men vote with their feet and their wallets, there will be another

G.I. Joe film. And if Washington's national security managers have anything to say about it, there will be what's already regularly referred to as "the next war." Film and war, however, are likely to share little other than some snazzy weaponry, thanks to the generosity of the Department of Defense, and American kids who will pay good money to sit in the dark and then perhaps join up to fight in the all-too-real world. In this way, an entertainment era ends. The curtain has come down and the children have gone off elsewhere to play.

Meanwhile, behind that curtain, you can still faintly hear the whistle of incoming mortars, the rat-a-rat of machine guns, the sounds of actual war that go on and on and on.

Why Military Dreams Fail—and Why It Doesn't Matter

For drone freaks (and these days Washington seems full of them), here's the good news: drones are hot. Not long ago (2006 to be exact), the air force could barely get a few armed unmanned aerial vehicles (UAVs) in the air at once; in 2009, the number was thirty-eight; by 2011, it will reputedly be fifty, and beyond that, in every sense, the sky's the limit.

Better yet, for the latest generation of armed surveillance drones, whole new surveillance capabilities will soon be available. Their newest video system, due to be deployed next year, has been dubbed "Gorgon Stare" after the creature in Greek mythology whose gaze turned its victims to stone. According to Julian Barnes of the *Los Angeles Times*, Gorgon Stare will offer a "pilot" back in the Langley, Virginia, headquarters of the CIA, the ability to "stare" via twelve video feeds (where only one now exists) at a 1.5 square mile area, and then, with Hellfire missiles and bombs, assumedly turn any part of that area into rubble. Within the year, that viewing capacity is expected to double to three square miles.

What we're talking about here is the gaze of the gods, updated in corporate labs for the modern American war-fighter—a gaze that can be focused on whatever moves just about anywhere on the planet, 24/7, with an instant ability to blow it away. And what's true of video capacity will be no less true of the next generation of drone sensors—and, of course, of drone weaponry like that "5-pound missile the size of a loaf of French bread" meant in some near-robotic future to replace the present 100-pound Hellfire missile, possibly on the Avenger or Predator C, the next generation drone under development at General Atomics Aeronautical Systems. Everything, in fact, will be almost infinitely upgradeable, since we're still in the robotics equivalent of the age of the "horseless carriage," as Peter Singer of the Brookings Institution assures us. The first nano-drones will, according to Jane Mayer of the *New Yorker*, be able to "fly after their prey like a killer bee through an open window."

When it comes to drones, the air force and the CIA are no longer the only games in town. The navy wants in, too. Chief of Naval Operations Admiral Gary Roughead, reports Jason Paur of *Wired*'s Danger Room blog, is looking for "a robotic attack aircraft that can land and take off from a carrier." According to Paur, the X-47B, which theoretically should be able to do just that, could be checking out those carrier decks by 2011 and be fully operational by 2025.

Not only that, but drones are leaving the air for the high seas where they are called unmanned surface vehicles (USVs). In fact, Israel—which, along with the United States, is leading the way on drones—reportedly has already launched USVs off the coast of Hamas-controlled Gaza. The United States can't be far behind, and it seems that, like their airborne cousins, these ships, too, will be weaponized.

Taking the Measure of a Slam-Dunk Weapons System

Soon, it seems, the world will be a drone fest. In his first nine months, President Obama authorized more drone attacks in the Pakistani tribal borderlands than the Bush administration did in its last three years in office.

In Washington, drones are even considered the "de-escalatory" option for the Afghan War by some critics. Among the few people who don't adore them are hard-core war-fighters who don't want an armada of robot planes standing in the way of sending in more troops. Vice President Joe Biden, however, is a drone-atic. He reportedly wanted to up their missions, especially in Pakistan, rather than go the full boots-on-the-ground route.

Secretary of Defense Robert Gates jumped onto the drone bandwagon early. He has long been pressing the air force to invest less in expensive manned aircraft—he's called the F-35, still in development, the last manned fighter aircraft—but more in the robotic kind.

Coming back to earth for a moment, what drones do is put wings on the Bush-era Guantánamo principle that Washington has an inalienable right to act as a global judge, jury, and executioner, and in doing so remain beyond the reach of any court or law. Philip Alston, the UN special rapporteur on extrajudicial executions, has suggested that the U.S. drone attacks might constitute war crimes under international law: "[T]he CIA is running a program that is killing significant numbers of people and there is absolutely no accountability in terms of the relevant international laws." But that will matter little. When it comes to drones, you don't have to be a prophet to predict the future, since we've already experienced it with previous wonder weapons.

Militarily speaking, in fact, we might as well be in the film *Groundhog Day*, in which Bill Murray's character is forced to live out the same twenty-four hours again and again, with all the grimness of that idea and none of the charm of that actor. We've repeatedly seen advanced weapons systems, like the atomic bomb, or mind-boggling technologies of war hailed for opening near-utopian paths to victory and future peace. Take "the electronic battlefield" in Vietnam, which was supposed to be an antidote to brute and ineffective American airpower. That high-tech, advanced battlefield of invisible sensors was to bring an end to the impunity of guerrillas and infiltrating enemy armies. No longer capable of going anywhere undetected, they would have nowhere to hide.

In the 1980s, we had President Ronald Reagan's Strategic Defense Initiative, quickly dubbed "Star Wars" by its critics, a label that he accepted with amusement. "If you will pardon my stealing a film line—the Force is with us," he said in his usual genial way. His dream, as he told the American people, was to create an "impermeable" anti-missile shield over the United States—"like a roof protects a family from rain"—that would end the possibility of nuclear attack from the Soviet Union and so create peace in our time, or, if you were of a more critical turn of mind, offer the possibility of a freebie nuclear assault on the Soviets. In the Gulf War, "smart bombs" and smart missiles were praised as the military saviors of the moment. They were to give war the kind of "precision" that would lower

civilian deaths to the vanishing point and, as the neocons of the Bush administration would claim in the next decade, free the U.S. military to "de-
capitate" any regime we loathed. All this would be possible without so
much as touching the civilian population, which would, of course, then
welcome us as liberators. And later, there was "netcentric warfare," that
Rumsfeldian high-tech favorite. Its promise was that advanced informa-
tion-sharing technology would create an uplinked force so savvy about
changing battlefield realities and so crushing that a mere demo or two
would cow any "rogue" nation or insurgency into submission.

Of course, you know the results of this sort of magical thinking
about wonder weapons (or technologies) and their properties just as
well as I do. The atomic bomb ended nothing, but led to an almost half-
century-long nuclear superpower standoff, to nuclear proliferation, and
so to the possibility that, someday, even terrorists might possess such
weapons. The electronic battlefield was incapable of staving off defeat
in Vietnam. That impermeable anti-missile shield never came even
faintly close to making it into our skies, and yet has continued to fuel
the global arms race. Those "smart bombs" of the First Gulf War proved
remarkably dumb, while the fifty "decapitation" strikes the Bush administration launched against Saddam Hussein's regime on the first day
of the 2003 invasion of Iraq took out not a single Iraqi leader but killed
"dozens" of civilians. And the history of the netcentric military in Iraq
is well known. Its "success" sent Secretary of Defense Rumsfeld into retirement and ignominy.

In the same way, robot drones as assassination machines will prove
to be just another weapons system rather than a panacea for American
warriors. To date, in fact, there is at least as much evidence in Pakistan
and Afghanistan that the drones are helping to spread war as that they
are staunching it.

Yet, the above summary is, at best, only half the story. None of these
wonder weapons or technologies succeeded in their moment, or as ad-
vertised, but that fact stopped none of them. From the atomic bomb
came a whole nuclear landscape that included the Strategic Air Command, weapons labs, production plants, missile silos, corporate interests,
and an enormous world-destroying arsenal (as well as proliferating ver-

sions of the same, large and small, across the planet). Nor did the electronic battlefield go away. Quite the contrary, it came home and entered our everyday world in the form of sensors, cameras, surveillance equipment, and the like, now implanted from our borders to our cities. While it's true that Reagan's impermeable shield was the purest of nuclear fantasies, it fueled a decades-long binge of way-out research, space warfare plans and commands, and boondoggles of all sorts, including the staggeringly expensive, still not operational anti-missile system that the Bush and now Obama administrations have struggled to base somewhere in Europe. Similarly, ever newer generations of smart bombs and ever brighter missiles have been, and are being, developed ad infinitum.

Rarely do wonder weapons or wonder technologies disappoint enough to disappear. Each of these is, in fact, now surrounded by its own miniversion of the military-industrial complex, with its own set of corporate players, special lobbyists in Washington, specific interests, and congressional boosters. Each has installed a typical revolving door that the relevant Pentagon officials and officers can spin through once their military careers are in order. This is no less true for that wonder weapon of our moment, the robot drone. In fact, you can already see the military-industrial-drone-robotics complex in formation.

As the Obama administration ups the ante on drone use in Pakistan and Afghanistan, it will be ensuring not the end of al-Qaeda or the Taliban, but the long life of robot war within our ever more militarized society. And by the time this set of robotic dreams fails to pan out, it won't matter. Yet another minisector of the military-industrial complex will be etched into the American grain.

Whatever the short-term gains from introducing drone warfare in these last years, we are now locked into the 24/7 assassination trade, with our own set of non-suicide bombers on the job into eternity. This may pass for sanity in Washington, but it's surely helping to pave the road to hell. If this is the latest game in town, it won't remain mainly an American one for long. Just wait until the first Iranian drone takes out the first Baluchi guerrilla supported by American funds somewhere in Pakistan. Then let's see what we think about the right of any nation to summarily execute its enemies—and anyone else in the vicinity—by drone.

The Afghan Speech Obama Should (But Won't) Give

[Note: This was written in November 2009, more than a month before President Obama addressed the nation from the U.S. Military Academy at West Point on the Afghan War.]

It's common knowledge that a president—but above all a Democratic president—who tried to de-escalate a war like the one now expanding in Afghanistan and parts of Pakistan, and withdraw American troops, would be so much domestic political dead meat. This everyday bit of engrained Washington wisdom is, in fact, based on not a shred of evidence in the historical record. We do know something about what could happen to a president who escalates a counterinsurgency war: Lyndon Johnson comes to mind for expanding his inherited war in Vietnam out of fear that he would be labeled the president who "lost" that country to the Communists. And then there was Vice President Hubert Humphrey, incapable of rejecting Johnson's war policy, who lost the 1968 election to Richard Nixon, a candidate pushing a fraudulent "peace with honor" formula for downsizing the war.

Still, we have no evidence about how American voters would deal with a president who didn't take the Johnson approach to a losing war. We do know that there would be those on the right, and quite a few war-fightin' liberals as well, who would go nuclear over any presidentially approved withdrawal from Afghanistan. And we know that a media storm would certainly follow. But when it comes to how voters would react, especially at a moment when unhappiness with the Afghan War (as well as the president's handling of it) is on the rise, there is no evidence.

While we don't know what exactly is going through Obama's mind, or just when or in what form he will address us, we do know something about what his conclusions are likely to be; we do know that he's not going to recommend a "minus option." We have long been assured that any proposals for the withdrawal of U.S. troops from Afghanistan were never "on the table."

In any case, we—the rest of us—have had all the disadvantages of essentially being in on the president's councils these last months, and none of the advantages of offering our own advice. Personally, I prefer not to leave the process to speechwriters and advisers.

What follows, then, is my version of the president's Afghan announcement. I've imagined it as a challenging prime-time address to the American people, doing what no American president has yet done.

The White House
Office of the Press Secretary

A New Way Forward:
The President's Address to the American People
on Afghan Strategy

Oval Office
For Immediate Release—December 2, 2009

8:01 P.M. EDT

My fellow Americans,

On March 28, I outlined what I called a "comprehensive, new strategy for Afghanistan and Pakistan." It was ambitious. It was also an attempt to fulfill a campaign promise that was heartfelt. I believed—and still believe—that, in invading Iraq, a war this administration is now ending, we took our eye off Afghanistan. Our well-being and safety, as well as that of the Afghan people, suffered for it.

I suggested then that the situation in Afghanistan was already "perilous." I announced that we would be sending seventeen thousand more American soldiers into that war zone, as well as four thousand trainers and advisers whose job would be to increase the size of the Afghan security forces so that they could someday take the lead in securing their own country. There could be no more serious decision for an American president.

Eight months have passed since that day. This evening, after a comprehensive policy review of our options in that region that has involved commanders in the field, the joint chiefs of staff, National Security Adviser James Jones, Secretary of Defense Robert Gates,

Secretary of State Hillary Clinton, Vice President Joe Biden, top intelligence and State Department officials and key ambassadors, Special Representative on Afghanistan and Pakistan Richard Holbrooke, and experts from inside and outside this administration, I have a very different kind of announcement to make.

I plan to speak to you tonight with the frankness Americans deserve from their president. I have recently noted a number of pundits who suggest that my task here should be to reassure you about Afghanistan. I don't agree. What you need is the unvarnished truth just as it's been given to me. We all need to face a tough situation, as Americans have done so many times in the past, with our eyes wide open. It doesn't pay for a president or a people to fake it or, for that matter, to kick the can of a difficult decision down the road, especially when the lives of American troops are at stake.

During the presidential campaign I called Afghanistan "the right war." Let me say this: with the full information resources of the American presidency at my fingertips, I no longer believe that to be the case. I know a president isn't supposed to say such things, but he, too, should have the flexibility to change his mind. In fact, more than most people, it's important that he do so based on the best information available. No false pride or political calculation should keep him from that.

And the best information available to me on the situation in Afghanistan is sobering. It doesn't matter whether you are listening to our war commander, General Stanley McChrystal, who, as press reports have indicated, believes that with approximately eighty thousand more troops—which we essentially don't have available—there would be a reasonable chance of conducting a successful counterinsurgency war against the Taliban, or our ambassador to that country, Karl Eikenberry, a former general with significant experience there, who believes we shouldn't send another soldier at present. All agree on the following seven points:

1. We have no partner in Afghanistan. The control of the government of Afghan president Hamid Karzai hardly extends

beyond the embattled capital of Kabul. He himself has just been returned to office in a presidential election in which voting fraud on an almost unimaginably large scale was the order of the day. His administration is believed to have lost all credibility with the Afghan people.

2. Afghanistan floats in a culture of corruption. This includes President Karzai's administration up to its highest levels and also the warlords who control various areas and, like the Taliban insurgency, are to some degree dependent for their financing on opium, which the country produces in staggering quantities. Afghanistan, in fact, is not only a narco-state, but the leading narco-state on the planet.

3. Despite billions of dollars of American money poured into training the Afghan security forces, the army is notoriously understrength and largely ineffective; the police forces are riddled with corruption and held in contempt by most of the populace.

4. The Taliban insurgency is spreading and gaining support largely because the Karzai regime has been so thoroughly discredited, the Afghan police and courts are so ineffective and corrupt, and reconstruction funds so badly misspent. Under these circumstances, American and NATO forces increasingly look like an army of occupation, and more of them are only likely to solidify this impression.

5. Al-Qaeda is no longer a significant factor in Afghanistan. The best intelligence available to me indicates—and again, whatever their disagreements, all my advisers agree on this—that there may be perhaps one hundred al-Qaeda operatives in Afghanistan and another three hundred in neighboring Pakistan. As I said in March, our goal has been to disrupt, dismantle, and defeat al-Qaeda in Pakistan and Afghanistan, and on this we have, especially recently, been successful. Osama bin Laden, of course, remains at large,

and his terrorist organization is still a danger to us, but not a $100 billion–plus danger.

6. Our war in Afghanistan has become the military equivalent of a massive bailout of a firm determined to fail. Simply to send another 40,000 troops to Afghanistan would, my advisers estimate, cost $40–$54 billion extra; 80,000 troops, more than $80 billion. Sending more trainers and advisers in an effort to double the size of the Afghan security forces, as many have suggested, would cost another estimated $10 billion a year. These figures are over and above the present projected annual costs of the war—$65 billion— and would ensure that the American people will be spending $100 billion a year or more on this war, probably for years to come. Simply put, this is not money we can afford to squander on a failing war thousands of miles from home.

7. Our all-volunteer military has for years now shouldered the burden of our two wars in Iraq and Afghanistan. Even if we were capable of sending 40,000–80,000 more troops to Afghanistan, they would without question be servicepeople on their second, third, fourth, or even fifth tours of duty. A military, even the best in the world, wears down under this sort of stress and pressure.

These seven points have been weighing on my mind over the last weeks as we've deliberated on the right course to take. Tonight, in response to the realities of Afghanistan as I've just described them to you, I've put aside all the subjects that ordinarily obsess Washington, especially whether an American president can reverse the direction of a war and still have an electoral future. That's for the American people, and them alone, to decide.

Given that, let me say as bluntly as I can that I have decided to send no more troops to Afghanistan. Beyond that, I believe it is in the national interest of the American people that this war, like the Iraq War, be drawn down. Over time, our troops and resources will be brought home in an orderly fashion, while we ensure that we provide adequate security for the men and women of our armed forces. Ours will be an administration that will stand or fall, as of today, on this essential position: that we ended, rather than extended, two wars.

This will, of course, take time. But I have already instructed Ambassador Eikenberry and Special Representative Holbrooke to begin discussions, however indirectly, with the Taliban insurgents for a truce in place. Before year's end, I plan to call an international conference of interested countries, including key regional partners, to help work out a way to settle this conflict. I will, in addition, soon announce a schedule for the withdrawal of the first American troops from Afghanistan.

For the counterinsurgency war that we now will not fight, there is already a path laid out. We walked down that well-mined path once in recent American memory and we know where it leads. For ending the war in another way, there is no precedent in our recent history and so no path—only the unknown. But there is hope. Let me try to explain.

Recently, comparisons between the Vietnam War and our current conflict in Afghanistan have been legion. Let me, however, suggest a major difference between the two. When Presidents John F. Kennedy and Lyndon Johnson faced their crises involving sending more troops into Vietnam, they and their advisers had little to rely on in the American record. They, in a sense, faced the darkness of the unknown as they made their choices. The same is not true of us.

In the White House, for instance, a number of us have been reading a book on how the United States got itself ever more disastrously involved in the Vietnam War. We have history to guide us here. We know what happens in counterinsurgency campaigns. We have the experience of Vietnam as a landmark on the trail behind us. And if that weren't enough, of course, we have the path to defeat already well cleared by the Russians in their Afghan fiasco of the 1980s, when they had just as many troops in the field as we would have if I had chosen to send those extra forty thousand Americans. That is the known.

On the other hand, peering down the path of de-escalation, all we can see is darkness. Nothing like this has been tried before in Washington. But I firmly believe that this, too, is deeply in the American grain. American immigrants, as well as slaves, traveled to this country as if into the darkness of the unknown. Americans have long braved the unknown in all sorts of ways.

To present this more formulaically, if we sent the troops and trainers to Afghanistan, if we increased air strikes and tried to strengthen the Afghan Army, we basically know how things are likely to work out: not well. The war is likely to spread. The insurgents, despite many losses, are likely to grow in strength. Hatred of Americans is likely to increase. Pakistan is likely to become more destabilized.

If, however, we don't take such steps and proceed down that other path, we do not know how things will work out in Afghanistan, or how well.

We do not know how things will work out in Pakistan, or how well.

That is hardly surprising, since we do not know what it means to end such a war now.

But we must not be scared. America will not—of this, as your president, I am convinced—be a safer nation if it spends many hundreds of billions of dollars over many years, essentially bankrupting itself and exhausting its military on what looks increasingly like an unwinnable war. This is not the way to safety, but to national penury—and I am unwilling to preside over an America heading in that direction.

Let me say again that the unknown path, the path into the wilderness, couldn't be more American. We have always been willing to strike out for ourselves where others would not go. That, too, is in the best American tradition.

It is, of course, a perilous thing to predict the future, but in the Afghanistan/Pakistan region, war has visibly only spread war. The beginning of a negotiated peace may have a similarly powerful effect, but in the opposite direction. It may actually take the wind out of the sails of the insurgents on both sides of the Afghan/Pakistan border. It may actually encourage forces in both countries with which we might be more comfortable to step to the fore.

Certainly, we will do our best to lead the way with any aid or advice we can offer toward a future peaceful Afghanistan and a future peaceful Pakistan. In the meantime, I plan to ask Congress to take some of the savings from our two wars winding down and put them into a genuine jobs program for the American people.

The way to safety in our world is, I believe, to secure our borders against those who would harm us, and to put Americans back to work. With this in mind, next month I've called for a White House Jobs Summit, which I plan to chair. And there I will suggest that, as a start, and only as a start, we look at two programs that were not only popular across the political spectrum in the desperate years of the Great Depression, but were remembered fondly long after by those who took part in them—the Civilian Conservation Corps and the Works Progress Administration. These basic programs put millions of Americans back to work on public projects that mattered to this nation and saved families, lives, and souls.

We cannot afford a failing war in Afghanistan and a 10.2 percent official unemployment rate at home. We cannot live with two Americas, one for Wall Street and one for everyone else. This is not the path to American safety.

As president, I retain the right to strike at Al-Qaeda or other terrorists who mean us imminent harm, no matter where they may be, including Afghanistan. I would never deny that there are dangers in the approach I suggest today, but when have Americans ever been averse to danger, or to a challenge either? I cannot believe we will be now.

It's time for change. I know that not all Americans will agree with me and that some will be upset by the approach I am now determined to follow. I expect anger and debate. I take full responsibility for whatever may result from this policy departure. Believe me, the buck stops here, but I am convinced that this is the way forward for our country in war and peace, at home and abroad.

I thank you for your time and attention. Goodnight and God bless America.

END 8:35 P.M. EDT

A Symbolic Surrender of Civilian Authority

On December 1, 2009, from the U.S. Military Academy at West Point, in his first prime-time presidential address to the nation, speaking of his plans for Afghanistan, Barack Obama surrendered. There were no surrender documents. He wasn't on the deck of the USS *Missouri*. He never bowed his head. Still, from that moment on, think of him not as the commander in chief, but as the commanded in chief.

Give credit to the victors. Their campaign was nothing short of brilliant. Like the policy brigands they were, they ambushed the president, held him up with their threats, brought to bear key media players and Republican honchos, and in the end made off with the loot. The campaign began with a strategic leak of Afghan War commander General Stanley McChrystal's grim review of the situation in that country, including demands for sizeable troop escalations and a commitment to a counterinsurgency war. It came to include rumors of potential retirements in protest if the president didn't deliver, as well as clearly insubordinate policy remarks by General McChrystal, not to speak of an impressive citizen-mobilization of inside-the-Beltway former neocon or fighting liberal think-tank experts, and a helping hand from an admiring media. In the process, the U.S. military succeeded in boxing in a president who had already locked himself into a conflict he had termed both "the right war" and a "necessary" one. After more than two months of painfully overreported deliberations, President Obama ended up essentially where General McChrystal began.

Counterinsurgency (COIN) doctrine was dusted off from the moldy Vietnam archives and made spanking new by General David Petraeus in 2006, applied in Iraq (and Washington) in 2007, and first put forward for Afghanistan in late 2008. It has now been largely endorsed, and a major escalation of the war—a new kind of military-led nation-building is to be cranked up and set in motion. COIN is being billed as a "population-centric," not "enemy-centric," approach in which U.S. troops are distinctly to be "nation-builders as well as warriors."

The additional thirty thousand troops Obama promised in his speech to surge into Afghanistan are more than the United States had there as late as summer 2008. In less than two years, in fact, U.S. troop strength in that country will have more than tripled to approximately one hundred thousand troops. We're talking about near-Vietnam-level escalation rates. If you include the thirty-eight thousand NATO forces also there (and a possible five thousand more to come), total allied troop strength will be significantly above what the Soviets deployed during their devastating Afghan War of the 1980s in which they fought some of the same insurgents now arrayed against us.

Think of the West Point speech, then, as Barack Obama's anti-MacArthur moment. In April 1951, in the midst of the Korean War, President Harry Truman relieved Douglas MacArthur of command of U.S. forces. He did so because the general, a far grander public figure than either McChrystal or CentCom commander Petraeus (and with dreams of his own about a possible presidential run), had publicly disagreed with, and interfered with, Truman's plans to "limit" the war after the Chinese intervened. Obama, too, has faced what Robert Dreyfuss in *Rolling Stone* calls a "generals' revolt"—amid fears that his Republican opposition would line up behind the insubordinate field commanders and make hay in the 2010 and 2012 election campaigns. Obama, too, has faced a general, Petraeus, who might well have presidential ambitions, and who has played a far subtler game than MacArthur ever did. After more than two months of what right-wing critics termed "dithering" and supporters called "thorough deliberations," Obama dealt with the problem quite differently. He essentially agreed to subordinate himself to the publicly stated wishes of his field commanders. (Not that his Republican critics will give him much credit for doing so, of course.) This is called "politics" in our country and, for a Democratic president in our era, the end result was remarkably predictable.

Monty Python in Afghanistan

There was surprisingly little discussion about the president's decision to address the American people on Afghanistan not from the Oval

Office, but from West Point. It was there, in 2002, that George W. Bush gave a speech before the assembled cadets in which he laid out his aggressive strategy of preventive war, which would become the cornerstone of the Bush Doctrine:

> If we wait for threats to fully materialize, we will have waited too long....
> Our security will require transforming the military you will lead—a military that must be ready to strike at a moment's notice in any dark corner of the world. And our security will require all Americans to be forward-looking and resolute, to be ready for preemptive action when necessary to defend our liberty and to defend our lives.

But keep in mind that this was still a graduation speech and presidents have traditionally addressed one of the military academies at graduation time.

Obama is not a man who appears in prop military jackets with "commander in chief" hand-stitched across his heart before hoo-aahing crowds of soldiers, as our last president loved to do, and yet he has increasingly appeared at military events and associated himself with things military. Has a president ever, in fact, given a non-graduation speech, no less a major address to the American people, at West Point? Certainly, the choice of venue, and so the decision to address a military audience first and other Americans second, not only emphasized the escalatory military path chosen, but represented a kind of symbolic surrender of civilian authority.

For his American audience, and undoubtedly his skittish NATO allies as well, the president did put a significant emphasis on an exit strategy from the war. That off-ramp strategy was, however, placed in the context of the training of the woeful Afghan security forces to take control of the struggle themselves and of the woeful government of Afghan president Hamid Karzai turning over a new nation-building leaf. Like the choice of West Point, this, too, seemed to eerily echo George W. Bush's regularly intoned mantra: "As Iraqis stand up, we will stand down."

In his address, Obama offered July 2011 as the date to begin withdrawing the first U.S. troops from Afghanistan. ("After 18 months, our troops will begin to come home.") However, according to the Washing-

ton-insider "Nelson Report," a White House on-background press briefing made it far clearer that the president was talking about a "conditions
based withdrawal" that would depend "on objective conditions on the
ground," on whether the Afghans had met the necessary "benchmarks."
When asked about "scaling back" the American war effort, General Mc-
Chrystal suggested a more conservative timeline—"sometime before
2013." Secretary of Defense Robert Gates referred vaguely to the "thin-
ning out" of U.S. forces.

In fact, there's no reason to put faith in any of these hazy deadlines.
After all, this is the administration that came into office announcing a
firm one-year closing date for the U.S. prison in Guantánamo (officially
missed), a firm sunshine policy for an end-of-2009 release of millions of
pages of historical documents from the archives of the CIA and other intelligence and military services (officially delayed, possibly for years), and
of course a firm date for the withdrawal of U.S. combat troops, followed
by all U.S. forces from Iraq (possibly slipping).

Finish the job in Afghanistan? Based on the plans of the field commanders to whom the president has bowed, on the administration's
record of escalation in the war so far, and on the quiet reassurances to
the Pakistanis that we aren't leaving in any imaginable future, this war
looks to be all job and no finish.

If it weren't so grim, despite all the upbeat benchmarks and encouraging words in the president's speech, this would certainly qualify as
Monty Python in Afghanistan. After all, three cabinet ministers and
twelve former ministers are under investigation in Afghanistan on corruption charges. And that barely scratches the surface of the problems
in a country that one Russian expert recently referred to as an "international drug firm," where at least one-third of the gross national product
comes from the drug trade. The Taliban now reportedly take a cut of the
billions of dollars in U.S. development aid flowing into the country, much
of which is otherwise squandered, and of the American money that goes
into "protecting" the convoys that bring supplies to U.S. troops throughout the country. One out of every four Afghan soldiers has quit or deserted the Afghan National Army, while the ill-paid, largely illiterate,
hapless Afghan police with their "well-deserved reputation for stealing

and extorting bribes," not to speak of a drug abuse rate estimated at 15 percent, are, as it's politely put, "years away from functioning independently." Meanwhile, the insurgency is spreading to new areas of the country and reviving in others.

Airless in Washington

Not that Washington, which obviously feels it has much to impart to the Afghan people about good governance and how to deal with corruption, has particularly firm ground to stand on. After all, in 2008, the United States completed its first billion-dollar presidential election in a $5 billion election season, and two administrations just propped up some of the worst financial scofflaws in the history of the world and got nothing back in return. Meanwhile, the money flowing into Washington political coffers from Wall Street, the military-industrial complex, the pharmaceutical and health care industries, real estate, legal firms, and the like might be thought of as a kind of drug in itself. At the same time, according to *USA Today*, at least 158 retired generals and admirals, many already pulling in military pensions in the range of $100,000 to $200,000, have been hired as "senior mentors" by the Pentagon "to offer advice under an unusual arrangement": they also work for companies seeking Defense Department contracts.

In Congress, a rare Senate maneuver—needing a sixty-vote super-majority to pass anything of significance—has, almost without comment, become a commonplace for the passage of just about anything. This means Congress is eternally in a state of gridlock. And that's just for starters when it comes to ways in which the U.S. government, so ready to surge its military and its civilian employees into Afghanistan in the name of good governance, is in need of repair, if not nation-building, itself.

It's nonetheless the wisdom of this Washington and of this military that Obama has not found wanting, at least when it comes to Afghanistan. So why did he listen to them? Stop for a moment and consider the cast of characters who offered the president the full range of advice available in Washington, all of it, as far as we can tell, from Joe Biden's "counterter-rorism-plus" strategy to McChrystal's COIN and beyond, escalatory in nature. Just a cursory glance at the Obama team's collective record should at least make you wonder:

- Secretary of State Hillary Clinton is now said to be the official with the best ties to Afghan president Hamid Karzai, and therefore the one in charge of "coaxing" him into a round of reasonable nation-building, of making "a new compact" with the Afghan people by "improving governance and cracking down on corruption." Yet, in the early 1990s, in her single significant nation-building experience at home, she botched the possibility of getting a universal health-care bill through Congress. She also had the "wisdom" to vote in 2003 to authorize the invasion of Iraq.

- Secretary of Defense Robert Gates, reputedly deeply trusted by the president and in charge of planning out our military future in Afghanistan, was in the 1980s a supposed expert on the Soviet Union, as well as deputy CIA director and later deputy to National Security Adviser Brent Scowcroft. Yet, in those years, he couldn't bring himself to believe that the Soviets were done for, even as that empire was disappearing from the face of the earth. In the words of former National Security Council official Roger Morris, Gates "waged a final battle against the Soviets, denying at every turn that the old enemy was actually dying." Former CIA official Melvin Goodman writes: "Gates was wrong about every key intelligence question of the 1980s…. A Kremlinologist by training, Gates was one of the last American hardliners to comprehend the changes taking place in the Soviet Union. He was wrong about Mikhail Gorbachev, wrong about the importance of reform, wrong about Moscow's pursuit of arms control and détente with the United States. He was wrong about the Soviet withdrawal from Afghanistan."

- Vice President Joe Biden, described by James Traub in the *New York Times* as potentially "the second-most powerful vice president in history," as well as "the president's all-purpose adviser and sage" on foreign policy, was during the Bush years a believer in nation-building in Afghanistan, voted to authorize the invasion of Iraq, and later promoted the idea—like Caesar with Gaul—of dividing that country into three parts (without, of course, bothering to ask the Iraqis), while leaving 25,000 to 30,000 American troops based there in perpetuity.

- General Stanley McChrystal, our war commander in Afghanistan and now the poster boy for counterinsurgency warfare, had his skills honed purely in the field of counterterrorism. The man who is now to "protect" the Afghan people previously won his spurs as the head of the Joint Special Operations Command (JSOC) in Iraq and Afghanistan.

- General David Petraeus, who has practically been deified in the U.S. media, is perhaps the savviest and most accomplished of this crew. His greatest skill, however, has been in fostering the career of David Petraeus. He is undoubtedly an adviser with an agenda and in his wake come a whole crew of military and think-tank experts, with almost unblemished records of being wrong in the Bush years, but to whom the surge in Iraq gave new legitimacy.

- Karl Eikenberry, our ambassador to Kabul, in his previous career in the U.S. military served two tours of duty in Afghanistan, and as the commander of Combined Forces Command–Afghanistan was the general responsible for building up the Afghan army and "reforming" that country's police force. We know how effective those attempts proved.

- And then there are key figures with well-padded Washington CVs like Admiral Mike Mullen, chairman of the joint chiefs of staff, or James Jones, present national security adviser and former commandant of the Marine Corps, as well as the Supreme Allied Commander, Europe, as well as a close friend of Senator John McCain, and a former revolving-door board member of Chevron and Boeing. Remind me just what sticks in your mind about their accomplishments?

So, when you think about Barack Obama's Afghan decisions, remember first that the man considered the smartest, most thoughtful president of our era chose to surround himself with these people. He chose, that is, not fresh air, or fresh thought in the field of foreign and war policy, but the airless precincts where the combined wisdom of Washington and the Pentagon now exists, and the remarkable lack of accomplishment that goes with it. In short, these are people whose credentials largely consist of not having been right about much over the years.

Admittedly, this administration has called in practically every Afghan expert in sight. Unfortunately, the most essential problem isn't in Afghanistan; it's in Washington where knowledge is slim, egos large, and conventional national security wisdom deeply imprinted on a system bleeding money and breaking down. The president campaigned on the slogan, "Change we can believe in." He then chose as advisers—in the economic sphere as well, where a similar record of gross error, narrow and unimaginative thinking, and overidentification with the powerful could easily be compiled—a crew who had never seen a significant change or an out-of-the-ordinary thought it could live with.

As a result, the Iraq War has yet to begin to go away, the Afghan War is being escalated in a major way, the Middle East is in some turmoil, Guantánamo remains open, black sites are still operating in Afghanistan, the Pentagon's budget has grown yet larger, and supplemental demands on Congress for yet more money to pay for George W. Bush's wars will, despite promises, continue.

Obama has ensured that Afghanistan, the first of Bush's disastrous wars, is now truly his war, as well.

The Nine Surges of Obama's War

In his West Point speech, President Obama offered Americans some specifics to back up his new "way forward in Afghanistan." He spoke of the "additional 30,000 U.S. troops" he was sending into that country. He brought up the "roughly $30 billion" it would cost us to get them there and support them for a year. And finally, he spoke of beginning to bring them home by July 2011. Those were striking enough numbers, even if larger and, in terms of time, longer than many in the Democratic Party would have cared for. Nonetheless, they don't faintly cover just how fully the president has committed us to an expanding war and just how wide it is likely to become.

Despite the seeming specificity of the speech, it gave little sense of just how big and expensive this surge will be. In fact, what is being portrayed in the media as the "surge" is but a modest part of an ongoing expansion of the war effort in many areas. Looked at another way, the media's focus on the president's speech as the crucial moment of decision, and on those thirty thousand new troops as the crucial piece of information, has distorted what's actually under way.

In reality, the U.S. military, along with its civilian and intelligence counterparts, has been in an almost constant state of surge since the last days of the Bush administration. Unfortunately, while information on this is available, and often well reported, it's scattered in innumerable news stories on specific aspects of the war. You have to be a media jockey to catch it all, no less put it together. What follows, then, is my attempt to make sense of the nine fronts on which the Unites States has been surging as part of Obama's widening war.

1. *The troop surge*: Let's start with those "30,000" new troops the president announced. First of all, they represent phase two of Obama's surge. As the president pointed out in his speech, there were "just over 32,000 Americans serving in Afghanistan" when he took office in January 2009. In March 2009, Obama announced that he was ordering in 21,000 additional troops. By December 2009, there were already approximately 68,000 to 70,000 U.S. troops in Afghanistan. However, if you add the 32,000 already there in January and the 21,700 dispatched after the March announcement, you only get 53,700, leaving another 15,000 or so to be accounted for. According to Karen DeYoung of the *Washington Post*, 11,000 of those were "authorized in the waning days of the Bush administration and deployed this year," bringing the figure to between 64,000

and 65,000. In other words, the earliest stage of the present Afghan "surge" was already under way when Obama arrived. It also seems that at least a few thousand more troops managed to slip through the door without notice or comment. Similarly, DeYoung reports that the president quietly granted Secretary of Defense Robert Gates the right to "increase the [30,000] number by 10 percent, or 3,000 troops, without additional White House approval or announcement." That already potentially brings the most recent surge numbers to 33,000, and an unnamed "senior military official" told DeYoung that "the final number could go as high as 35,000 to allow for additional support personnel such as engineers, medevac units and route-clearance teams, which comb roads for bombs."

Now, add in the 7,500 troops and trainers that administration officials reportedly strong-armed various European countries into offering. More than 1,500 of these are already in Afghanistan and simply not being withdrawn as previously announced. The cost of sending some of the others, like the 900-plus troops Georgian president Mikhail Saakashvili promised, will undoubtedly be absorbed by Washington. Nonetheless, add most of them in and, miraculously, you've surged up to, or beyond, Afghan War commander General Stanley McChrystal's basic request for at least 40,000 troops to pursue a counterinsurgency war in that country.

2. *The contractor surge*: Given our heavily corporatized and privatized military, it makes no sense simply to talk about troop numbers in Afghanistan. You also need to know about the private contractors who have taken over so many formerly military duties, from KP and driving supply convoys to providing security on large bases.

There's no way of even knowing who is responsible for the surge of (largely Pentagon-funded) private contractors in Afghanistan. They certainly went unmentioned in Obama's West Point speech. Yet a modest-sized article by August Cole in the *Wall Street Journal* the day after gave us the basics, if you went looking for them. Headlined "U.S. Adding Contractors at Fast Pace," Cole's article reported: "The Defense Department's latest census shows that the number of contractors increased about 40 percent between the end of June and the end of September, for a total of 104,101. That compares with 113,731 in Iraq, down 5 percent in the same period.... Most of the contractors in Afghanistan are locals, accounting for 78,430 of the total." In other words, there are already more private contractors on the payroll in Afghanistan than there will be U.S. troops when the latest surge is complete.

Though many of these contractors are local Afghans hired by outfits like DynCorp International and Fluor Corporation, the website TPM Muckraker managed to get a further breakdown of these figures from the Pentagon and found that there were 16,400 "third country nationals" among the contractors, and among those 9,300 Americans. This is a formidable crew, and its numbers are evidently still surging, as are the Pentagon contracts doled out to private outfits that go with them. Cole, for instance, writes of the contract that DynCorp and Fluor share to support U.S. forces in Afghanistan, "which could be worth as much as $7.5 billion to each company in the coming years."

3. *The militia surge*: U.S. Special Forces are now carrying out pilot programs for a minisurge in support of local Afghan militias that are, at least theoretically, anti-Taliban. The idea is evidently to create a movement along the lines of Iraq's Sunni Awakening movement that, many believe, ensured the "success" of George W. Bush's 2007 surge in that country. For now, as far as we know, U.S. support takes the form of offers of ammunition, food, and possibly some Kalashnikov rifles, but in the future we'll be ponying up more arms and, undoubtedly, significant amounts of cash.

This is, after all, to be a national program, the Community Defense Initiative, which, according to Jim Michaels of *USA Today*, will "funnel millions of dollars in foreign aid to villages that organize 'neighborhood watch'–like programs to help with security." Think of this as a "bribe" surge. Such programs are bound to turn out to be essentially money-based and designed to buy "friendship."

4. *The civilian surge*: The State Department now claims to be "on track" to triple the U.S. civilian component in Afghanistan from 320 officials in January 2009 to 974 by early 2010. Of course, that means another mini-surge in private contractors: more security guards to protect civilian employees of the U.S. government, including "diplomats and experts in agriculture, education, health and rule of law sent to Kabul and

to provincial reconstruction teams across the country." A similar civilian surge is evidently under way in neighboring Pakistan, just the thing to go with a surge of civilian aid and a plan for that humongous new, nearly billion-dollar embassy compound to be built in Islamabad.

5. *The CIA and special forces surge*: Noah Shachtman of *Wired*'s Danger Room blog had it right when he wrote: "The most important escalation of the war might be the one the President didn't mention at West Point," referring to the CIA's "covert" (but openly discussed) drone war in the Pakistani tribal borderlands. In fact, the CIA's drone attacks there have been escalating in numbers since the Obama administration came into office. Now, it seems, paralleling the civilian surge in the Af-Pak theater of operations, there is to be a CIA one as well. While little information on this is available, David E. Sanger and Eric Schmitt of the *New York Times* report that the CIA has delivered a plan to the White House "for widening the campaign of strikes against militants by drone aircraft in Pakistan, sending additional spies there and securing a White House commitment to bulk up the CIA's budget for operations inside the country." In addition, Scott Shane of the *Times* reports, "The White House has authorized an expansion of the CIA's drone program in Pakistan's lawless tribal areas, officials said...to parallel the president's decision... to send 30,000 more troops to Afghanistan. American officials are talking with Pakistan about the possibility of striking in Baluchistan for the first time—a controversial move since it is outside the tribal areas—because that is where Afghan Taliban leaders are believed to hide."

The Pakistani southern border province of Baluchistan is a complex tinderbox of a region with its own sets of separatists and religious extremists, as well as a (possibly U.S.-funded) rebel movement aimed at the Baluchi minority areas of Iran. The Pakistani government is powerfully opposed to drone strikes in the area of the heavily populated provincial capital Quetta where, Washington insists, the Afghan Taliban leadership largely resides. If such strikes do begin, they could prove the most destabilizing aspect of the widening of the war that the present surge represents.

In addition, thanks to the *Nation* magazine's Jeremy Scahill, we know that, from a secret base in Karachi, Pakistan, the U.S. Army's Joint Special

Operations Command, in conjunction with the private security contractor Xe (formerly Blackwater), operates "a secret program in which they plan targeted assassinations of suspected Taliban and Al Qaeda operatives, 'snatch and grabs' of high-value targets and other sensitive action inside and outside Pakistan." Since so many U.S. activities in Pakistan involve secretive, undoubtedly black-budget operations, we may only have the faintest outlines of what the "surge" there means.

6. *The base-building surge*: Like the surge in contractors and in drone attacks, the surge in base building in Afghanistan significantly preceded Obama's latest troop-surge announcement, but he has continued it. A December 5, 2009, NBC *Nightly News* report on the ever-expanding U.S. base at Kandahar Airfield, which it aptly termed a "boom town," shows just how ongoing this part of the overall surge is, and at what a staggering level. As in Iraq from 2003 on, billions of dollars are being sunk into bases, the largest of which—especially the old Soviet site, Bagram Air Base, with more than $200 million in construction projects and upgrades under way—are beginning to look like ever more permanent fixtures on the landscape.

As Nick Turse of TomDispatch.com has reported, forward operating bases and smaller combat outposts have been sprouting all over southern Afghanistan. "Forget for a moment the 'debates' in Washington over Afghan War policy," he wrote, "and, if you just focus on the construction activity and the flow of money into Afghanistan, what you see is a war that, from the point of view of the Pentagon, isn't going to end any time soon. In fact, the U.S. military's building boom in that country suggests that, in the ninth year of the Afghan War, the Pentagon has plans for a far longer-term, if not near-permanent, garrisoning of the country, no matter what course Washington may decide upon."

7. *The training surge*: In some ways, the greatest prospective surge may prove to be in the training of the Afghan National Army and police. Despite years of U.S. and NATO "mentoring," both are in notoriously poor shape. The Afghan army is riddled with desertions, running at a rate of at least 25 percent of those trained annually, and the Afghan police are reportedly a hapless, ill-paid, corrupt, drug-addicted lot. Nonetheless, Washington (with the help of NATO reinforcements) is planning to bring

an army whose numbers officially stand at approximately 94,000 (but may actually be as low as 40-odd thousand) to 134,000 reasonably well-trained troops by fall 2010 and 240,000 a year later. Similarly, the Obama administration hopes to take the police numbers from an official 93,000 to 160,000.

8. *The cost surge*: This is a difficult subject to pin down in part because the Pentagon is, in cost-accounting terms, one of the least transparent organizations around. What can be said for certain is that Obama's $30 billion figure won't faintly hold when it comes to the real surge. There is no way that figure will cover anything like all the troops, bases, contractors, and the rest. Just take the plan to train an Afghan security force of approximately 400,000 in the coming years. We've already spent more than $15 billion on the training of the Afghan army, and another $7 billion has gone into police training, staggering figures for a far smaller combined force with poor results. Imagine, then, what a massive bulking up of the country's security forces will actually cost. In congressional testimony, Centcom commander General David Petraeus suggested a possible price tag of $10 billion a year. And if such a program works, which seems unlikely, try to imagine how one of the poorest countries on the planet will support a 400,000-person force. Afghan president Hamid Karzai has suggested that it will take at least fifteen to twenty years before the country can actually pay for such a force itself. In translation, what we have here is undoubtedly a version of Colin Powell's Pottery Barn rule ("You break it, you own it"). In this case, you build it, you own it. If we create such security forces, they will be, financially speaking, ours into the foreseeable future. And this is even without adding in those local militias we're planning to invest "millions" in.

9. *The endlessly receding horizon surge*: By all accounts, the president tried to put some kind of limit on his most recent Afghan surge, not wanting "an open-ended commitment." With that in mind, he evidently insisted on a plan in which some of the surge troops would start to come home in July 2011. This was presented in the media as a case of giving something to everyone (the Republican opposition, his field commanders, and his own antiwar Democratic Party base). In fact, he gave his commanders and the Republican opposition a very real surge in numbers. In

this regard, a *Washington Post* headline said it all: "McChrystal's Afghanistan Plan Stays Mainly Intact." On the other hand, what he gave his base was only the vaguest of drawdown promises. Moreover, within hours of the speech, even that commitment was being watered down by the first top officials to speak on the subject. Soon enough, as the right wing began to blaze away about the mistake of announcing a withdrawal date "to the enemy," there was little short of a stampede of high officials eager to make that promise ever less meaningful. In what Mark Mazzetti of the *Times* called a "flurry of coordinated television interviews," the top civilian and military officials of the administration marched onto the Sunday morning talk shows "in lockstep" to reassure the Right (and they were reassured) by playing "down the significance of the July 2011 target date." The United States was, Secretary of Defense Gates and others indicated, going to be in the region in strength for years to come. ("July 2011 was just the beginning, not the end, of a lengthy process. That date, [national security adviser] General [James] Jones said, is a 'ramp' rather than a 'cliff.'")

When it came to the spreading Taliban insurgency in Afghanistan, the president in his speech spoke of his surge goal this way: "We must reverse the Taliban's momentum and deny it the ability to overthrow the government." This seemed a modest enough target, even if the means of reaching it are proving immodest indeed. After all, we're talking about a relatively lightly armed minority Pashtun insurgency. Against them and a minuscule number of al-Qaeda operatives, the Pentagon has launched an unbelievably costly buildup of forces over vast distances, along fragile, overextended supply lines, and in a country poorer than almost any other on the planet. The State Department has followed suit, as has the CIA across the border in Pakistan. This is the reality the president and his top officials didn't bother to explain to the American people.

And yet, confoundingly, as the United States bulks up, the war only grows fiercer both within the country and in parts of Pakistan. As Andrew Bacevich, author of *The Limits of Power*, has written, "Sending U.S. troops to fight interminable wars in distant countries does more to inflame than to extinguish the resentments giving rise to violent anti-Western jihadism." Whatever the Obama administration does in Afghanistan and

Pakistan, however, give it some credit: the ability to mount a sustained operation of this size in one of the most difficult places on the planet, when it can't even mount a reasonable jobs program at home, remains a strange wonder of the world.

Pentagon Time: Tick...Tick...Tick...

Back in 2007, when General David Petraeus was the surge commander of U.S. forces in Iraq, he had a penchant for clock imagery. In an interview in April of that year, he typically said: "I'm conscious of a couple of things. One is that the Washington clock is moving more rapidly than the Baghdad clock, so we're obviously trying to speed up the Baghdad clock a bit and to produce some progress on the ground that can perhaps give hope to those in the coalition countries, in Washington, and perhaps put a little more time on the Washington clock." And he wasn't alone. Military spokespeople and others in the Bush administration right up to the president regularly seemed to hear one, two, or sometimes as many as three clocks ticking away ominously and out of sync.

Hearing some discordant ticking myself of late, I decided to retrieve Petraeus's image from the dustbin of history. So imagine three ticking clocks, all right here in the United States, one set to Washington time, a second to American time, and the third to Pentagon time.

In Washington—with even the *New York Times* agreeing that a "majority" of one hundred is sixty (not fifty-one) and that the Senate's forty-first vote settles everything—the clock seems to be ticking erratically, if at all. On the other hand, that American clock, if we're to believe the good citizens of Massachusetts, is ticking away like a bomb. Americans are impatient, angry, and "in revolt" against Washington time. That's what the media continue to tell us in the wake of the Senate upset in which Republicans won the long-safe Democratic seat opened up by the death of Edward Kennedy. Depending on which account you read, they were outraged by a nearly trillion-dollar health-care reform that was also a giveaway to insurance companies, and annoyed by Democratic candidate Martha Coakley calling Boston Red Sox pitcher Curt Schilling a "Yankees fan." They were anxious about an official Massachusetts unemployment rate of 9.4 percent (and a higher real one), an economy that has re-bounded for bankers but not for regular people, soaring deficits, stagger-ing foreclosure rates, mega-banking bonuses, the Obama administration's bailout of those same bankers, and its coziness with Wall Street. They were angry and impatient about a lot of things, blind angry you might say, since they were ready to vote back into office the party not in office, even if be-hind that party's "new face" were ideas that would take us back to the ori-gins of the present disaster.

It's worth noting, however, that they weren't angry about every-thing—and that the Washington clock, barely moving on a wide range of issues, is still ticking away when it comes to one institution. The good citizens of Massachusetts may be against free rides and bailouts for many types, but not for everybody. I'm speaking, of course, about the Pentagon, for which Congress in 2010 passed a record budget of $626 billion. This happened without real debate, much public notice, or even a touch of anger in Washington or Massachusetts. And keep in mind that the Pentagon's real budget is undoubtedly closer to a trillion dol-lars, without even including the full panoply of support for our national security state.

The Tea Party crews don't rail against Pentagon giveaways, nor do American voters. Unfettered Pentagon budgets pass in the tick-tock of a Washington clock and no one seems fazed when the *Wall Street Journal* reveals that military aides accompanying globe-hopping parties of con-gressional representatives regularly spend thousands of taxpayer dollars on snacks, drinks, and other "amenities" for them, even while, like some K Street lobbying outfit, promoting their newest weaponry. Think of it, in financial terms, as Pentagon peanuts shelled out for actual peanuts, and no one gives a damn.

It was hardly news—and certainly nothing to get angry about—when the secretary of defense met privately with the nation's top military-industrial contractors, called for an even "closer partnership," and pledged to further their mutual interests by working "with the White House to se-cure steady growth in the Pentagon's budgets over time." Nor did it cause a stir among the denizens of inside-the-Beltway Washington or Americans generally when the top ten defense contractors spent more than $27 million lobbying the federal government, as in the last quarter of 2009, just as plans for the president's Afghan surge were being prepared.

However, it's not just the angry citizens of Massachusetts, or those Tea Party organizers, or Republican stalwarts who see no link between our military-industrial outlays, our perpetual wars, and our economic woes. When, for instance, was the last time you saw a bona fide liberal economist and columnist like Paul Krugman include the Pentagon and our wars in the litany of things potentially bringing this country down?

Striking percentages of Americans attend the church (temple, mosque) of their choice, but when it comes to American politics and the economy, the U.S. military is our church, "national security" our bible, and nothing done in the name of either can be wrong. It's as if the military, already the most revered institution in the country, existed on the other side of a Star-Trekkian financial wormhole.

Which brings us to Pentagon time. Yes, that third clock is ticking, but at a very different tempo from those in Washington or Massachusetts.

Americans are evidently increasingly impatient for "change" of whatever sort, whether you can believe in it or not. The Pentagon, on the other hand, is patient. It's opted for making counterinsurgency the central strategy of its war in Central and South Asia, the sort of strategy that, even if successful, experts claim could easily take a decade or two to pull off. But no problem—not when the Pentagon's clock is ticking on something like eternal time.

And here's the thing: because the mainstream media are no less likely to give the Pentagon a blank check than Americans generally, it's hard indeed to grasp the extent to which that institution, and the military services it represents, are planning and living by their own clock. Though major papers have Pentagon "beats," they generally tell us remarkably little, except inadvertently and in passing, about Pentagon time.

Take, for example, a January 6, 2010, story from the inside pages of the *New York Times*. Reporter Eric Schmitt began it this way: "The military's effort to build a seasoned corps of expert officers for the Afghan war, one of the highest priorities of top commanders, is off to a slow start, with too few volunteers and a high-level warning to the armed services to steer better candidates into the program, according to some senior officers and participants." At stake was an initiative "championed" by Afghan War commander General Stanley McChrystal to create a "912-member corps of mostly officers and enlisted service members who will work on Afghanistan and Pakistan issues for up to five years."

As Schmitt saw it, a program in its infancy was already faltering because it didn't conform to one of the normal career paths followed in the U.S. military. But what caught my eye was that phrase "up to five years." Imagine what it means for the war commander, backed by key figures in the Pentagon, to plan to put more than nine hundred soldiers, including top officers, on a career path that would leave them totally wedded, for five years, to war in the Af-Pak theater of operations. (After all, if that war were to end, the State Department might well take charge.) In other words, McChrystal was creating a potentially powerful interest group within the military whose careers would be wedded to an ongoing war with a time line that extended into 2015, and who would have something to lose if it ended too quickly. What does it matter then that President Obama was proclaiming his desire to begin drawing down the war in July 2011?

Or consider the plan being proposed by special forces major Jim Gant, and now getting a most respectful hearing inside the military, according to Ann Scott Tyson of the *Washington Post*. Gant wants to establish small special forces teams that would "go native," move into Afghan villages and partner up with local tribal leaders, "One Tribe at a Time," as an influential paper he wrote on the subject was entitled. "The U.S. military," reported Tyson, "would have to grant the teams the leeway to grow beards and wear local garb, and enough autonomy in the chain of command to make rapid decisions. Most important, to build relationships, the military would have to commit one or two teams to working with the same tribe for three to five years, Gant said." She added that Gant has "won praise at the highest levels for his effort to radically deepen the U.S. military's involvement with Afghan tribes—and is being sent back to Afghanistan to do just that." Again, another "up to five year" commitment in Afghanistan and a career path to go with it on a clock that, in Gant's case, has yet to start ticking.

Or just to run through a few more examples:

- In August 2009, the superb Walter Pincus of the *Washington Post* quoted air force brigadier general Walter Givhan, in charge of training the Afghan National Army Air Corps, as saying: "Our goal is by 2016 to have an air corps that will be capable of doing those operations and the things that it needs to do to meet the security requirements of this country." Of course, that six-year timeline includes the American advisers training that air force. (And note that Givhan's 2016 date may actually represent slippage. In January 2008, when air force brigadier general Jay H. Lindell, who was then commander of the Combined Air Power Transition Force, discussed the subject, he spoke of an "eight-year campaign plan" through 2015 to build up the Afghan Air Corps.)

- In a January 13, 2010, piece on Pentagon budgeting plans, Anne Gearan and Anne Flaherty of the Associated Press reported: "The Pentagon projects that war funding would drop sharply in 2012, to $50 billion" from the present at least $159 billion (mainly thanks to a projected massive drawdown of forces in Iraq), "and remain there through 2015." Whether the financial numbers are accurate or not, the date is striking: again a five-year window.

- Or take the "train and equip" program aimed at bulking up the Afghan military and police, which will be massively staffed with U.S. military advisers (and private security contractors) and is expected to cost at least $65 billion. It's officially slated to run from 2010 to 2014, by which time the combined Afghan security forces are projected to reach four hundred thousand.

- Or consider a couple of the long-term contracts already being handed out for Afghan War work like the $158 million the air force has awarded to Evergreen Helicopters, Inc., for an "indefinite delivery/indefinite quantity (IDIQ) contract for rotary wing aircraft, personnel, equipment, tools,

material, maintenance and supervision necessary to per-
form passenger and cargo air transportation services. Work
will be performed in Afghanistan and is expected to start
Apr. 3, 2009, to be completed by Nov. 30, 2013." Or the Pentagon contract awarded to the private contractor SOS International primarily for translators, which has an
estimated completion date of September 2014.

Of course, this just scratches the surface of long-term Afghan War
planning in the Pentagon and the military, which rolls right along, seemingly barely related to whatever war debates may be taking place in Washington. Few in or out of that city find these timelines strange, and indeed
they are just symptomatic of an organization already planning for "the
next war" and the ones after that, not to speak of the next generation
bomber of 2018, the integrated U.S. Army battlefield surveillance system
of 2025, and the drones of 2047.

This, in short, is Pentagon time, and it's we who fund that clock that
ticks toward eternity. If the Pentagon gets in trouble, fighting a war or
otherwise, we bail it out without serious debate or any of the anger we
saw in the Massachusetts election. No one marches in the streets, or demands that Pentagon bailouts end, or votes 'em (or at least their supporters) out of office.

In this way, no institution is more deeply embedded in American life
or less accountable for its acts. Pentagon time exists enswathed in an almost religious glow of praise and veneration, what might once have been
known as "idolatry." Until the Pentagon is forced into our financial universe, the angry, impatient one where most Americans now live, we're in
trouble. Until candidates begin losing because angry Americans reject
our perpetual wars, and the perpetual war planning that goes with them,
this sort of thinking will simply continue, no matter who the "commander in chief" is or what he thinks he's commanding. Americans need to
stop saluting and end the Pentagon's free ride before our wars kill us.

EPILOGUE

Premature Withdrawal

We've now been at war with, or in, Iraq for almost twenty years, and intermittently at war in Afghanistan for thirty years. Think of it as nearly half a century of experience, all bad. And what is it that Washington seems to have concluded? In Afghanistan, where one disaster after another has occurred, that we Americans can finally do more of the same, somewhat differently calibrated, and so much better. In Iraq, where we had, it seemed, decided that enough was enough and we should simply depart, the calls from a familiar crew for us to stay are growing louder by the week.

The Iraqis, so the argument goes, need us. After all, who would leave them alone, trusting them not to do what they've done best in recent years: cut one another's throats?

Modesty in Washington? Humility? The ability to draw new lessons from long-term experience? None of the above is evidently appropriate for "the indispensable nation," as former Secretary of State Madeleine Albright once called the United States, and to whose leaders she attributed the ability to "see further into the future." None of the above is part of the American arsenal, not when Washington's weapon of choice, repeatedly consigned to the scrap heap of history and repeatedly rescued, remains a deep conviction that nothing is going to go anything but truly, deeply, madly badly without us, even if, as in Iraq, things have for years gone truly, deeply, madly badly with us.

An expanding crew of Washington-based opiners is now calling for the Obama administration to alter its plans, negotiated in the last months of the Bush administration, for the departure of all American troops from Iraq by the end of 2011. They seem to have taken Albright's belief in American foresight—even prophesy—to heart and so are basing their arguments on their ability to divine the future.

The problem, it seems, is that, whatever may be happening in the present, Iraq's future prospects are terrifying, which makes leaving, if not inconceivable, then as massively irresponsible (as former *Washington Post* correspondent and bestselling author Tom Ricks wrote in a *New York Times* op-ed) as invading in the first place. Without the U.S. military on hand, we're told, the Iraqis will almost certainly deep-six democracy, while devolving into major civil violence and ethnic bloodletting, possibly of the sort that convulsed their country in 2005–06 when, by the way, the U.S. military was present in force.

The various partial winners of Iraq's much delayed March 7, 2010, election would, we were assured beforehand, jockey for power for months trying to cobble together a functioning national government. During that period, violence, it was said, would surely escalate, potentially endangering the marginal gains made thanks to the U.S. military "surge" of 2007. The possibilities remain endless and, according to these doomsayers, none of them are encouraging: Shiite militias could use our withdrawal to stage a violence-filled comeback. Iranian interference in Iraqi affairs is likely to increase and violently so, while al-Qaeda-in-Iraq could move into any post-election power void with its own destructive agenda.

The Warrior-Pundits Occupy the Future

Such predictions are now dribbling out of the world of punditry and into the world of news reporting, where the future threatens to become fact long before it makes it onto the scene. Already it's reported that the anxious U.S. commander in Iraq, General Ray Odierno, "citing the prospects for political instability and increased violence," is talking about "plan B's" to delay the agreed upon withdrawal of all "combat troops" from the country this August. He has, Ricks reported on *Foreign Policy*'s website, officially requested that a combat brigade remain in or near the troubled northern city of Kirkuk after the deadline.

As 2009 ended, Secretary of Defense Robert Gates was suggesting that new negotiations might extend the U.S. position into the post-2011 years. ("I wouldn't be a bit surprised to see agreements between ourselves and the Iraqis that continue a train, equip, and advise role beyond the end of 2011.") Centcom commander General David Petraeus agreed. More recently, Gates added that a "pretty considerable deterioration" in the country's security situation might lead to a delay in withdrawal plans (and Iraqi prime minister Nouri al-Maliki has agreed that this is a possibility). Vice President Joe Biden is already talking about relabeling "combat troops" not sent home in August because, as he put it in an interview with Helene Cooper and Mark Landler of the *New York Times*, "we're not leaving behind cooks and quartermasters." The bulk of the troops remaining, he insisted, "will still be guys who can shoot straight and go get bad guys."

And a chorus of the usual suspects, Washington's warrior-pundits and "warrior journalists" (as Tom Hayden calls them), have been singing ever-louder versions of a song warning of that greatest of all dangers: premature withdrawal. Ricks, for instance, recommended in the *Times* that, having scuttled the "grandiose original vision" of the Bush invasion, the Obama administration should still "find a way" to keep a "relatively small, tailored force" of thirty thousand to fifty thousand troops in Iraq "for many years to come." (Those numbers, oddly enough, bring to mind the thirty-four thousand U.S. troops that, according to Ricks in his 2006 bestseller *Fiasco*, Deputy Secretary of Defense Paul Wolfowitz projected as the future U.S. garrison in Iraq in the weeks before the invasion of 2003.)

Kenneth Pollack, a drumbeater for that invasion, is now wary of removing "the cast"—his metaphor for the U.S. military presence—on the "broken arm" of Iraq too soon, since states that have "undergone a major inter-communal civil war have a terrifying rate of recidivism." For Kimberly and Frederick Kagan, drumbeaters *extraordinaire*, writing for the *Wall Street Journal*, the United States must start discussing "a long-term military partnership with Iraq beyond 2011," especially since that country will not be able to defend itself by then.

Why, you might well ask, must we stay in Iraq, given our abysmal record there? Well, say these experts, we are the only force all Iraqis now accept, however grudgingly. We are, according to Pollack, the "peacekeepers...the lev[ee] holding back violence...Iraq's security blanket, and the broker of political deals...we enforce the rules." According to Ricks, we are the only "honest brokers" around. According to the Kagans, we were the "guarantor" of the recent elections, and have a kind of "continuing leverage" not available to any other group in that country, "should we choose to use it."

Today, Iraq is admittedly a mess. On our watch, the country crashed and burned. No one claims that we've put it back together. Multibillions of dollars in reconstruction funds later, the United States has been incapable of delivering the simplest things like reliable electricity or potable water to significant parts of the country. Now, the future sits empty and threatening before us. So much time in which so many things could happen, and all of them horrifying, all calling out for us to remain because *they* just can't be trusted, *they* just don't deliver.

The Sally Fields of American Foreign Policy

Talk about blaming the victim. An uninvited guest breaks into a lousy dinner party, sweeps the already meager meal off the table, smashes the patched-together silverware, busts up the rickety furniture, and then insists on staying ad infinitum because the place is such a mess that someone responsible has to oversee the cleanup process.

What's remained in all this, remarkably enough, is our confidence in ourselves, our admiration for us, our—well, why not say it?—narcissism. Nothing we've done so far stops us from staring into that pool and being struck by what a kindly, helpful face stares back at us. Think of those gathering officials, pundits, journalists, and military figures seemingly eager to imagine the worst and so put the brakes on a full-scale American withdrawal as the Sally Fields of foreign policy. ("I can't deny the fact that you like me, right now, you like me!")

When you have an administration that has made backpedaling its modus operandi, this rising chorus in Washington and perhaps among the military in Iraq could prove formidable in an election year (here, not there).

What, of course, makes their arguments particularly potent is the fact that they base them almost entirely on things that have yet to happen, that may, in fact, never happen. After all, humans have such a lousy track record as predictors of the future. History regularly surprises us, and yet their dismal tune about that future turns out to be an effective cudgel with which to beat those in favor of getting all U.S. troops out by the end of 2011.

Few remember anymore, but we went through a version of this forty years ago in Vietnam. There, too, Americans were repeatedly told that the United States couldn't withdraw because, if we left, the enemy would launch a "bloodbath" in South Vietnam. This future bloodbath of the imagination appeared in innumerable official speeches and accounts. It became so real that sometimes it seemed to put the actual, ongoing bloodbath in Vietnam in the shade, and for years it provided a winning explanation for why any departure would have to be interminably and indefinitely delayed. The only problem was, when the last American took that last helicopter out, the bloodbath didn't happen.

In Iraq, only one thing is really known: After our invasion and with U.S. and allied troops occupying the country in significant numbers, the Iraqis did descend into the charnel house of history, into a monumental bloodbath. It happened in our presence, on our watch, and in significant part thanks to us.

But why should the historical record—the only thing we can, in part, rely on—be taken into account when our pundits and strategists have such privileged access to an otherwise unknown future? Based on what we're seeing now, such arguments may intensify. Terrible prophesies about Iraq's future without us may multiply. And make no mistake, terrible things could indeed happen in Iraq. They could happen while we are there. They could happen with us gone. But history delivers its surprises more regularly than we imagine—even in Iraq.

In the meantime, it's worth keeping in mind that not even Americans can occupy the future. It belongs to no one.

Note on the Text

If, soon after 9/11, you had told me that I would, in the coming years, write hundreds of thousands of words on America's wars, the Pentagon, its garrisoning of the planet, and the militarization of the United States, I would, to say the least, have been surprised. I surely would have thought you had no knack for predicting the future. That this actually happened still surprises me. My only explanation is that I couldn't help myself, that this was the way the world looked to me and I found myself continually amazed that it didn't look similarly to hordes of reporters, pundits, and analysts.

Mind you, I was never in the military and I certainly think of myself as the most peaceable of guys. Sometimes, however, it takes a complete outsider to see that what's in front of us all is a forest, not a random grouping of trees, or, in the case of this book, an identifiable American way of war rather than a set of disparate political and military acts full of sound and fury but signifying little.

The twenty-nine pieces that make up this book were written between March 2004 and the early months of 2010. They span the tumultuous era in which my website, TomDispatch.com, was born and has lived its relatively short life. However, I thought it important to acknowledge here that the essays you have just read are not simply the ones I originally wrote. Most have been trimmed, and the tell-tale signs of the immediate moment—the recentlys and next weeks, along with examples that were gripping at the time but are forgotten today—have been removed; so have most of the thematic repetitions that are bound to pop up in any set of weekly responses to ongoing events. In a few cases, the essays have even been very modestly updated. Nothing basic about them has, however, been changed, including my conclusions, which, on the whole, still hold up well.

Generally speaking, the book moves chronologically from the moment before 9/11, through the disastrous Bush years and year one of the Obama administration, right up to late last night (thanks to the ability of a small independent press these days to put out a book with remarkable speed). For the sake of whatever flow this book may have, I decided not to include in the text the original date on which each piece was posted. But for the record, and in case readers should wish to check out any of the essays in their original form at TomDispatch.com, here is a list of them with their original titles and the dates they were posted. In each case below, the title of a piece in this book is followed by the original title and date, unless of course the title remained the same:

The World Before September 11—Shark-bit World, December 8, 2005

9/11 in a Movie-Made World—September 7, 2006

The Billion-Dollar Gravestone—May 16, 2006

Looking Forward, Looking Backward—Don't Turn the Page on History, July 23, 2009

Twenty-First-Century Gunboat Diplomacy—March 30, 2004

Wonders of the Imperial World—The Colossus of Baghdad, May 29, 2007

How to Garrison a Planet (and Not Even Notice)—Going on an Imperial Bender, September 4, 2008

Icarus (Armed with Vipers) Over Iraq—December 5, 2004

The Barbarism of War from the Air—Degrading Behavior, July 28, 2006

An Anatomy of Collateral Damage—The Value of One, the Value of None, September 11, 2008

Launching the Drone Wars—Terminator Planet, April 7, 2009

Which War Is This Anyway?—Are We in World War IV? March 10, 2005

The Imperial Unconscious—March 1, 2009

Fixing What's Wrong in Washington…in Afghanistan—February 21, 2010

This book has no footnotes. The original posts at TomDispatch.com were, however, heavily footnoted in the style of the Internet—through links that led readers to my sources and also sometimes offered directions for further exploration. Linking is, in fact, the first democratic form of footnoting, making sources instantly accessible to normal readers who, unlike scholars, may not have quick access to a good library. URLs in a book, however, are both cumbersome and useless. So if you want to check my sources, you'll need to go to the originals online at TomDispatch.com. Fair warning, however: One of the debits of linking is that links regularly die, so the older the piece, the greater the chance that some of the links won't work.

Acknowledgments

I've been a book editor for almost forty years now and lived in a world of editors. I know good editing—a rare enough commodity—when I stumble across it. Anthony Arnove, who works at Haymarket Books, is a superb editor (as well as a jack-of-all-trades, the fate of any independent book publisher). If this collection is now really a book, it's thanks to his ministrations. He made me work, which—having been on the other side of the process—I consider one of the best things you can say about an editor. A special bow to him. Thanks go as well to Mikki Smith, copyeditor extraordinaire, Dao Tran, eagle-eyed proofer, and to the hardworking duo, Rachel Cohen and Julie Fain, also of Haymarket.

TomDispatch.com has been the odyssey of my later life and for its existence and ongoing health I have a number of people to thank: Ham Fish of The Nation Institute, who made it an institute project and me a fellow; Taya Kitman, also of the institute, who's been remarkably supportive through the years; Joe Duax, who offers youth for my age and savvy about an Internet and computer world I don't faintly grasp; Chris Holmes, who wandered into my life from Tokyo (as can only happen in the world of the Web), and defined generosity for me even as he stopped endless small mistakes and errors from entering the world; and Tam Turse, whose eagle eye has made such a difference. Another kind of gratitude is reserved for Nick Turse, who has worked with me all these years, lived through my endless phone calls, and helped make TomDispatch such an adventure for me.

I also want to thank all those authors (and friends) who have written for TomDispatch. You add spice to my day, and sometimes a sense of collective joy as well. And let me offer a bow to those at other websites and blogs I've run into online (and sometimes in person). Dealing with, working with, exchanging ideas with you has been dizzying and wonderful. You include: David Swanson and Chip Yost of After Downing Street, Tony Allison of *Asia Times*, Jan Frel of AlterNet, Eric Garris of Antiwar.com, Mark Karlin of Buzzflash, Jon Queally and Andrea Germanos of Commondreams, Rick Shenkman of History News Network, David Weiner and Cara Parks of the Huffington Post, Juan Cole of Informed Comment, Mamoon Alabbasi of Middle East Online, Sam Baldwin and Nikki Gloudeman of *Mother Jones* magazine, Tony Karon of Rootless Cosmopolitan, Victoria Harper of Truthout, and Paul Woodward of the War in Context, among others. You have helped keep a world of critical and oppositional thinking alive through the worst of times. My gratitude to all of you.

Finally, I want to offer thanks and love to my wife, Nancy, who lived her own life unflappably and wonderfully in the midst of my craziness.

Index

Feith, Douglas, 12, 42–43
Filkins, Dexter, 62
Flaherty, Anne, 203
Fleischer, Ari, 23
Franklin, H. Bruce, 61–62
Franks, Tommy, 121
Frantz, Douglas, 14
Fratto, Tony, 81–82
Freedland, Jonathan, 48
Freedom Tower, 26–27, 30–31
Friedman, Tom, 13, 22

G

Gabler, Neal, 19
Gall, Carlotta, 77–78, 80
Gant, Jim, 202
Garlasco, Marc, 76
Gates, Robert, 103, 111, 142, 145–46,
    158–59, 172–73, 187, 189, 207
Gearan, Anne, 203
Gibbs, Robert, 114
G.I. Joe, 163–68
G.I. Joe: The Rise of Cobra (2009), 165–71
Givhan, Walter, 203
Global War on Terror, 6, 12, 33–34, 75,
    77, 123–28
Goodman, Melvin, 189
"Gorgon Stare" video system, 90, 107, 171
Gorman, Siobhan, 105
Graham, Bradley, 43
Graham, Robert (Bob), 22
Ground Zero, 19, 25–30
Grozny (Chechnya), 94–96, 98–101
gunboat diplomacy, 37–44

H

Hayden, Tom, 207
Hekmatyar, Gulbuddin, 96, 102
Hersh, Seymour, 73, 141
Hiroshima, 16, 18, 20, 59–60, 62, 67–68, 71
Hirsh, Michael, 142
Hitchens, Theresa, 45
Holbrooke, Richard, 143
Hollywood movie, war as, 16–19,

25–26, 68, 84, 158–61, 163–71.
    See also Dr. Strangelove (1964);
    G.I. Joe: The Rise of Cobra (2009);
    Pearl Harbor (2001); *Terminator*
    movies
homeland security, 16, 21, 126–27,
    130–31, 160
Humphrey, Hubert, 176
Hussein, Saddam, 23–25, 46–47, 51, 69,
    71, 148, 154–55, 174
Hutton, James, 88–89

I

Ignatius, David, 142–43
imprisonment, 33, 118, 132, 155, 187. *See
    also* torture
Israel, 12, 64–66, 69–70, 72–73, 172

J

Jamail, Dahr, 100
James, Caryn, 17
Johnson, Chalmers, 40, 53
Johnson, Lyndon, 176
Jones, James, 105, 115, 146, 190–91, 198

K

Kagan, Frederick, 152, 207–08
Kagan, Kimberly, 207–08
Kandahar Airfield, 54, 86–87, 196
Karzai, Hamid, 78, 80, 83, 113–15, 189,
    197
Khalilzad, Zalmay, 83
Khan, Awal, 136–37, 140
Khan, Reza, 77–78
Kilian, Michael, 43–44
Kraft, Joseph, 97
Krauthammer, Charles, 21, 109
Krugman, Paul, 201
Kurtz, Howard, 112

L

LaFraniere, Sharon, 99
Landler, Mark, 207
Laos, 35, 61, 71, 108–9, 120

About Haymarket Books

Haymarket Books is a nonprofit, progressive book distributor and publisher, a project of the Center for Economic Research and Social Change. We believe that activists need to take ideas, history, and politics into the many struggles for social justice today. Learning the lessons of past victories, as well as defeats, can arm a new generation of fighters for a better world. As Karl Marx said, "The philosophers have merely interpreted the world; the point, however, is to change it."

We take inspiration and courage from our namesakes, the Haymarket Martyrs, who gave their lives fighting for a better world. Their 1886 struggle for the eight-hour day reminds workers around the world that ordinary people can organize and struggle for their own liberation.

For more information and to shop our complete catalog of titles, visit us online at www.haymarketbooks.org.

Also from Haymarket Books

Hopes and Prospects
Noam Chomsky

Breaking the Sound Barrier
Amy Goodman, edited by Denis Moynihan

Field Notes on Democracy: Listening to Grasshoppers
Arundhati Roy

War Without End: The Iraq War in Context
Michael Schwartz

Winter Soldier: Iraq and Afghanistan
Iraq Veterans Against the War and Aaron Glantz

Between the Lines: Readings on Israel, the Palestinians, and the U.S. "War on Terror"
Tikva Honig-Parnass and Toufic Haddad

About TomDispatch

Tom Engelhardt launched TomDispatch.com in October 2001 as an e-mail publication offering commentary and collected articles from the world press. In December 2002, it gained its name, became a project of The Nation Institute, and went online as "a regular antidote to the mainstream media." The site now features three articles a week, all original to the site. These include Engelhardt's regular commentaries, as well as the work of authors ranging from Rebecca Solnit, Chalmers Johnson, Bill McKibben, Andrew Bacevich, Barbara Ehrenreich, and Mike Davis to Michael Klare, Adam Hochschild, Noam Chomsky, Anand Gopal, and Karen J. Greenberg. Nick Turse, who also writes for the site, is its associate editor and research director.

TomDispatch is intended to introduce readers to voices and perspectives from elsewhere (even when the elsewhere is here). Its mission is to connect some of the global dots regularly left unconnected by the mainstream media and to offer a clearer sense of how this imperial globe of ours actually works.

About Tom Engelhardt

Tom Engelhardt created and runs the TomDispatch.com website, a project of The Nation Institute, where he is a fellow. He is the author of a highly praised history of American triumphalism in the cold war, *The End of Victory Culture*, and of a novel, *The Last Days of Publishing*. Many of his TomDispatch interviews were collected in *Mission Unaccomplished: TomDispatch Interviews with American Iconoclasts and Dissenters*. He also edited *The World According to TomDispatch: America in the New Age of Empire*, a collection of pieces from his site that functions as an alternative history of the mad Bush years.

TomDispatch is the sideline that ate his life. Before that he worked as an editor at Pacific News Service in the early 1970s, and, these last four decades, as an editor in book publishing. For fifteen years, he was Senior Editor at Pantheon Books, where he edited and published award-winning works ranging from Art Spiegelman's *Maus* and John Dower's *War Without Mercy* to Eduardo Galeano's *Memory of Fire* trilogy. He is now Consulting Editor at Metropolitan Books, as well as the cofounder and coeditor of Metropolitan's the American Empire Project, where he has published bestselling works by Chalmers Johnson, Andrew Bacevich, and Noam Chomsky, among others. Many of the authors whose books he has edited and published over the years now write for TomDispatch.com. For a number of years, he was also a Teaching Fellow at the Graduate School of Journalism at the University of California, Berkeley. He is married to Nancy J. Garrity, a therapist, and has two children, Maggie and Will.